LEGENDARY LOCALS

OF

BANGOR

MAINE

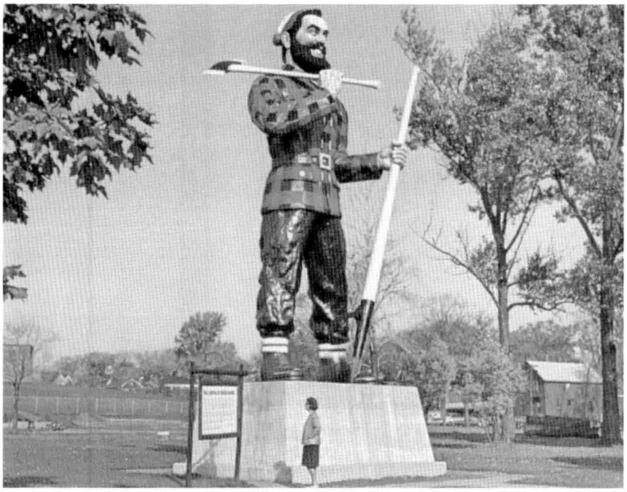

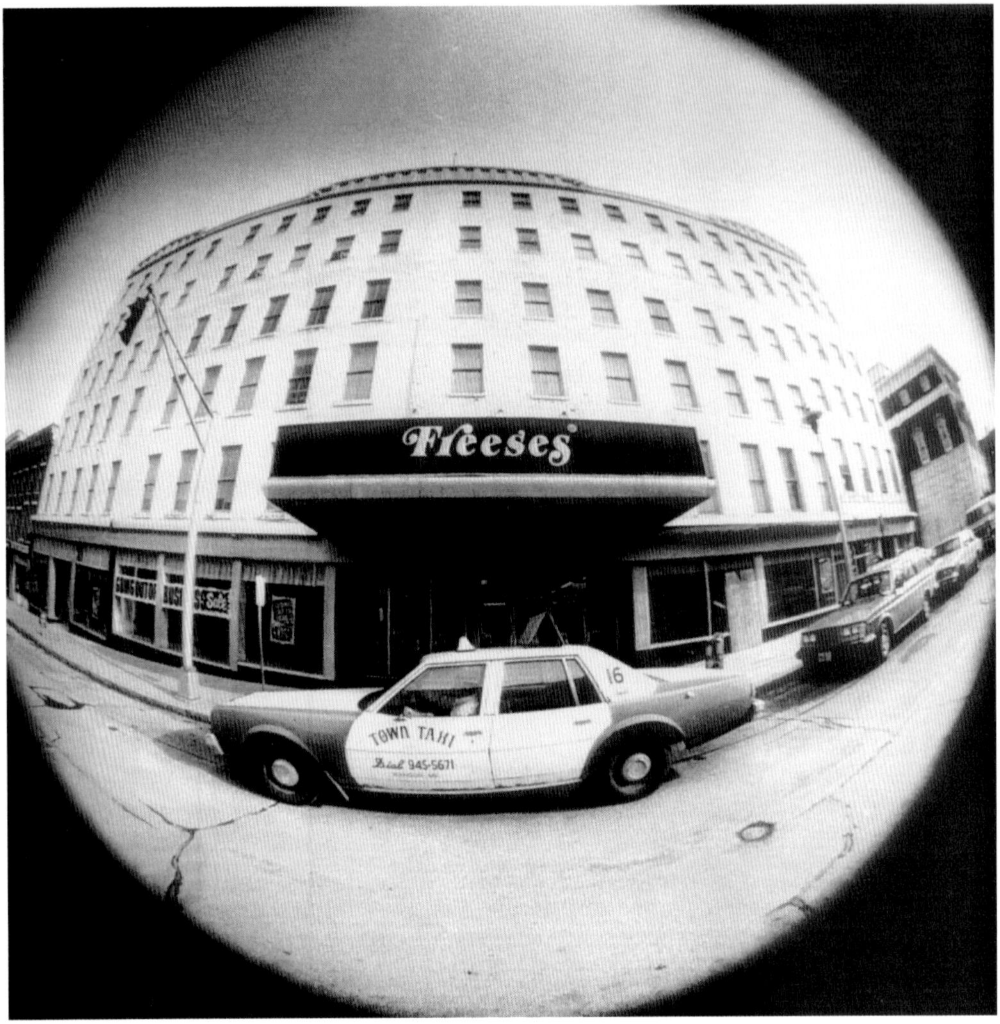

Freese's

Freese's Department Store was a downtown shopping mecca from 1892 to 1985. (Courtesy of *Bangor Daily News.*)

Page 1: Paul Bunyan Statue

The 37-foot-high fiberglass-over-metal Paul Bunyan statue, built in 1959 to honor Bangor's 125th birthday, overlooks the city's Main Street. (Courtesy of Richard R. Shaw.)

LEGENDARY LOCALS

OF

BANGOR

MAINE

RICHARD R. SHAW AND BRIAN F. SWARTZ

LEGENDARY LOCALS

ISBN 978-1-4671-0073-1

Legendary Locals is an imprint of Arcadia Publishing
Charleston, South Carolina

Printed in the United States of America

Library of Congress Control Number: 2012954945

For all general information, please contact Arcadia Publishing:
Telephone 843-853-2070
Fax 843-853-0044
E-mail sales@arcadiapublishing.com
For customer service and orders:
Toll-Free 1-888-313-2665

Visit us on the Internet at www.arcadiapublishing.com

Dedication
This book is dedicated to the librarians, historians, and others who have shared the photographs in this book. Bangor's history is told through their stories.

On the Front Cover: Clockwise from top left:
Stephen King, author (Courtesy of *Bangor Daily News*; see pages 70, 71), Nathan and Rosa Cohen, peddlers (Courtesy of Bangor Public Library; see page 50), J. Normand Martin, Paul Bunyan designer (Courtesy of *Bangor Daily News*; see pages 73 and 124), Alonzo Johnson, businessman (Courtesy of Bangor Historical Society; see page 50), James B. Vickery, historian (Courtesy of *Bangor Daily News*; see page 75), Michael Daley, boxer (Courtesy of Gary W. Woolson; see page 80), Nelle Penley, reporter (Courtesy of Bangor Public Library; see page 69), Edward "Zip" Kellogg, canoeist (Courtesy of Zip Kellogg; see page 52), Dick Curless, country music performer (Courtesy of *Bangor Daily News*; see page 81).

On the Back Cover: From left to right:
L. Felix Ranlett, librarian (Courtesy of Bangor Public Library; see page 103), Clara and Reuben Cohen, bakers (Courtesy of *Bangor Daily News*; see page 56).

CONTENTS

ACKNOWLEDGMENTS

Legendary Locals of Bangor could not have happened without the assistance of many people. The authors particularly wish to extend their gratitude to the following: *Bangor Daily News*, particularly Anthony Ronzio, Jeanne Luetjen, Ardeana Hamlin, and publisher Richard J. Warren; Bangor Historical Society; Bill Sawtell; Cynthia Immonen, Paris Cape Historical Society; David Cheever, Maine State archivist; David M. Fitzpatrick; Desiree Butterfield-Nagy, archivist/special collections librarian at Raymond H. Fogler Library, University of Maine; Dana Lippitt and Jennifer Pictou; Dr. William Hopkins; Elizabeth Stevens and William Cook, Local History and Special Collections librarians at the Bangor Public Library; Erin Vosgien, editor at Arcadia Publishing; Mark Tuck; Rod Tenney; Tara C. Craig, reference services supervisor, Rare Book & Manuscript Library, Columbia University; Tony Caruso and Risteen Bahr at Bangor International Airport; Walter McDougal; Dorothy Cole Warren; and Xiaorong Horton, Realty of Maine, Brownville.

Images in *Legendary Locals of Bangor* appear courtesy of the *Bangor Daily News* (BDN), Bangor Public Library (BPL), Bangor Historical Society (BHS), *The History of Penobscot County, Maine* (HPCM), Library of Congress (LOC), Richard R. Shaw (RRS), and Brian F. Swartz (BFS), among other sources.

INTRODUCTION

I think the best stories always end up being about the people rather than the event, which is to say character-driven.

—Stephen King
On Writing: A Memoir of the Craft

Many harrowing events have shaped Bangor, Maine, since Jacob Buswell, the first white settler, decided to call the riverfront burgh his home in 1769. Floods in the 19th and 20th centuries forced merchants and homeowners to regroup and rebuild. So did infernos like the great fire of 1911, which claimed two lives and inflicted $3 million in damages on the city's downtown.

The voter-approved urban renewal seemed like a fine way to wipe out urban blight, but 50 years and many lost landmarks later, it remains a point of controversy. When Dow Air Force Base left town in 1968, skeptics said the population loss would thrust Bangor into economic chaos. But typical of the city's spirit, planners converted the base into a thriving international airport.

Behind every event in the Queen City's history have been people whose lives were forever changed by circumstances beyond their control. The authors, both former *Bangor Daily News* staff writers and editors, learned that with every historical moment is a human being whose story is waiting to be told.

Newspaper readers wanted to know all about the Civil War widows whose husbands' bodies were shipped back home from Gettysburg and about the neighbors of the Brewer men, John Scribner and George Abbott, who perished in the 1911 fire. And they wanted details of the lives of Louis Lacrosse and Shep Hurd (see page 107), Dakin's Sporting Goods Co. employees who were caught up in the 1937 Brady Gang massacre on Central Street.

People like to read about people, and that is what this book is all about. All of the faces captured in photographs and paintings are true locals. Many, such as teacher Bernard Mann (see page 120), were born in the Queen City; others, like Lt. James Dow (see page 41), namesake of the city's Air Force base, did not live here, but their names will forever be intertwined with the city's fabric.

The authors strived to locate legends of all stripes. You can imagine that the list is endless . . . enough to fill 100 books. People rattled off their own lists of businessmen, politicians, artists, musicians—even a few scoundrels who shall remain nameless—whom they thought should make it into the book. Our challenge was to present Bangor's story in the lives of its people, starting with its earliest days and ending with the present.

Eight chapters seemed like a logical size to fill 125 pages with text and pictures. Based on the hundreds of images made available to us by the *Bangor Daily News*, Bangor Public Library, Bangor Historical Society, Raymond H. Fogler Library, private individuals, and various other sources, the chapter breakdown came into focus.

The city's strong legacy of wartime sacrifice certainly deserved a chapter. Civil War heroes such as Charles Jameson and Daniel Chaplin found a home in Chapter 2, "Military Achievers," as did lesser-known figures such as the Army Air corpsman Willard Orr, who died December 7, 1941, in the Japanese attack on Pearl Harbor.

Other legends featured are candy-maker George F. Burton (see page 106); country singer Dick Curless (see page 81); librarian Mary Curran (see page 104); and Penobscot Indian Molly Molasses (see page 114).

Some of our legends qualify for more than one chapter. Molly Molasses lived to "A Ripe Old Age" (Chapter 8), but she also was a household name in the mid-1800s, as a fixture on the city's streets and steamboats. Television veterans Eddie Driscoll (see page 83) and George Hale (see page 89), found in Chapter 5, "Entertainment and Sports," are also household names.

While the majority of the book's people are deceased, it was important to feature living legends, as well. All were truly honored, and at times surprised, to be in such esteemed company as Vice Pres. Hannibal Hamlin (see page 48), Congressman Charles Boutelle (see page 29), and Bangor's philanthropist and horror master, Stephen King (see pages 70, 71).

One of the advantages of living locally all of our lives was actually knowing some of the book's legends. The authors, individually and collectively, personally know or knew Bernard Mann, Catherine Lebowitz (see page 121), Bob Cimbollek (see page 87), J. Normand Martin (see pages 73 and 124), Clara Swan (see pages 118, 119), and Zip Kellogg (see page 52), along with others. Maybe there is something in the city's air or water that has produced so many memorable characters, including the Baldacci, McKernan, and Cohen political dynasties represented in this book.

A word about the images—all were carefully selected with an eye for variety, diversity, and quality. When our capable editor, Erin Vosgien, said none had been rejected for any reason, we were a little surprised and happy. That meant retaining the wonderfully grainy images of Charlie Howard (see page 61) and Willard Orr (see pages 36 and 37).

Most photographers' names have been lost to time, but a few survive. The *Bangor Daily News'* bow tie–wearing veteran Carroll Hall, a legend in his own right, snapped the classic shot of Stephen King that graces the book's front cover.

But maybe the photographers' names are less important than their subjects, such as those featured on the front and back covers. Among the legends on the covers of the book are businessman Alonzo Johnson, canoeist Zip Kellogg, reporter Nelle Penley (see page 69), librarian L. Felix Ranlett (see page 103), and bakers Reuben and Clara Cohen (see page 56).

Some legends never actually lived, or did they? Stephen King's book characters and Paul Bunyan, who has overlooked Main Street since 1959, are members of Bangor's family.

Perhaps the greatest tribute is not to be forgotten but for others to know that your life was well lived. Hopefully, *Legendary Locals of Bangor* will rekindle memories of memorable characters and introduce readers to others they never knew.

How many more legendary locals can you name for future books? Maybe people not yet born will make the short list. Budding writers, artists, athletes, or politicians may be in the lineup and not even know it.

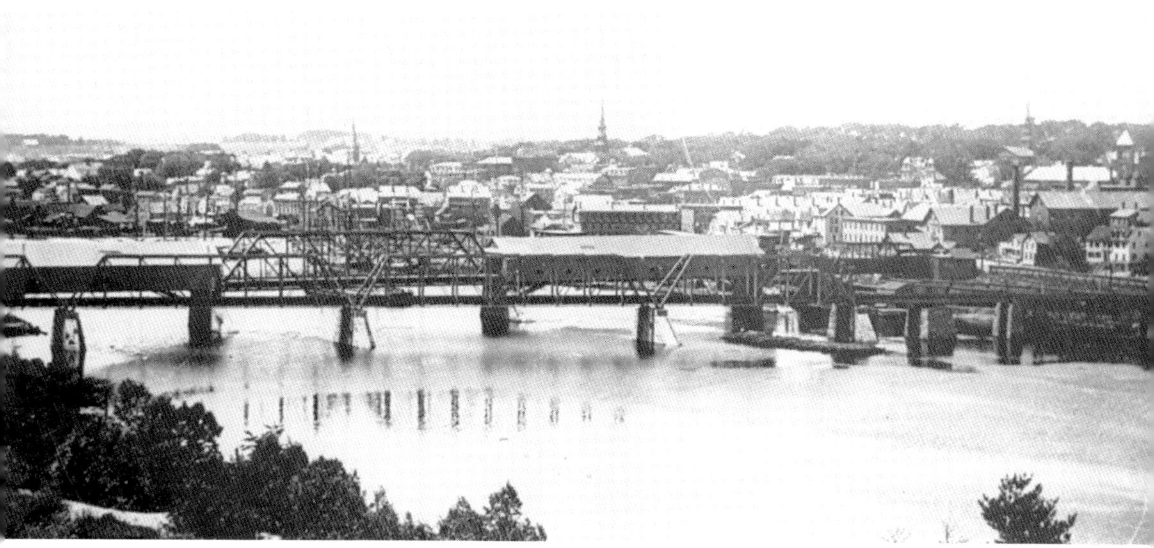

Penobscot River

Penobscot River panoramas give a sense of what Bangor was like more than a century ago. The long covered bridge that once linked the city to Brewer was damaged in a 1902 flood and rebuilt with two iron spans. Boston steamboats linked Bangor to Bean Town from 1835 to 1935. (Both, courtesy of RRS.)

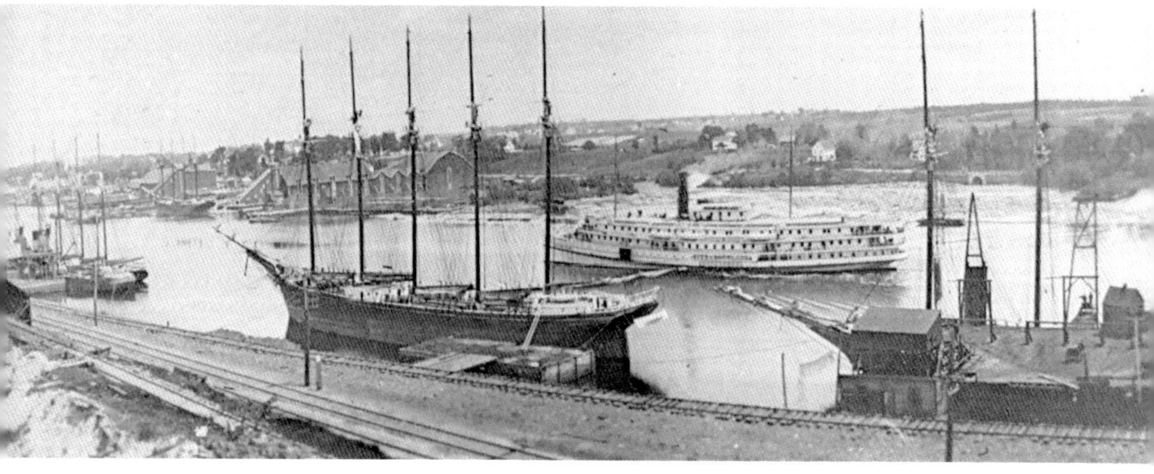

Amelia Earhart

Amelia Earhart appeared at the Bangor House in 1933 during the first of two visits to the city to promote the local airport and women in flight. Flanking the celebrated aviator are civic leaders and curious onlookers. (Courtesy of RRS.)

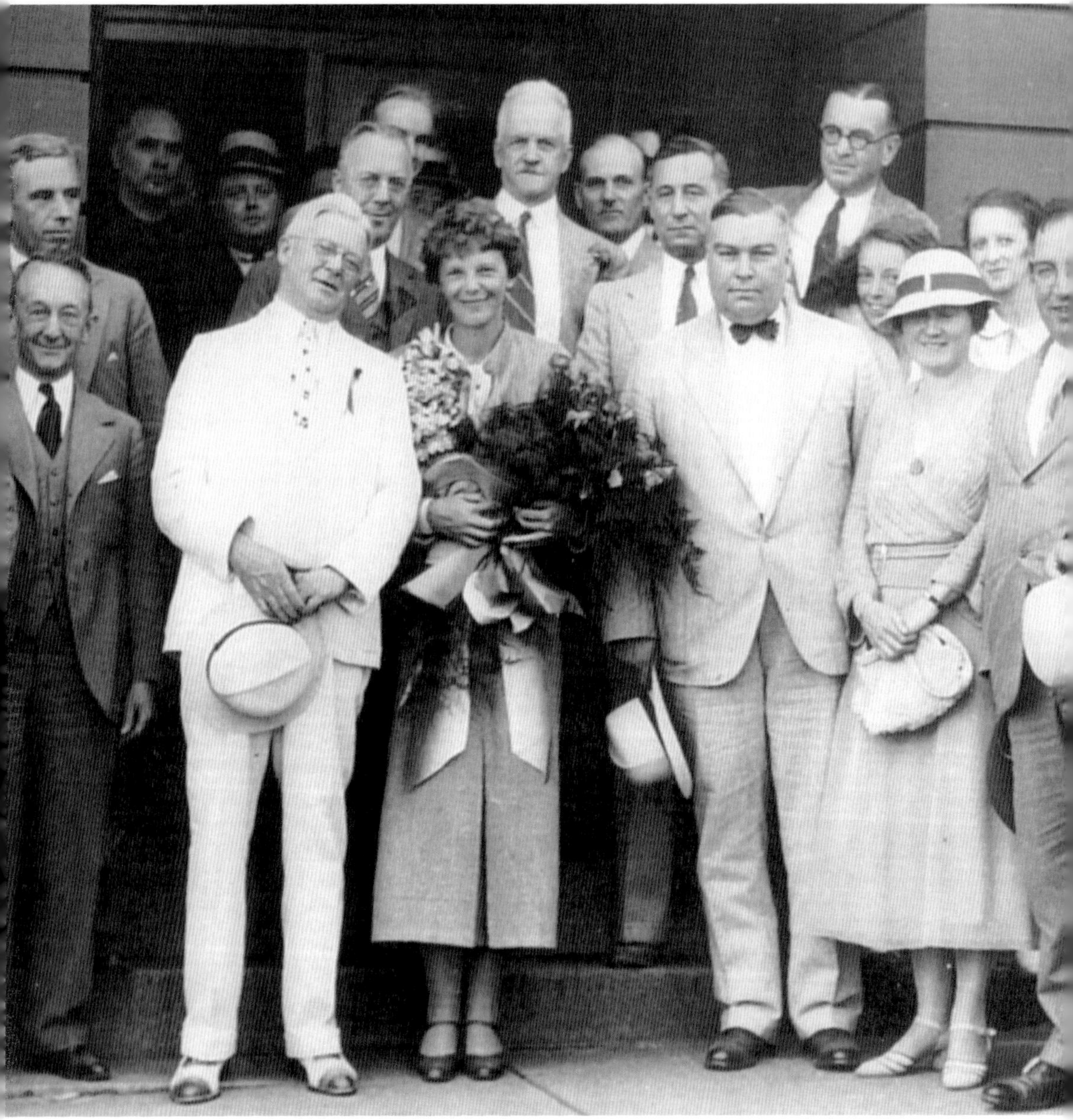

CHAPTER ONE

Queen City Pioneers

Ever since the Spanish-hired explorer Estevan Gómez navigated his ship "up" the Penobscot River in the spring of 1525, pioneers have either visited the Queen City or settled here. And what a group of eclectic people they were!

After Gómez came itinerant French explorer Samuel de Champlain (1604), Massachusetts soldier and trader Robert Treat (1774), and the legendary Rev. Seth Noble (1786), the first minister hired in "Kenduskeag Plantation," as Bangor was then called. Champlain sailed away to explore the New England coast, but Treat liked what he saw and stayed.

And did Noble surreptitiously change the official name of Bangor, as local lore insists?

From the American Revolution through the mid-1800s, people came to Bangor from other parts of Maine and New England to build new lives in the new settlement (soon-to-be town) growing where the Kenduskeag Stream merged with the Penobscot River.

Despite the rugged terrain—rolling hills, fast-flowing streams, and thick, almost-trackless forests—and cold, snowy winters, within two generations the pioneering men and women had transformed the area around the Kenduskeag Stream and Penobscot River into a large town and a major seaport that specialized in shipping lumber, singles, bricks, and ice worldwide.

These hardy folk pioneered the "Queen City," as Bangor came to be known. Although exactly who first coined the phrase "Queen City" remains unclear, the *Bangor Daily Whig & Courier* referred to the "Queen City of the East" in 1859.

And what of those Queen City pioneers? Rumored to have the sharpest-looking horses and carriage in town, fashionable bachelor Rufus Dwinel made his fame and fortune as a lumber baron.

Charles Hayward proved that a grocer could do well in Bangor.

When Henry David Thoreau needed a traveling companion for his famous trip to Mount Katahdin, he tapped his cousin's husband, Bangor businessman George Thatcher. Imagine that, being written into history as Thoreau's companion?

There were doctors and lawyers; Sumner Laughton had to choose between the two professions, and the residents of Bangor benefited from that decision.

There were businessmen and politicians—and often the former were also the latter. Being a small town until the 1830s or so, Bangor needed every bit of local talent to make its government work; the lawyer arguing a case in the Penobscot County Courthouse in the morning and the entrepreneur operating a store or hotel by day would gather at night as selectmen, then as town councilors, and, finally (decades later), as city councilors to govern their fair city.

Those pioneers made Bangor what it is today: the Queen City, a great place to live and work.

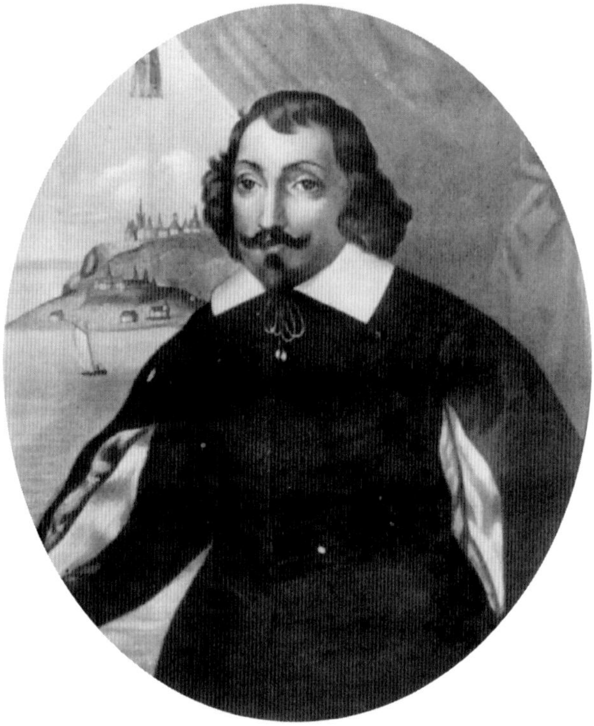

"Bon Jour" to Bangor

French explorer Samuel de Champlain extended a hearty "bon jour" to Bangor inhabitants in September 1604. Except the place was not Bangor—yet—and the inhabitants did not quite know what to make of the inquisitive Frenchman and his 18-ton sailing ship.

Champlain arrived in the New World earlier in 1604 to help establish a permanent French colony on St. Croix Island, located near present-day Calais in eastern Maine. Along with 12 French sailors and two Passamaquoddy guides, Champlain left the island on September 2 to explore the uncharted coast to the west. After "discovering" and naming Mount Desert Island, Champlain explored Penobscot Bay before entering the "Norembegue" (Penobscot) river in mid-September.

"From this narrow place which was the narrowest that we had found, after making about seven or eight leagues we came upon a little river (today's Kenduskeag Stream) near which we had to anchor" because "in front of us we saw a quantity of rocks visible at low tide," Champlain wrote. He and the Passamaquoddys canoed upriver, where Champlain noted the future site of the Bangor dam: "a waterfall . . . which came down a slope seven or eight feet" high. Champlain explored some distance beyond the waterfall.

On September 16, some 30 to 40 Indians (Champlain described them as "Etchemins") led by Chief Bessabez arrived and, somewhere near lower Oak Street in modern Bangor, "sat down . . . in a circle according to their custom," Champlain noted. Soon Chief Cabahis and another 20 to 30 Indians arrived "and greatly enjoyed looking at us, for it was the first time they had seen Christians," Champlain wrote.

Accompanied by two Frenchmen and the Passamaquoddys, Champlain joined the festivities. The Passamaquoddys interpreted Champlain's "bon jour" and subsequent speech for the benefit of the host Etchemins. Champlain smoked tobacco with Bessabez "and his companions," and the Indians welcomed the French to Kadesquit, as they called the future site of Bangor. Then, the Indians "made us presents of venison and game," and everyone partied; "they did nothing but sing, dance, and make good cheer" until dawn on September 17, Champlain recalled. He sailed away later that day.

The Knights of Columbus later erected a monument to Champlain on Kenduskeag Mall in Bangor. A statue of a French nobleman erected at St. Croix Island International Historic Site in Calais may resemble Champlain. (Clockwise from above, courtesy of LOC; Courtesy of BFS; Courtesy of BFS.)

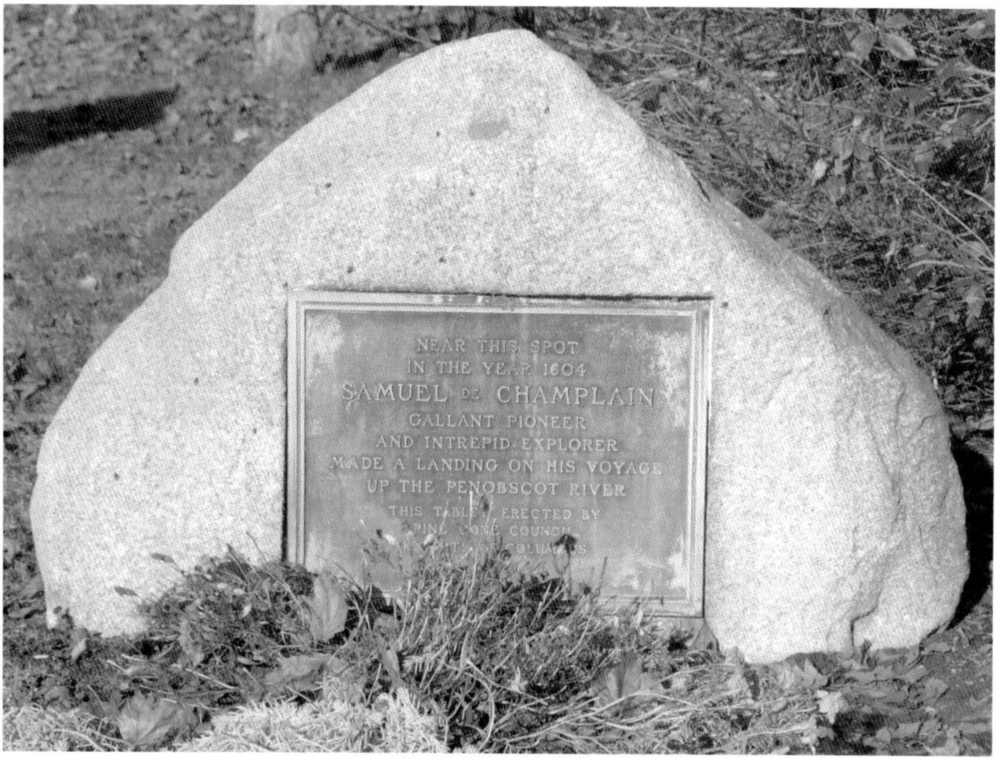
NEAR THIS SPOT
IN THE YEAR 1604
SAMUEL DE CHAMPLAIN
GALLANT PIONEER
AND INTREPID EXPLORER
MADE A LANDING ON HIS VOYAGE
UP THE PENOBSCOT RIVER
ERECTED BY

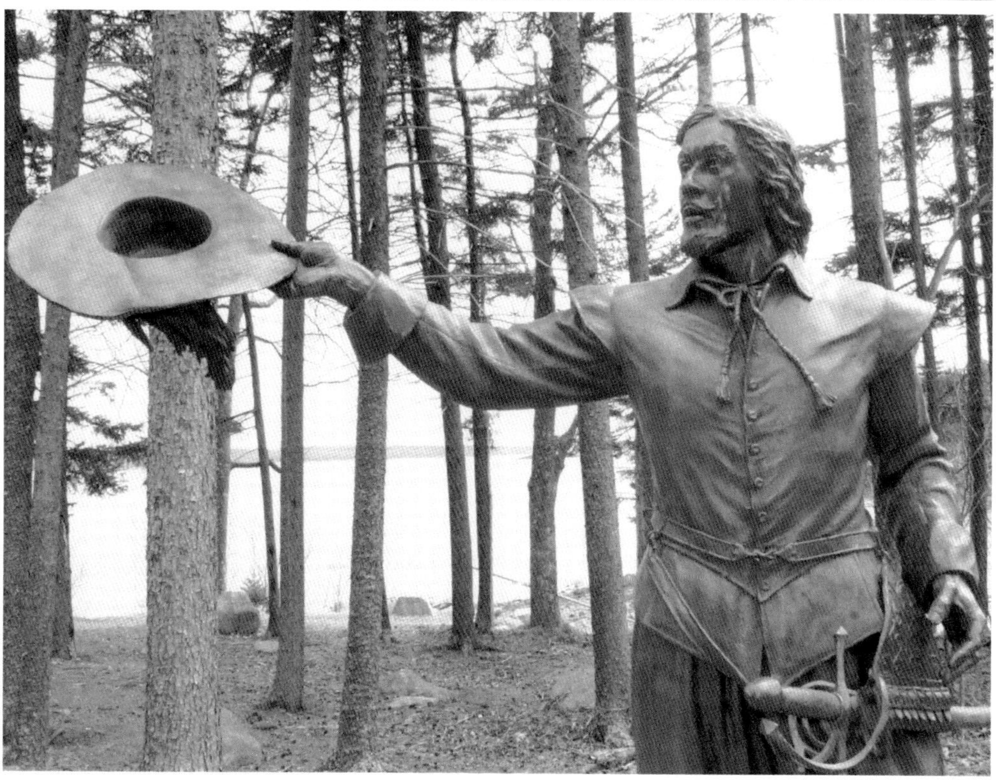

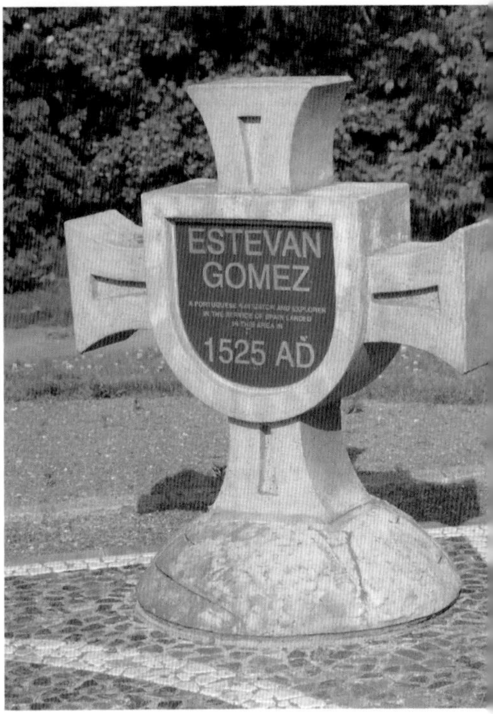

Monument to Bangor's "Discoverer"
In 1524, King Charles V of Spain hired Portuguese sailor Estevan Gómez to find the Northwest Passage. In the spring of 1525, Gómez explored the Maine coast aboard the *La Anunciada*, a caravel similar to this early 20th-century replica of the *Santa Maria*.

Gómez saw so many deer along the Penobscot River shore that he named it "Rio de las Gamas."

He reached the confluence of the Kenduskeag Stream and the Penobscot River in June. The first European to "discover" the region, he went ashore and met some Indians.

Gómez sailed away; history forgot his Bangor connection. In 1999, Portuguese Americans in New Bedford, Massachusetts, raised funds to build a Gómez monument in Bangor. Sculptor Julio Vasconcellos crafted the monument, which features a cross and a compass rose.

Bangor dedicated the monument on Columbus Day 1999. (Right, courtesy of BFS; below, courtesy of LOC.)

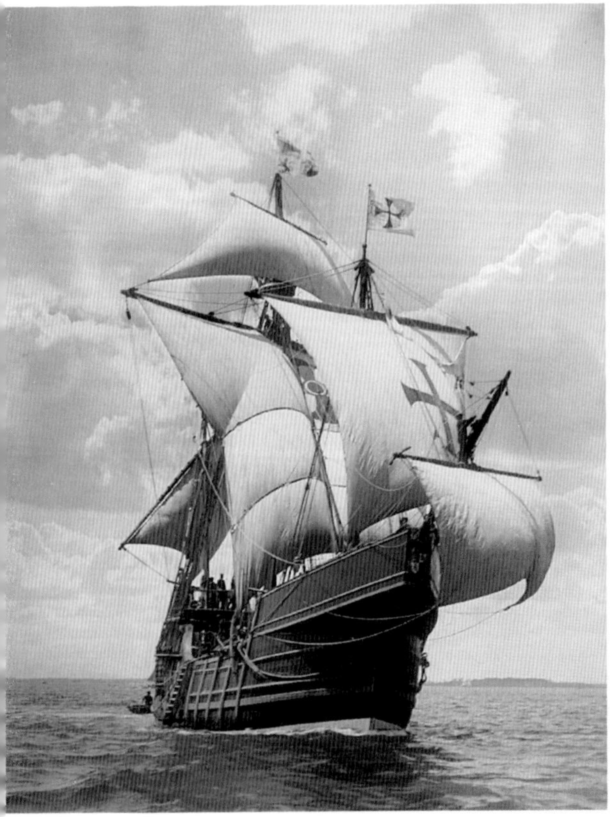

A Legend Became a City's Name

The legend persists that a Congregational minister officially named Bangor—and that is not what local residents wanted their town to be called.

Bangor lore recalls Seth Noble, born in Westfield, Massachusetts, in April 1743. Later ordained as a minister, he served a Congregational church in Nova Scotia in the 1770s. An ardent supporter of American independence, he was forced to flee to New England in 1777. On June 7, 1786, people living in Kenduskeag Plantation on the Penobscot River in the District of Maine hired Noble as the plantation's first permanent minister. His wife, Hannah Barker Noble, and their three children accompanied him when Noble started his new job on September 10, 1786. Hannah died in Kenduskeag Plantation in May 1790; Seth later married a local widow, Ruhama Emery. She would not be his last wife. Within a few years, the bloom went off the rose for Noble and his congregation. The good reverend liked to imbibe, and he apparently failed to focus as seriously on spiritual matters as his congregants would like.

So far, these are the facts involving Rev. Seth Noble. Now, the legend begins. When Kenduskeag Plantation residents decided to incorporate their plantation as a town in 1790, they authorized Noble to travel to Boston and petition the Massachusetts General Court to name the new town "Sunbury."

Noble "was a good singer and had a clear and pleasant voice," said William Boyd, a local deacon. Noble especially liked to sing the hymn "Bangor"; upon arriving in Boston—and before presenting the incorporation petition to the Massachusetts legislature—he alleged substituted the name "Bangor" for the name "Sunbury." And that, supposedly, is how Bangor got its name.

But legend is not always reality, particularly this legend involving Rev. Seth Noble. The petition composed at Kenduskeag Plantation on May 18, 1790, delineated the physical boundaries of the sought-after town and asked Bay State legislators to "incorporate" it "by the name of Bangor." So on February 25, 1791, the Massachusetts General Court passed "an act" that "incorporated . . . a town . . . by the name of Bangor." A 1798 map shows the property lines of the early settlers of the future city of Bangor. (Courtesy of HPCM.)

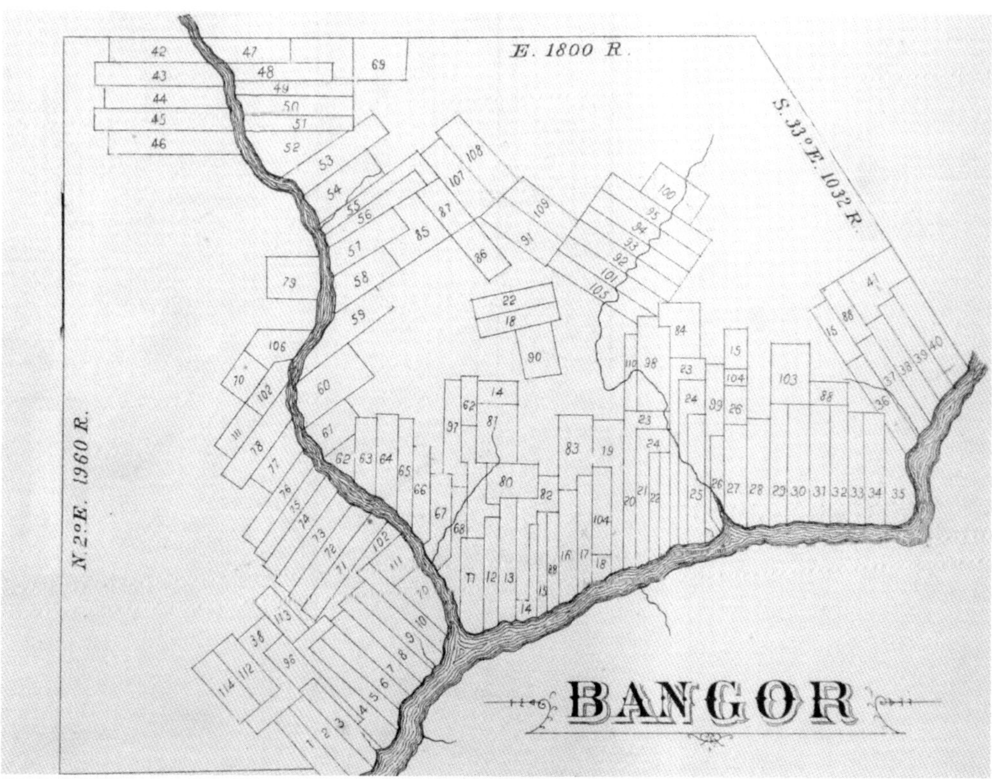

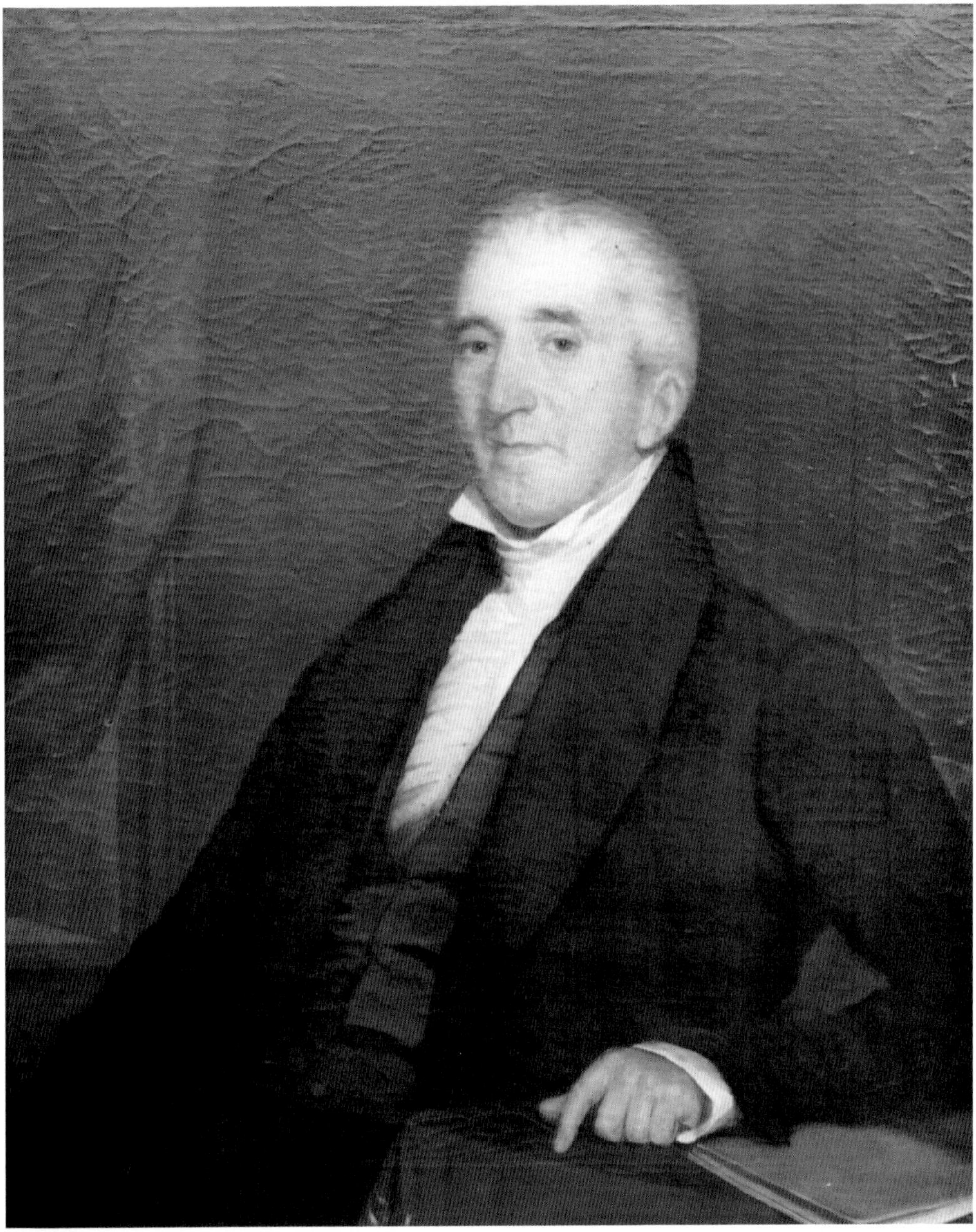

His Testament Still Stands

A five-story building at the corner of Main and Union Streets testifies to the commitment that William Emerson made to Bangor. He arrived in Bangor from New Hampshire in 1806, ran a general store, invested in real estate, and served in the Maine State Senate and on the influential governor's council. Emerson helped finance the brick-built Bangor House, which opened in 1834 and still stands today. (Courtesy of BPL.)

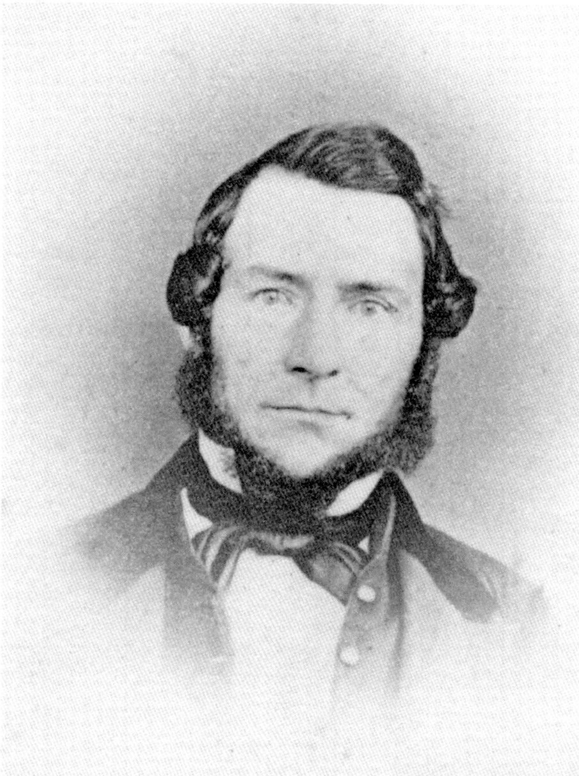

Bangor Lumber Baron

Rufus Dwinel arrived in Bangor in 1826. He originally ran a general store. Dwinel started buying and selling the commercial forests upriver from Bangor that would supply timber shipped worldwide. Dwinel became a successful Bangor lumber baron well known for his business acumen and fastidious dress. A confirmed bachelor, he was a partner in the first railroad that developers attempted to build in Bangor in 1832. (Courtesy of BPL.)

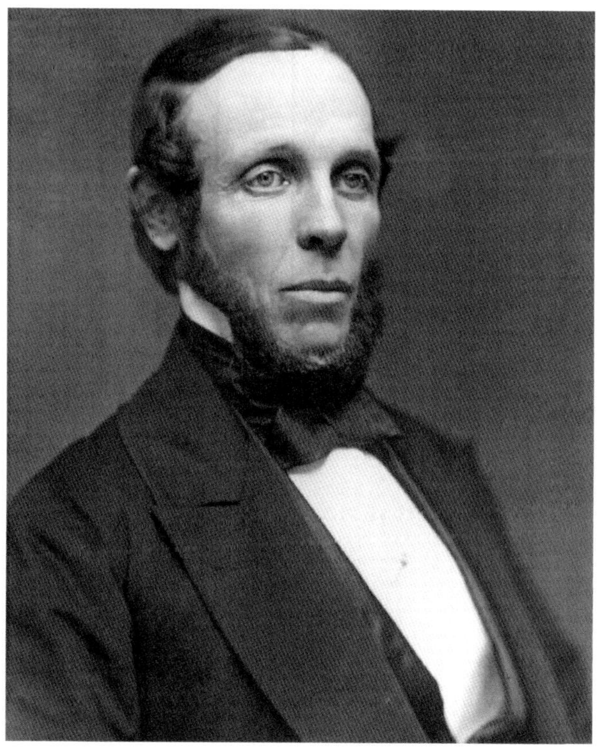

Homegrown Grocer

The grocery trade made Charles Hayward famous in Bangor, where he arrived in March 1832 to clerk at a retail grocery store. In August 1840, Hayward became a partner, and the business became Hayward & Harris in 1855. By the early 1880s, Hayward was a wholesale grocer, in business as Charles Hayward & Co. A longtime Bangor Savings Bank trustee, he held various municipal offices in Bangor. (Courtesy of BPL.)

A Hands-On Mayor

Bangor's first mayor was short in height but tall in his love for his adopted hometown.

Hailing from Exeter, New Hampshire, where he was born in 1773, Allen Gilman graduated from Dartmouth College 18 years later and hung up his lawyer's shingle in Hallowell, Maine, in 1796. He arrived in Bangor in 1801.

To better govern the District of Maine, Massachusetts officials established Penobscot County in 1816 and named Gilman its first register of probate. He was well known in Maine's legal circles.

When Bangor adopted a city charter in 1834, voters elected Gilman their first mayor and reelected him in 1835. *The History of Penobscot County, Maine* reveals that Gilman was literally a hands-on mayor, unafraid to work on a bridge construction project or legally duke it out with a scofflaw ignoring an early city ordinance. (Courtesy of BPL.)

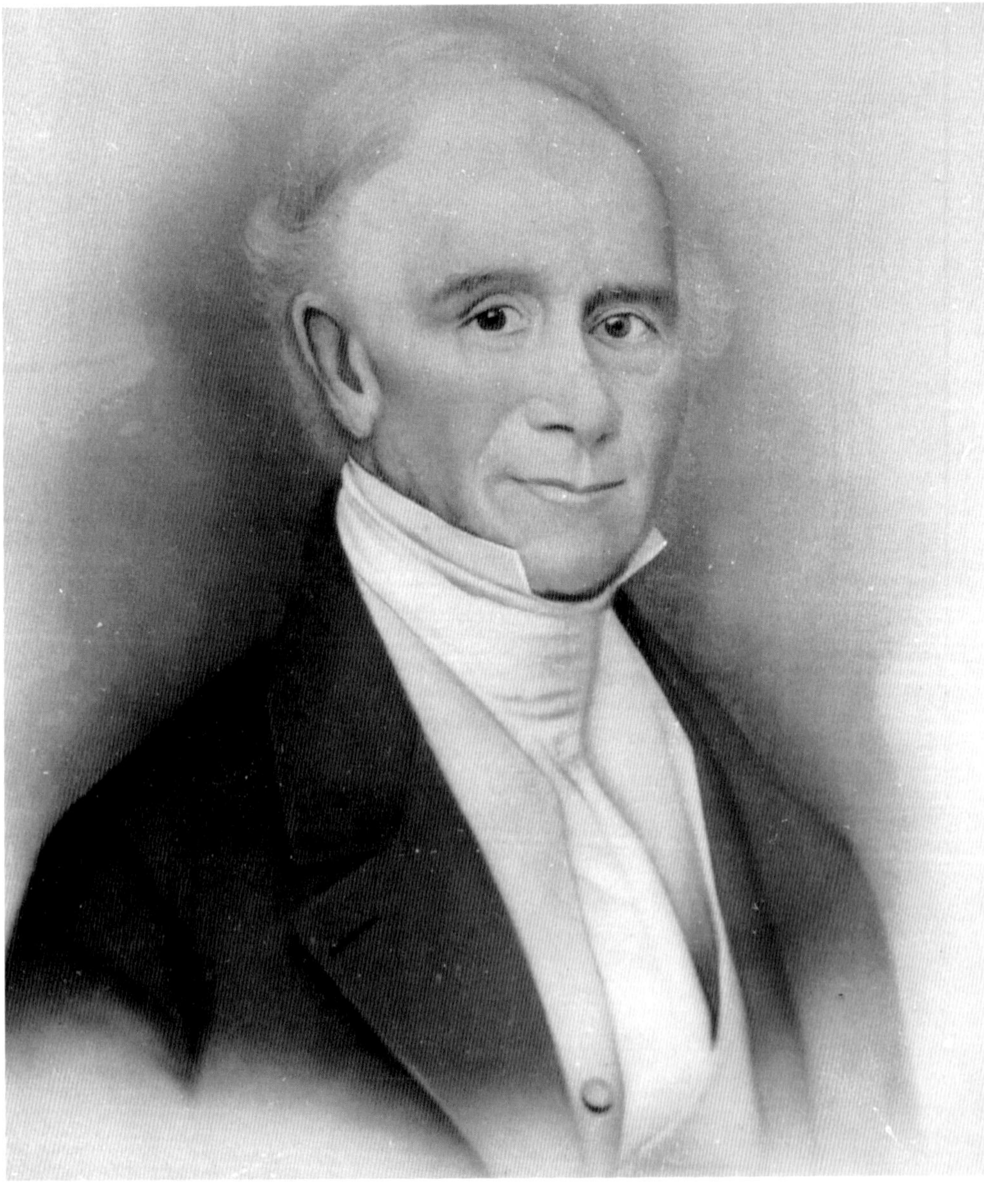

Conversant in the Penobscot Tongue

Robert Treat had a knack for languages, which helped him immensely after he arrived in Bangor in 1774 and constructed a log cabin near where Newbury Street intersects with Hancock Street today.

While stationed earlier at Fort Pownall in Stockton Springs, Treat had learned the Penobscot Nation tongue. After settling in Bangor, he later opened a business near the Penjajawock Stream where Native Americans could trade for Colonial goods. He was well known among the members of the Penobscot Nation—and perhaps trusted by them. Treat served as one of two interpreters during land negotiations held between Massachusetts officials and Penobscot Nation leaders at Bangor in late August 1786.

Treat died at Bangor in May 1824. (Courtesy of Stockton Springs Historical Society.)

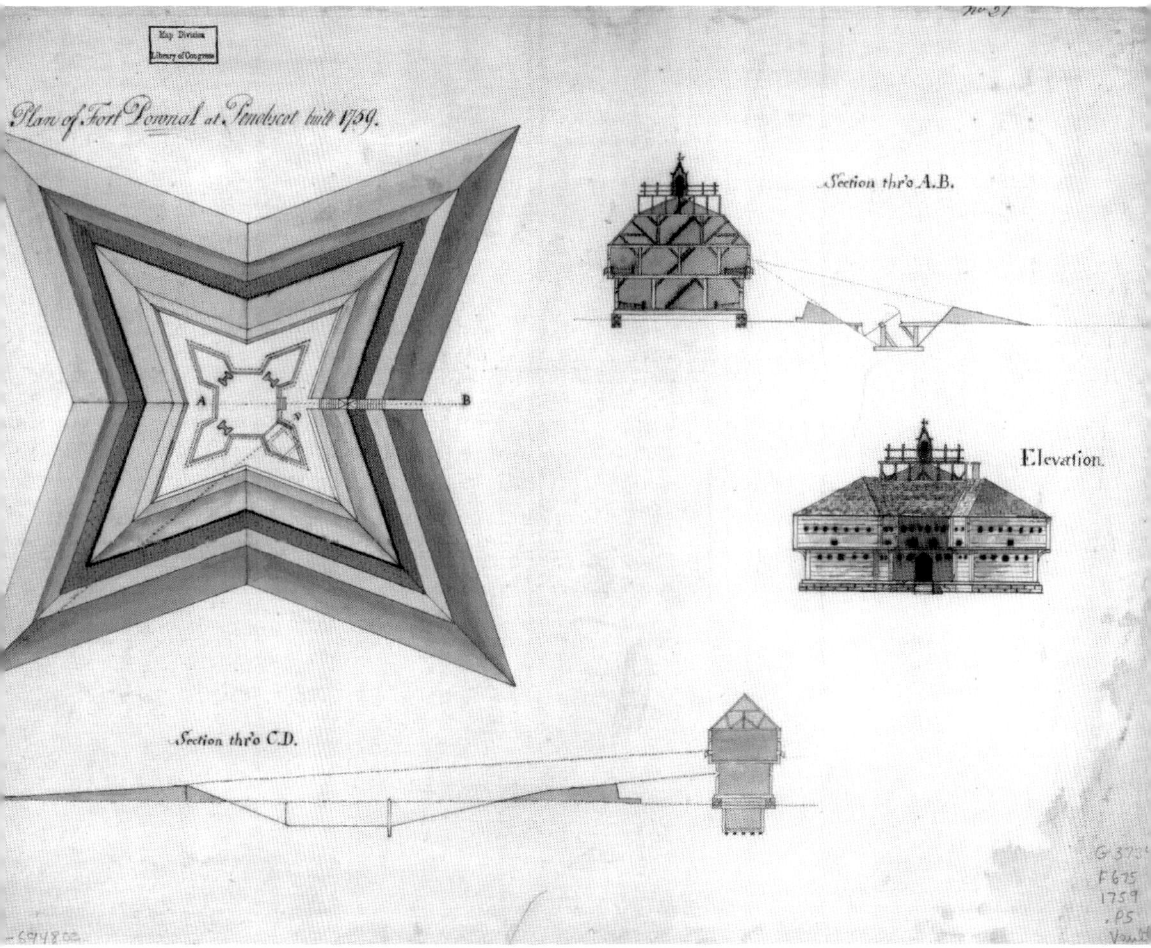

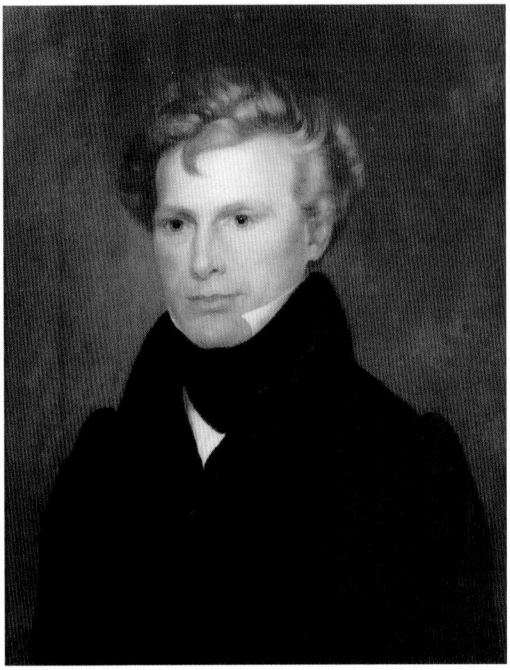

Thoreau's Travel Companion

Arriving in Bangor in 1822, George A. Thatcher immersed himself in the city's business, political, and social circles—but his adventures elsewhere earned him a place in state lore. Thatcher married Rebecca Jane Billings, a cousin to Henry David Thoreau. In his famous *In the Maine Woods*, Thoreau refers to "the relative" who traveled with him various places in Maine. That relative was George Thatcher. (Courtesy of BPL.)

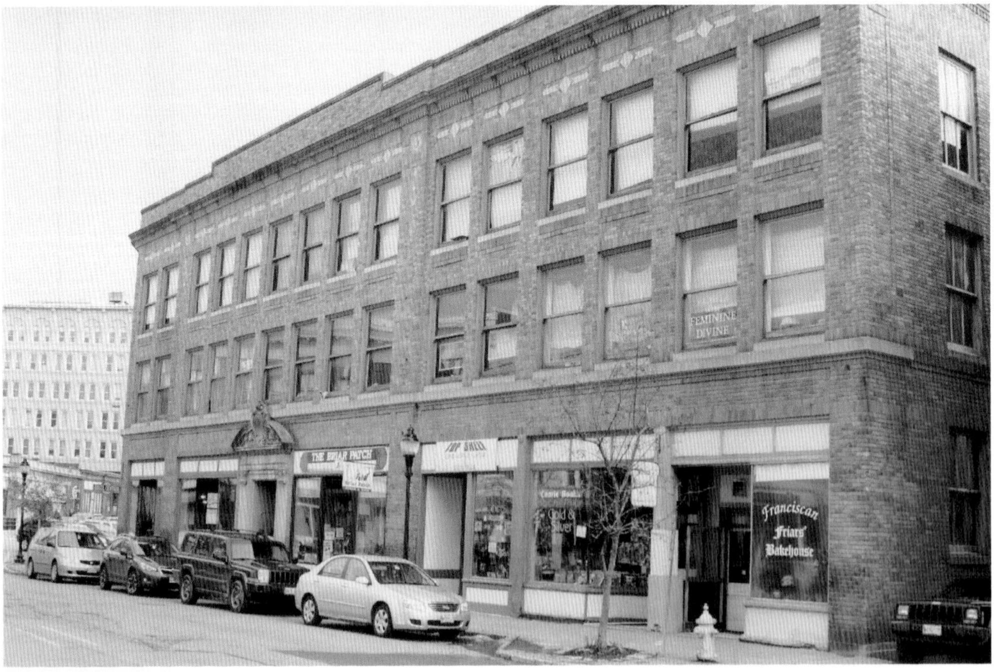

Well-Known Attorney

After graduating from Hampden Academy and Yale College, Charles Stetson was admitted to the bar in 1826. He relocated his law practice to Bangor in 1833. Stetson became Bangor's first municipal court judge in 1834. He held other local offices, served on the governor's executive council, and won election to Congress in 1849. His family's name lives on in the Stetson Block on Central Street in Bangor. (Courtesy of BFS.)

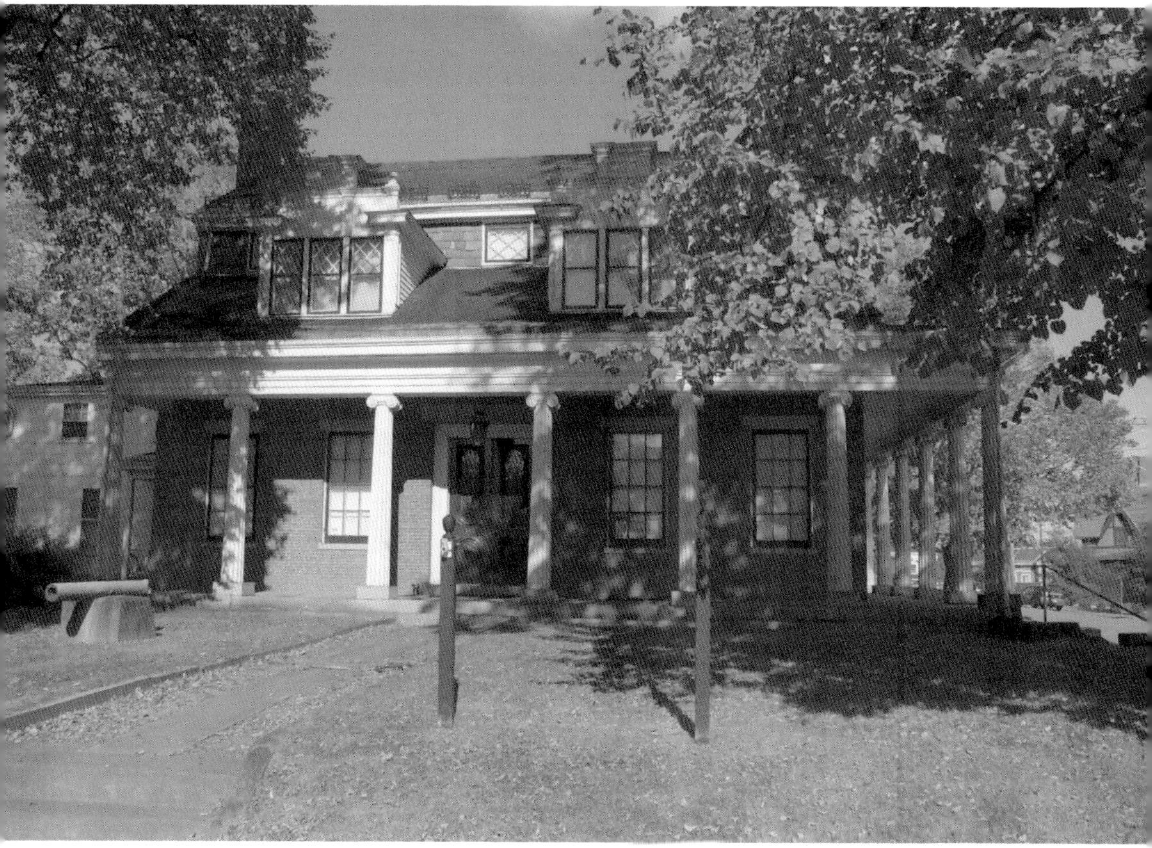

His Mansion Became a Museum

Attorney Thomas Adams Hill inadvertently left Bangor a museum.

Born in Sherburne, Massachusetts, in July 1783, Hill studied law in Vermont and gained admittance to the Massachusetts Bar at Augusta, District of Maine, in 1807. He moved to Bangor in 1810.

Hill was among the Bangor militiamen captured by British troops occupying the city in September 1814. Afterwards, Hill became a wealthy man by diligently practicing law and investing in real estate, including a Kenduskeag Stream toll bridge and the first brick stores erected on Bangor's West Side. He also helped start Bangor's first newspaper.

Hill built a stately brick mansion at High and Union Streets. He died in 1864; the Sons of Union Veterans acquired the mansion in 1944. Today, the Thomas A. Hill House is home to the Bangor Historical Society Museum. (Courtesy of BFS.)

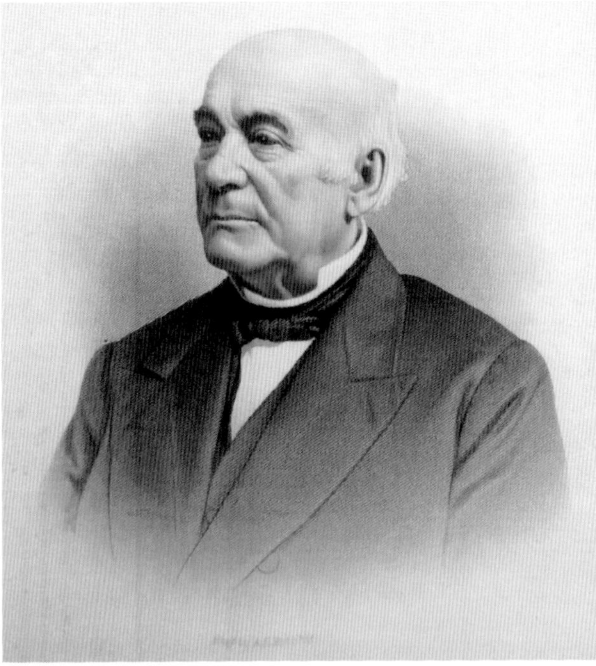

Law or Medicine?

Bangor benefited when Sumner Laughton decided to pursue medicine rather than the law. He was studying for both professions in 1830 when he decided to become a doctor. A graduate of the Bowdoin College Medical Department, Laughton practiced medicine elsewhere in the Penobscot Valley before opening a general practice in Bangor in 1849. He treated thousands of patients during his almost 50 years as a doctor. (Courtesy of HPCM.)

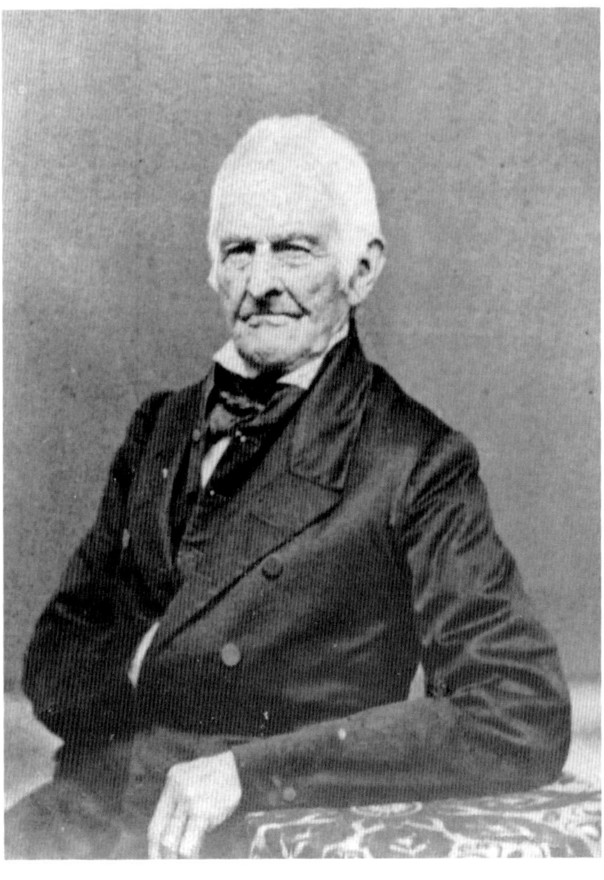

Two Brothers Backed Bangor

Brothers Amos and Moses Patten were deeply involved in Bangor's early development. Successful and hardworking businessmen, the Pattens lent their talents to governing the new town. Voters elected Amos town clerk in 1801 and selectman in 1802 and kept returning Moses (left) to office as a selectman from 1808 to 1818. Although the War of 1812 all but wiped them out financially, the Pattens prospered afterwards. (Courtesy of BPL.)

CHAPTER TWO

Military Achievers

In times of local, regional, or national trouble, Bangor residents have never looked far to find their heroes. Since Colonial times, men and women from Bangor have "rallied round the flag" to defend their homes, state, and country. When British troops landed at Winterport in September 1814 and marched north to capture a damaged American warship in Hampden, Bangor militiamen turned out to fight the red coats at the Battle of Hampden.

An American defeat, that battle led to enemy troops occupying Bangor and wreaking economic havoc on the town.

After Maine became a state, Bangor militiamen participated in the Bloodless Aroostook War of the 1830s. When Confederate troops fired on Fort Sumter in April 1861, Bangor men helped fill the ranks of the 2nd Maine Infantry Regiment and fought bravely at Manassas that July.

Surnames like Boutelle, Chaplin, Garnsey, Jameson, and Roberts became familiar to Bangoreans during the Civil War. Also a brilliant administrator, local attorney John Hodsdon served as Maine's adjutant general throughout the war. Bangor residents identified their slain heroes on the Soldiers' Monument erected at Mount Hope Cemetery in June 1864; the monument was the first such municipal monument to Civil War heroes.

Bangor's military achievers have appeared in every foreign war fought by the United States since the 1898 dust-up with the Kingdom of Spain. Called to active duty, National Guardsman Norman Dow was the first "Bangor boy" to die in far-off France during the Great War. Two Bangor sisters trained as nurses and cared for patients at an Allied hospital.

Two local brothers went to France, the older brother with the American Expeditionary Force and his younger sibling as a volunteer ambulance driver. The brothers' names might have been forgotten if the young brother had not become a world-famous painter in his own right.

America's involvement in World War II could not have occurred without military achievers from Bangor being present. While doing his job as an Army cook on Oahu on December 7, 1941, young Willard Orr of Bangor was killed in action.

A naval officer from Bangor was aboard a Navy battleship at Pearl Harbor that fateful Sunday morning. Surviving the Japanese attack, he went on to command a famous battleship in the various Pacific campaigns.

After graduating from a Bangor nursing school, Alice Zwicker joined the Army as a nurse. Captured by the Japanese in the Philippines, she endured years of captivity before gaining her freedom.

Killed in a mid-air collision not long before the United States joined the Allies in World War II, an Army pilot gave his name to a strategically located military airfield constructed in Bangor. That base later became Bangor International Airport.

The people introduced in this chapter are only representative of Bangor's heroic legends; many more military achievers have represented the Queen City in American history.

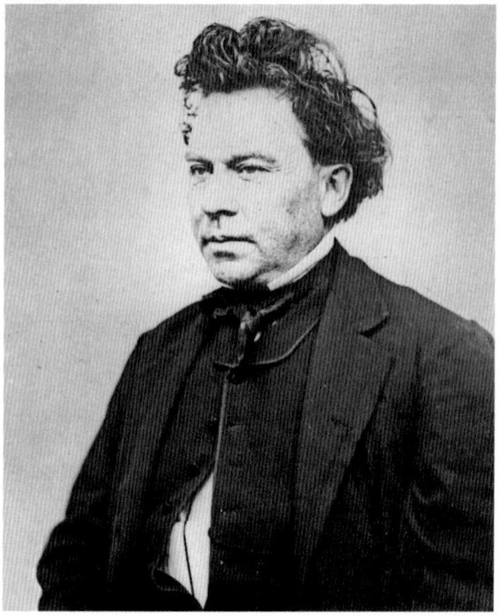

John Hodsdon Led Maine's War Effort

Four-year-old John Littlefield of Corinth was adopted by his stepfather, Capt. Isaac Hodsdon, and took his surname in 1820. Known forever afterwards as John L. Hodsdon, the boy became an attorney known for his integrity, work ethic, and attention to the details. All three attributes paid handsomely for Maine when the legislature named him adjutant general in 1861.

Hodsdon served with a local militia company and, later, practiced law in Bangor after moving there in 1834. Called up with the Maine militia, he gained valuable military administrative experience during the 1837 Aroostook War.

The Civil War found Maine almost totally unprepared for supplying even basic equipment, food, and shelter for the thousands of Mainers heading off to war. Militia supplies were kept in such old buildings as the arsenal located on Essex Street in Bangor (right, above). Based at the state house, Hodsdon and his talented clerical staff created almost overnight the administrative system needed to coordinate the state's extensive war efforts. Charged with procuring the clothing, weapons, and other gear needed by Maine soldiers, Hodsdon and his staff capably managed the huge amounts of correspondence engulfing the adjutant general's office. A typical day might see Hodsdon advertising to buy horses for a cavalry regiment, reading a general's report, and dictating or writing letters that dealt with mundane matters and heartbreak. A door knock might introduce a supplicant seeking an officer's commission or a heart-broken mother seeking news of a missing son. No matter who contacted him, even if from another state, Hodsdon turned no one away.

Some historians believe that Hodsdon filed away every bit of correspondence sent him; today the Maine State Archives preserves myriad reports and letters from Maine officers, politicians, ordinary soldiers, and civilians.

And out on the lines, Maine soldiers fighting in battles such as First Manassas (right, below) benefited as Hodsdon and his staff kept the administrative wheels turning as smoothly as possible. The legislature also named him the state's commissary general, paymaster general, acting quartermaster general, and inspector general.

Hodsdon worked diligently during the war. Despite his other duties, he compiled and published the annual Maine adjutant general's reports, which detailed the fates of the men and units that Maine sent to preserve the Union.

John L. Hodsdon lies buried in Mount Hope Cemetery. (Clockwise from above, courtesy of BPL; courtesy of RRS; courtesy of LOC.)

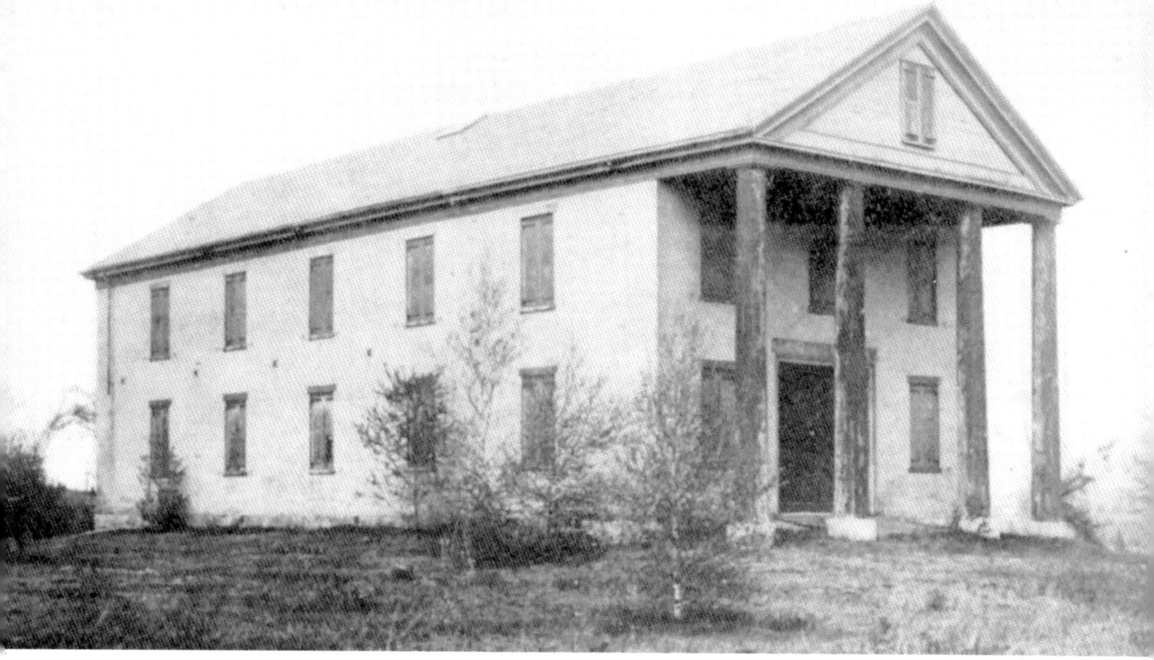

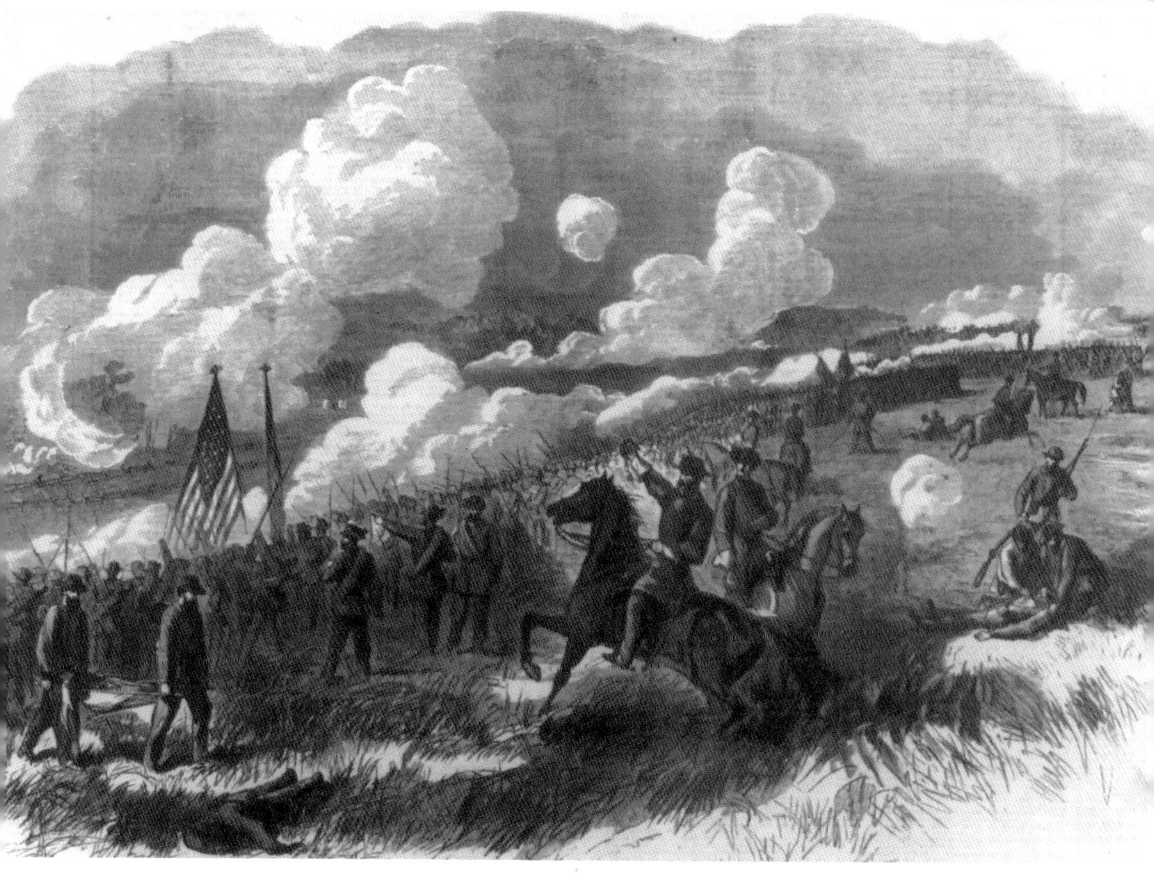

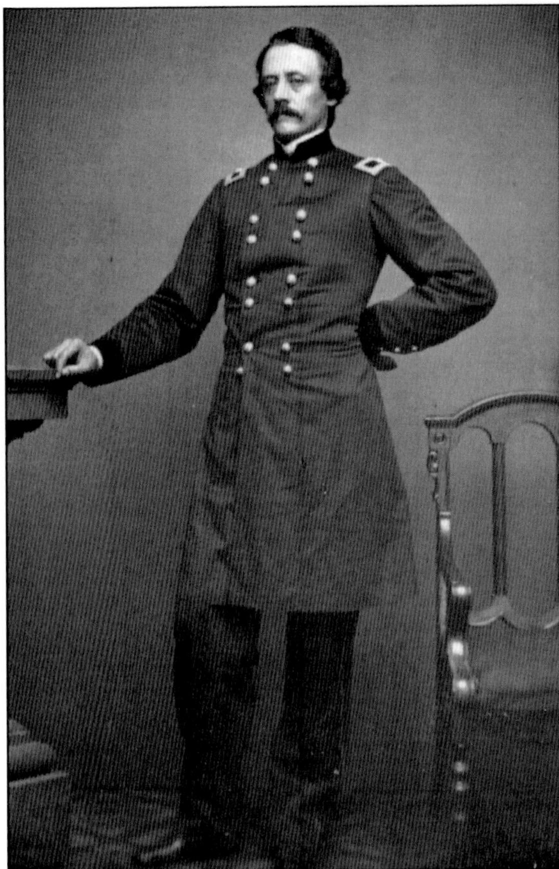

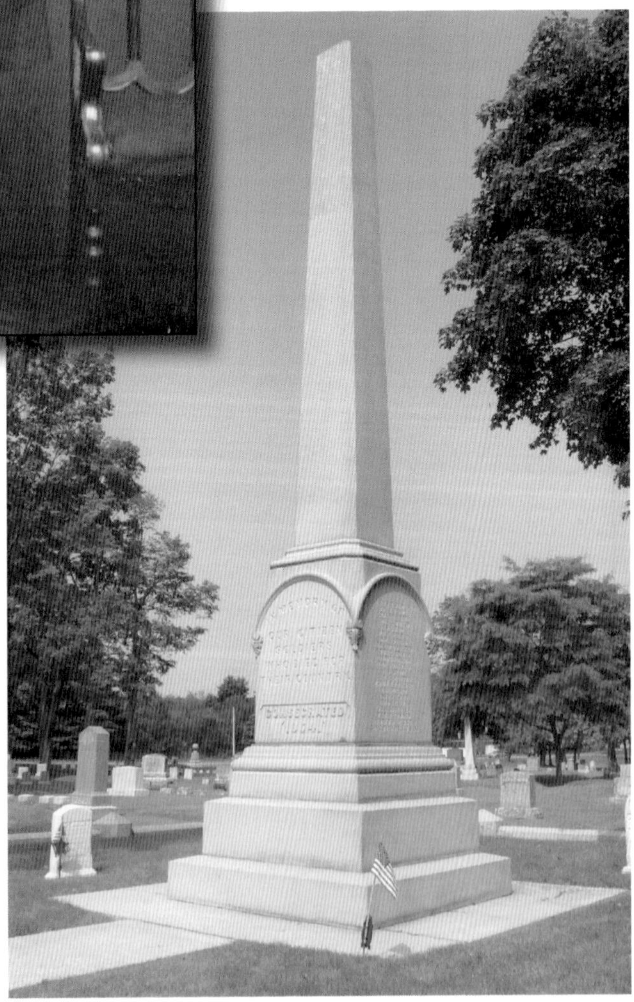

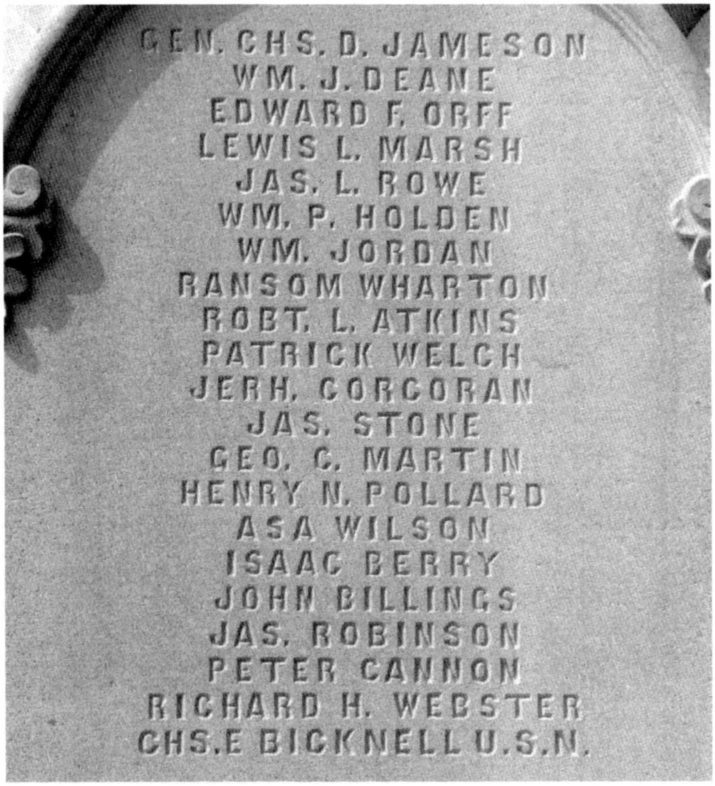

Brave as a Lion

Although he never was a Bangor boy, Charles Davis Jameson remains forever "etched" among the Queen City's heroes. Born in Gorham, Maine, on February 24, 1827, Jameson moved to Old Town while in his youth and, later, became involved in that city's extensive sawmill industry. In political inclinations a Democrat, he represented Maine at the April 1860 Democratic National Convention. In 1861, Jameson ran for governor as a "War Democrat" and lost to the Republican candidate.

Meanwhile, he helped form the 2nd Maine Infantry Regiment and, as its colonel, marched with it through the streets of Bangor as a pouring rain fell on May 14, 1861. The soldiers boarded a train in Bangor and headed south to war. Jameson so skillfully handled the 2nd Maine during the Battle of Bull Run in Virginia that he received a promotion to brigadier general. Taking command of a brigade of New York and Pennsylvania troops, he fought in the 1862 Peninsula Campaign.

At the Battle of Fair Oaks, a Pennsylvania captain saw Jameson "fighting like a tiger through that terrible afternoon, and passing through that storm of leaden hail, as if he never knew of danger." That fall, when Jameson fell seriously ill (likely with typhoid fever), that same captain noted that Jameson "looks very badly," and "I am afraid that we will may lose him. He is . . . as brave as a lion, and still as tender-hearted as a child." The brave general came home to die in Old Town on November 6, 1862. He lies buried there to this day.

But Bangor patriots never forgot Jameson. In 1863, they started raising funds to build a Soldiers' Monument at Mount Hope Cemetery on State Street. On a hot Friday, June 17, 1864, a long parade flowed along State Street from downtown Bangor to the cemetery, where ministers and politicians—including Vice Pres. Hannibal Hamlin—dedicated the monument.

The names of 55 Bangor men who died serving their country during the Civil War are etched on three sides of the monolith. The list begins on the north side, which faces upriver toward Old Town. At the top of the list is etched the name "Gen. Chs. D. Jameson." The brave general will be forever remembered in Bangor. (Clockwise from top left, courtesy of BPL; courtesy of BFS; courtesy of BFS.)

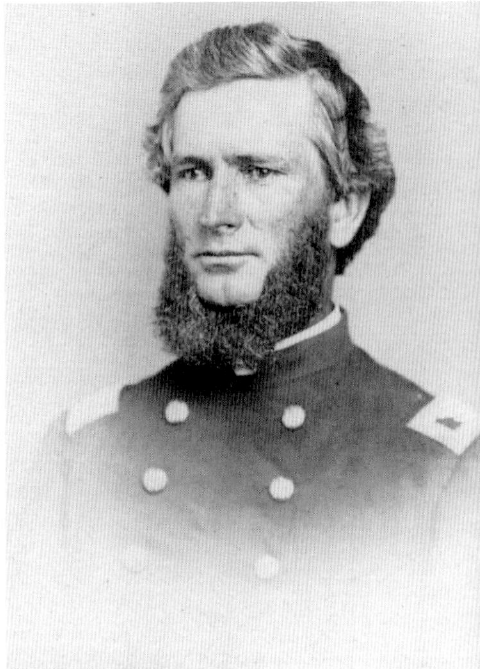

The Clerk Who Commanded Heroes

A Bangor store clerk, Daniel Chaplin quit his job and became a captain in the 2nd Maine Infantry Regiment. In 1862, he recruited men for the 18th Maine Infantry, which became the 1st Maine Heavy Artillery Regiment. Chaplin was its colonel.

On June 18, 1864, some 900 men from the 1st Maine charged Confederate defenses at Petersburg, Virginia. Within 10 minutes, 632 men were shot; afterwards, Chaplin cried over losing so many of his men. On August 17, while scanning enemy lines with his binoculars, he was fatally wounded by a bullet. "They have hit me this time," Chaplin said.

Regimental survivors later erected at Petersburg a monument at the site of their June 1864 charge. The monument lists the names of every 1st Maine HA soldier shot during that awful battle. (Right, courtesy of BPL; below, courtesy of BFS.)

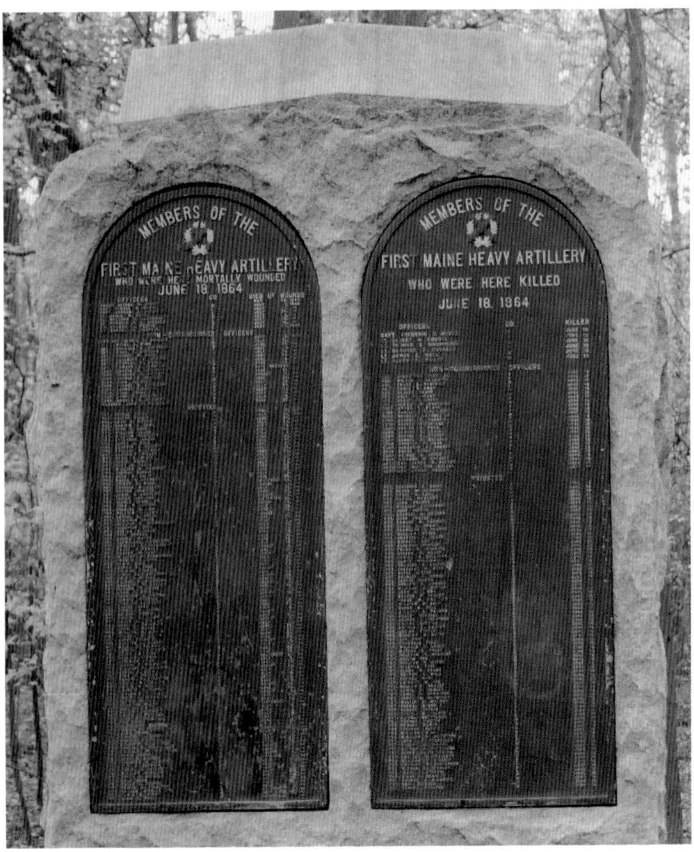

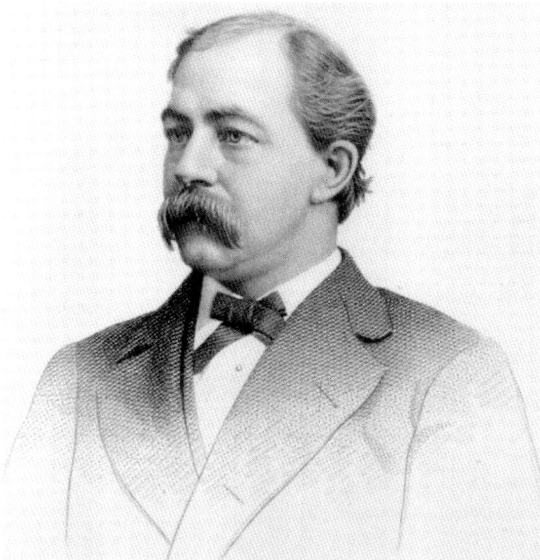

Sailor Turned Journalist

Born in Damariscotta in 1839, Charles A. Boutelle went to sea at age 15 with his shipmaster father. In 1862, he joined the Navy as an acting master aboard the USS *Paul Jones*. He later transferred to the USS *Sassacus*.

On May 5, 1864, the Confederate ironclad *Albemarle* attacked the Union fleet in Albemarle Sound. Boutelle oversaw the gun crews aboard the *Sassacus*, which rammed and almost sank the ironclad. He was cited in dispatches for his professionalism.

After working a few years in maritime shipping, Boutelle arrived in Bangor in 1870 as managing editor of the *Whig & Courier* newspaper. He and Benjamin Burr bought the newspaper in 1874. A *New York Telegram* article later described Boutelle's "style of writing" as "chaste and cultured, as it is pointed and vigorous." (Both, courtesy of BPL.)

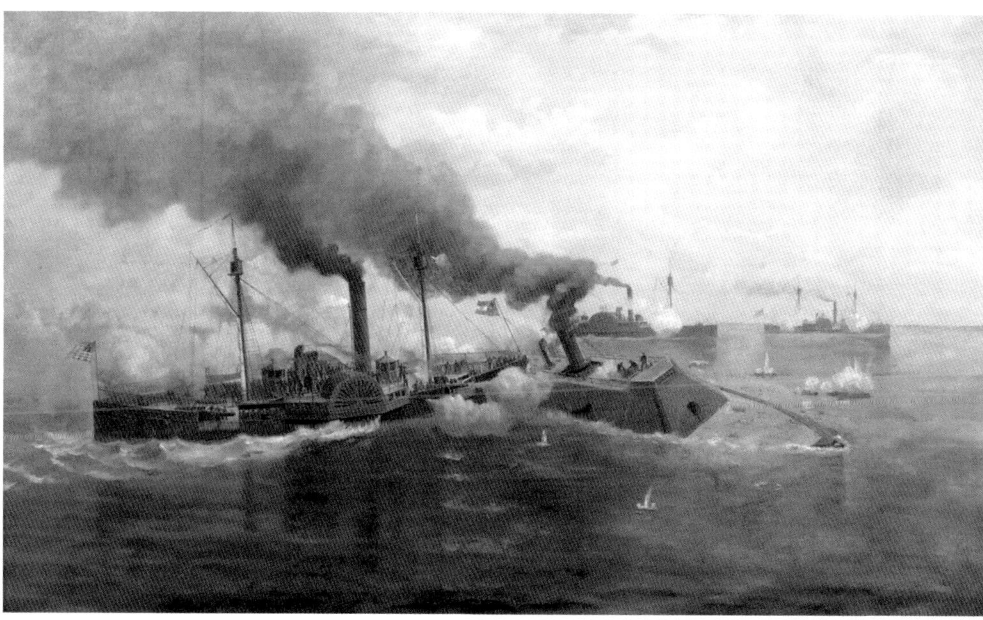

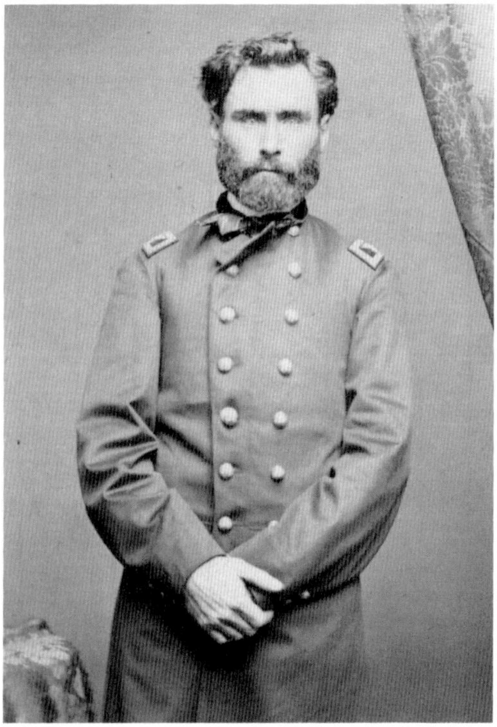

"Whizzing about and around Us"

When he had to choose between duty and self, Charles Wentworth Roberts decided to defend his country. Born into the family of wealthy Bangor lumber baron Amos Main Roberts, Charles W. Roberts studied at Bowdoin College in Brunswick. He was well respected in Bangor, where he worked as a merchant and served as a lieutenant colonel in a militia regiment.

When Adjutant General Hodsdon (see page 24) formed the 2nd Maine Infantry Regiment from several militia companies in the spring of 1861, Gov. Israel Washburn Jr. named Roberts as the unit's lieutenant colonel. Ironically, Washburn was a Republican, and Roberts was a so-called "War Democrat," a member of that faction of the Democratic Party that favored waging war to preserve the Union.

The soldiers of Company A, 2nd Maine Infantry Regiment (opposite page) were drawn from a Bangor militia company. These men knew Roberts quite well, and vice versa. Roberts survived the July 21 battle at Manassas, Virginia, unscathed, but a bullet knocked down the horse he was riding.

That August, Roberts was involved in putting down a major mutiny by many 2nd Maine Infantry soldiers. The innocent were punished along with the guilty, he believed, telling Governor Washburn that "some Sea Campers and Lazy Landlubbers, who have for a long time been stirring this question, like cowards returned to the ranks" and stirred trouble.

Promoted to colonel in the fall of 1861, Roberts commanded the 2nd Maine for more than 18 months. On Saturday, April 5, 1862, he led the regiment into action near Yorktown, Virginia.

Advancing along muddy roads, Roberts and men arrived opposite a Confederate fort about noon and deployed in a cornfield. During the noisy, but effectively harmless shooting that followed, Roberts noticed "several winged messages of death . . . whizzing about and around us," he later told his brigade commander.

On Wednesday, April 9, Roberts and his men enjoyed a pleasant break from the war after arriving "at our present safe and pleasant camping ground." Falling ill in spring 1863, Roberts resigned that June and returned to Bangor. The Second Empire–style house that he later built on State Street still stands. Roberts lost his one electoral bid to become Maine's governor. After his death in 1898, he was buried at Mount Hope Cemetery in Bangor. (Both, courtesy of BPL.)

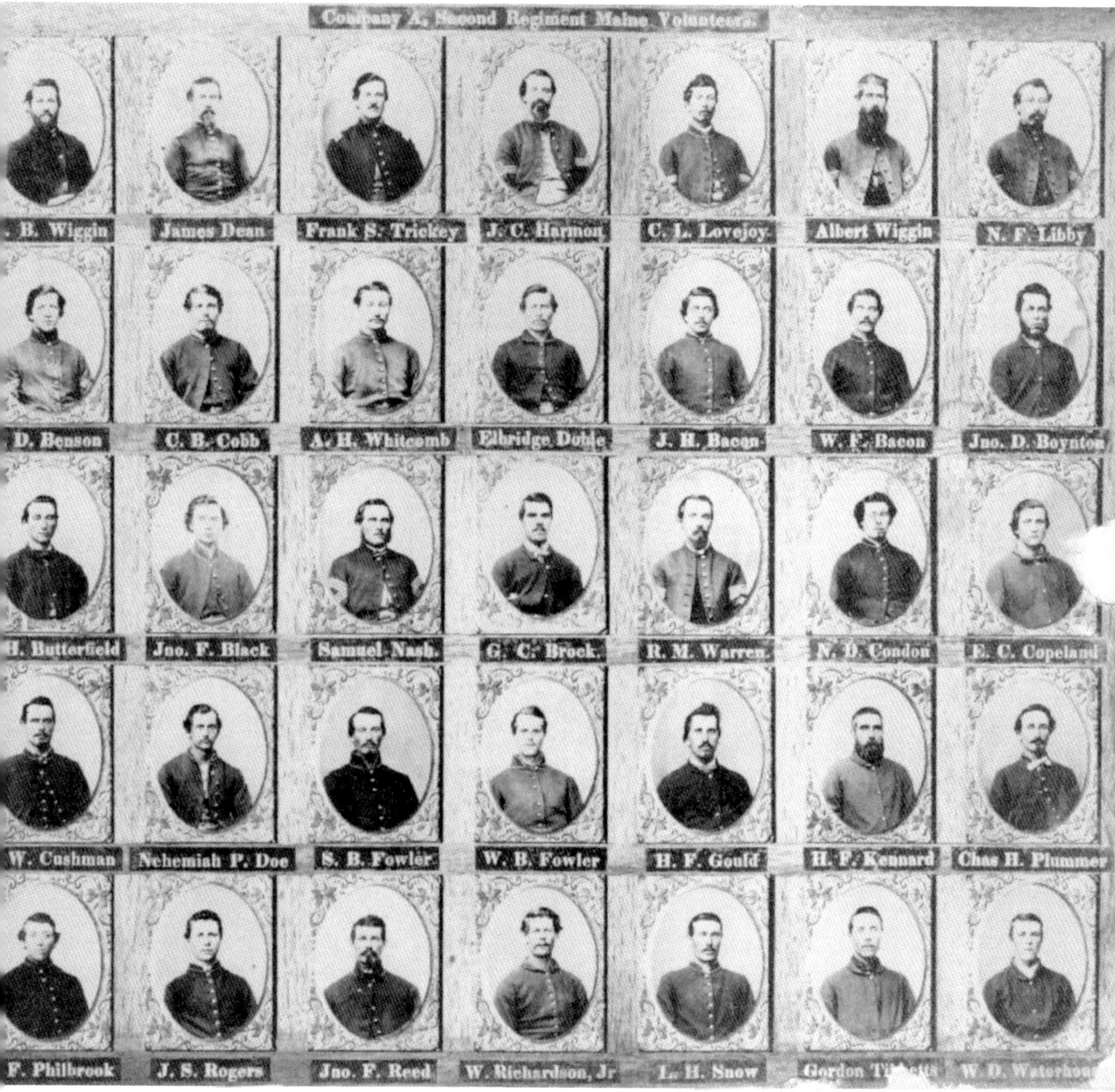
Company A, Second Regiment Maine Volunteers.
B. Wiggin
James Dean
Frank S. Trickey
J. C. Harmon
C. L. Lovejoy
Albert Wiggin
N. F. Libby
D. Benson
C. B. Cobb
A. H. Whitcomb
Elbridge Doble
J. H. Bacon
W. F. Bacon
Jno. D. Boynton
H. Butterfield
Jno. F. Black
Samuel Nash
G. C. Brock
R. M. Warren
N. D. Condon
E. C. Copeland
W. Cushman
Nehemiah P. Doe
S. B. Fowler
W. B. Fowler
H. F. Gould
H. F. Kennard
Chas H. Plummer
F. Philbrook
J. S. Rogers
Jno. F. Reed
W. Richardson, Jr
L. H. Snow
Gordon
W. D.

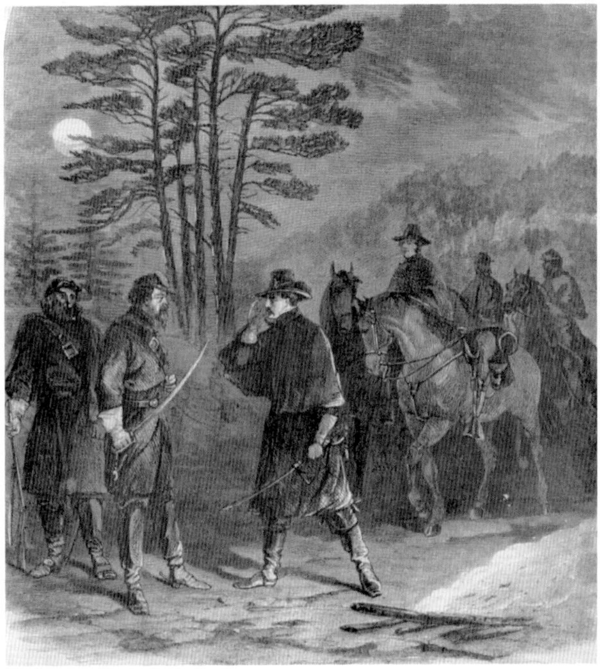

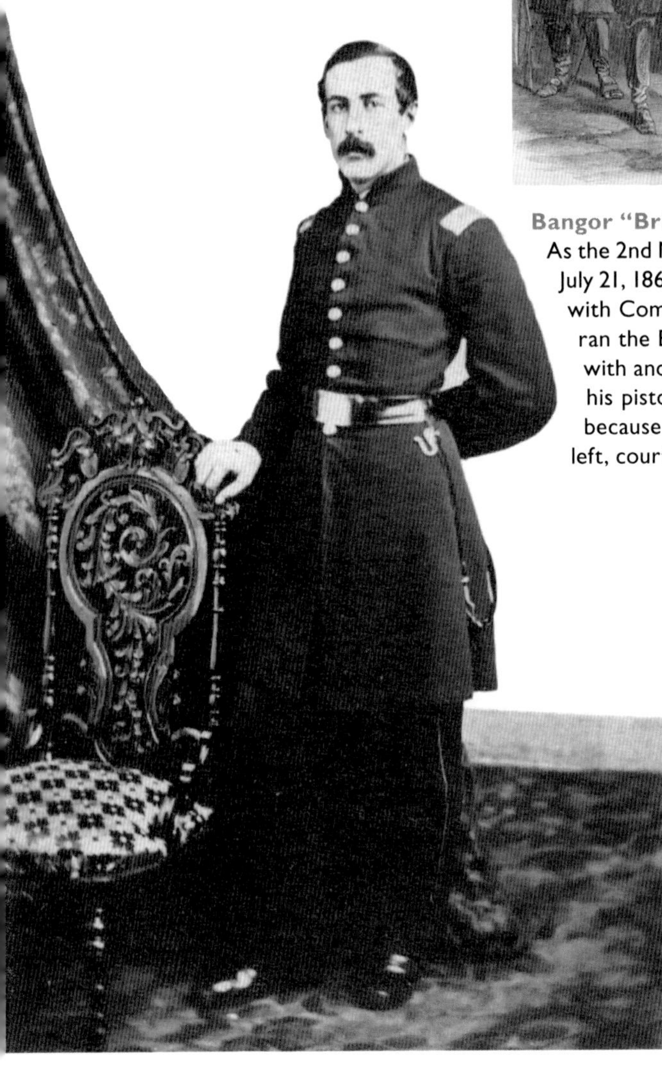

Bangor "Brick"

As the 2nd Maine Infantry fought at Manassas, Virginia, on July 21, 1861, Frank Garnsey served as a second lieutenant with Company G. He was a son of privilege; his father ran the Bangor House. Watching Garnsey (splattered with another soldier's blood) climb a rail fence to fire his pistol at the enemy, his men called him a "brick" because he was so steadfast. (Right, courtesy of LOC; left, courtesy of BPL .)

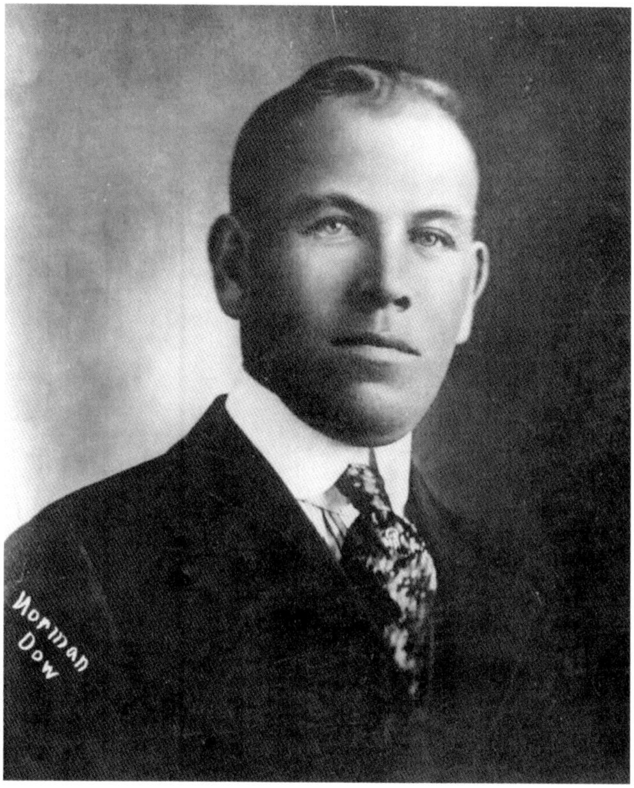

A Glorious Death

After the United States declared war on Germany in April 1917, many National Guard units were activated to flesh out the understrength Army. The 31-year-old Norman N. Dow, who worked for Swift & Company in Bangor, left home with the Bangor Machine Gun Company. He was originally from Princeton.

Dow went over to France with the 103rd Infantry Regiment, which traced its lineage to the 2nd Maine Infantry Regiment formed in Bangor in spring 1861. As part of the 26th Division, the regiment deployed into the trenches of France in early February 1918.

On Friday, May 10, Dow and his comrades were involved in "some big fighting," Bangor soldier Ruby Urban Leavitt wrote his mother seven days later. He was recuperating "in a hospital from the effect of [poison] gas."

During the attack, "every man (including Dow) stood by his [machine] gun," Leavitt wrote. German artillery pounded the positions held by the Bangor Machine Gun Company, which took casualties.

"I suppose you know by this time that Norman Dow has gone," Leavitt noted. "High explosives got him. He was right at his gun and in the thick of intense fire when he fell—he lived a few hours after, but did not regain consciousness."

Word soon reached Dow's four brothers (three were in the military) and four sisters (Dow's parents were dead) that he had been killed in action. Dow and Kenneth Klein, whose parents lived on Essex Street, were the first two Bangor men to die during World War I; their names appeared on the same casualty list released by the Army on Wednesday, May 15.

Dow "was well known and held in the highest regard by many friends, for his fine character, high integrity, [and] genial and cheerful disposition," the *Bangor Daily News* noted. Dow belonged to the Columbia Street Baptist Church and the Daniel Chaplin Chapter, Sons of Union Veterans.

"We all miss Normie—he was such a great pal, but, mother, his was a glorious death," Ruby Leavitt told his mother, who lived on Cottage Street in Bangor. The Veterans of Foreign Wars later named its Bangor post, No. 1761, for Norman N. Dow. (Courtesy of BPL.)

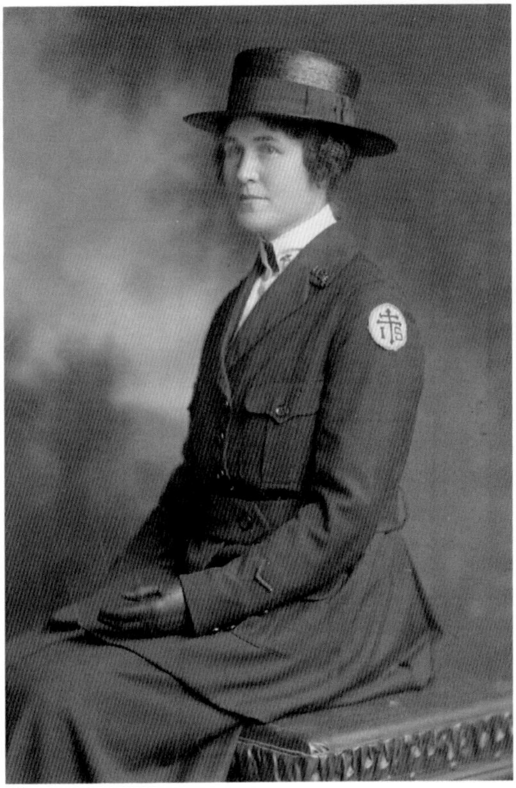

Sister Nurses

American men lived because sisters Alice and Sarah MacMullen left 11 Boynton Street in Bangor for France during World War I.

Born in New Brunswick—Alice in 1879 and Sarah in 1881—the MacMullens received their diplomas from the Eastern Maine General Hospital School of Nursing. As Red Cross nurses, they joined the Army at Fort Sam Houston in Texas in August 1917 and left for France a year later.

The MacMullens worked in a hospital complex where there were "20,000 Americans there at a time," Alice, pictured left, noted. "There never were such boys as those American soldiers, never."

Sarah, seen below, agreed. "There were never soldiers or men . . . half so eager to get well, so they could go back to fight again," she commented.

The sisters returned to Bangor on Wednesday, May 14, 1919. (Both, courtesy of BPL.)

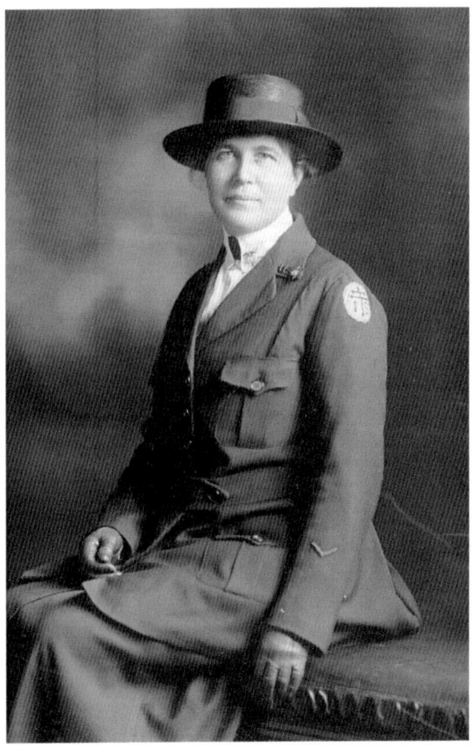

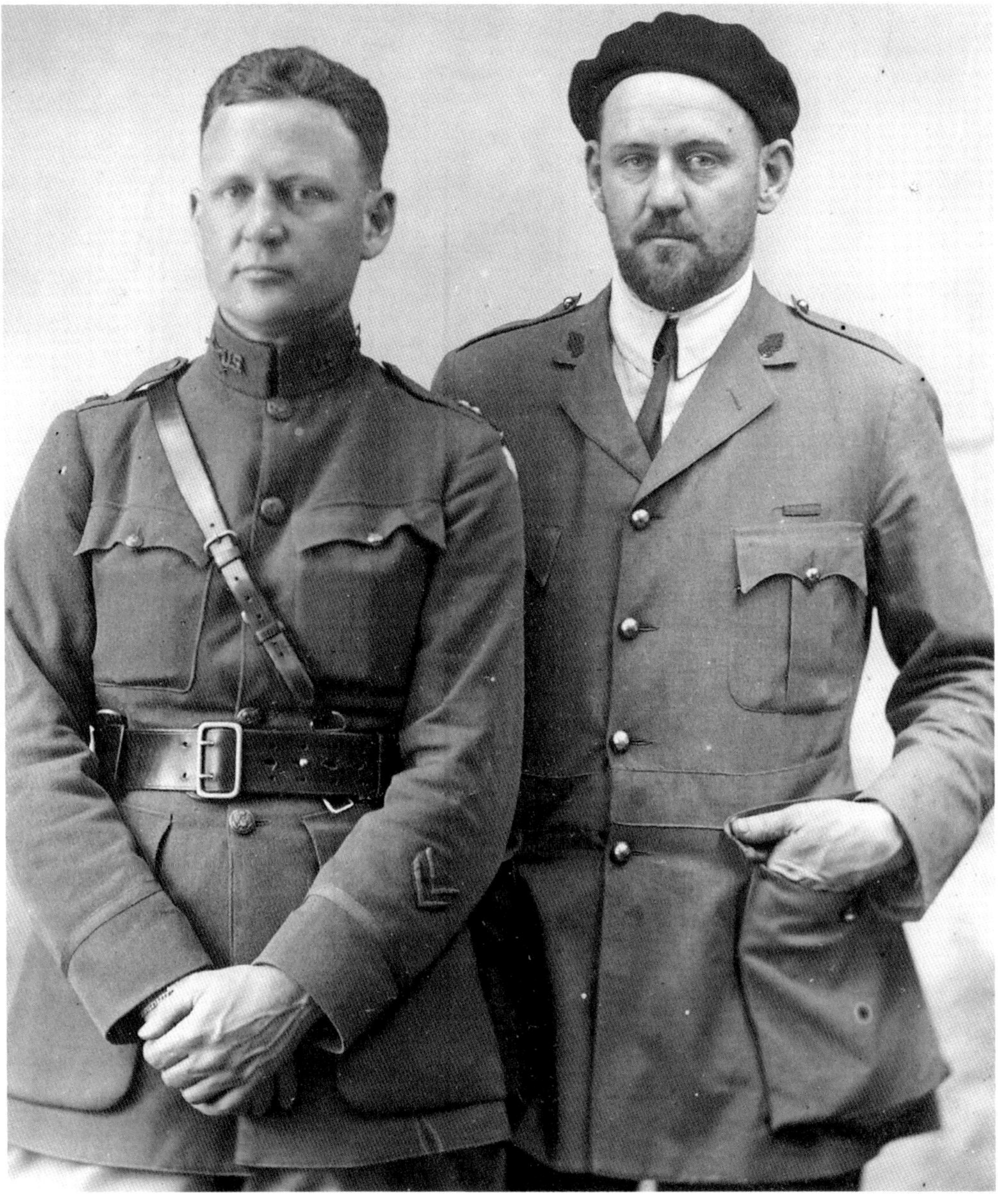

Peirce Brothers Served Their Country

Artist Waldo Peirce (right) and his older brother, Hayford, both served in France during World War I. The sons of Mellen and Anna Hayford Peirce, the brothers lived at 214 Cedar Street on Bangor's West Side. Both attended Bangor schools, Milton Academy, and Harvard University.

Hayford arrived at the American Expeditionary Force headquarters in France in December 1917. Commissioned a first lieutenant in March 1918, he oversaw intelligence efforts involving photographs provided by aerial reconnaissance. Promoted to captain, Hayford was sent to Berlin on assignment in 1919.

Waldo Peirce volunteered as an ambulance driver for the French army in 1915 and earned the Croix de Guerre for his services during the Battle of Verdun. He was attached to the French army in 1917 "for painting war notes at the front," according to his mother. (Courtesy of BPL.)

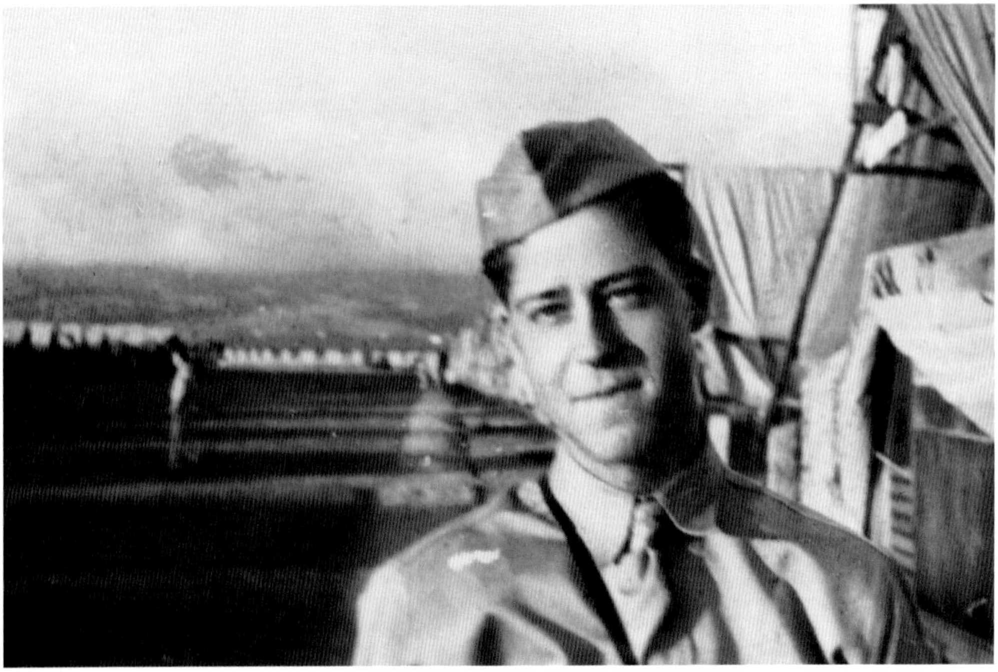

Supreme Sacrifice at Pearl Harbor

The supreme sacrifice made by Willard Carleton Orr helped propel the United States into World War II. Born in Bangor on April 12, 1920, "W. Carleton," as he identified himself, attended the Sherburne School from 1926 to 1932 and the Hannibal Hamlin School from 1932 to 1934. Then, he went to Bangor High School, located on Harlow Street. A debater and essayist, Orr also belonged to the National Honor Society.

According to Eva Orr, his mother, he "was active in the Dramatic Club and Latin Club" while at Bangor High, from which he graduated in 1939. "His principal [*sic*] love was debating and as class debater and tournament debater he was awarded a certificate of honor cum laude."

"He was a member of All Souls Congregational Church in Bangor" and was "very active in the young people's fellowship," Eva Orr remembered. Her son's hobbies included collecting poems and stamps, reading, fishing, swimming, and writing essays.

After high school, Orr worked briefly as a clerk for a local "market gardener" (or landscaper). He joined the US Army as a private on December 23, 1939. The Army trained him as a cook, promoted him to private first class about a year later, and then sent him to Hawaii (above).

Stationed at Hickam Field in Honolulu, Orr served as the head cook for the Headquarters and Headquarters Squadron, 17th Air Base Group. Island duty probably seemed like paradise for the young soldier from Bangor. Absent in Hawaii's balmy climate were the cold and snow of a Maine winter, and duty at Hickam Field was not that stressful.

All of that changed when Japanese naval aircraft (opposite, above) attacked American military bases on Oahu on Sunday, December 7, 1941. When torpedo bombers targeted the warships moored along "Battleship Row" at Pearl Harbor (opposite, below), dive-bombers attacked and strafed Army and Navy airfields.

Due to its proximity to Pearl Harbor, Hickam Field received extensive attention. Enemy bombs flattened the barracks and other facilities. Among the 139 Americans killed during the attack on Hickam was Willard Carleton Orr, serial No. 6149312-AC. The United States declared war on Japan on December 8, 1941.

Willard Carleton Orr was awarded a Purple Heart, a Certificate of Honor, and a Citation of Memorial. The City of Bangor later named a Kenduskeag Stream footbridge for him. (Clockwise from above, courtesy of BPL; courtesy of LOC; courtesy of LOC.)

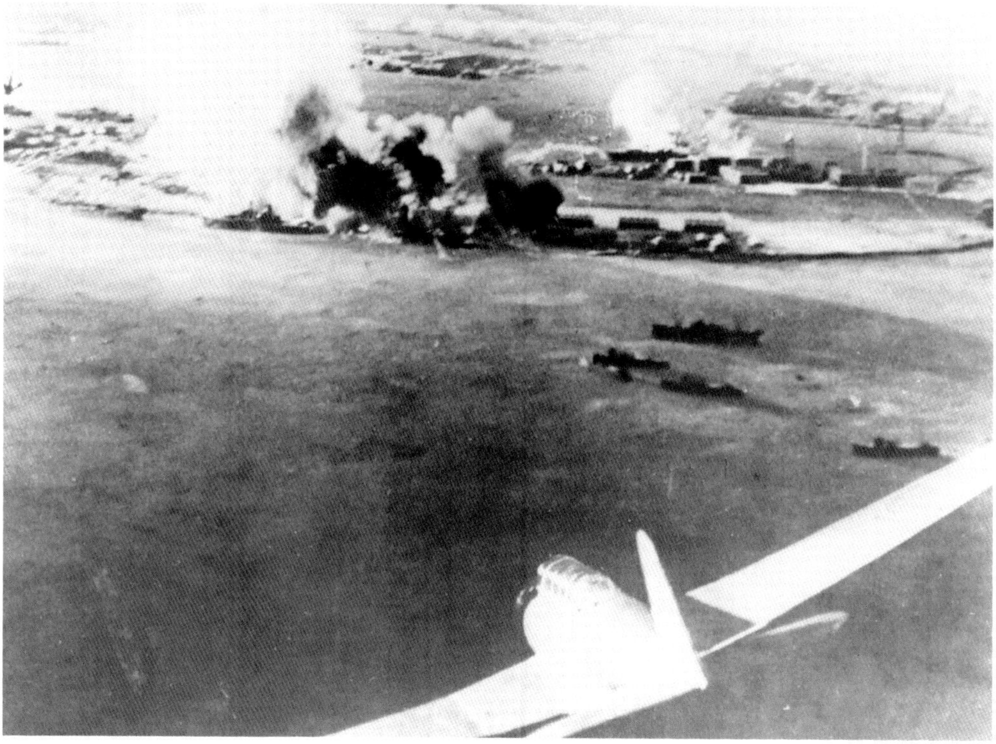

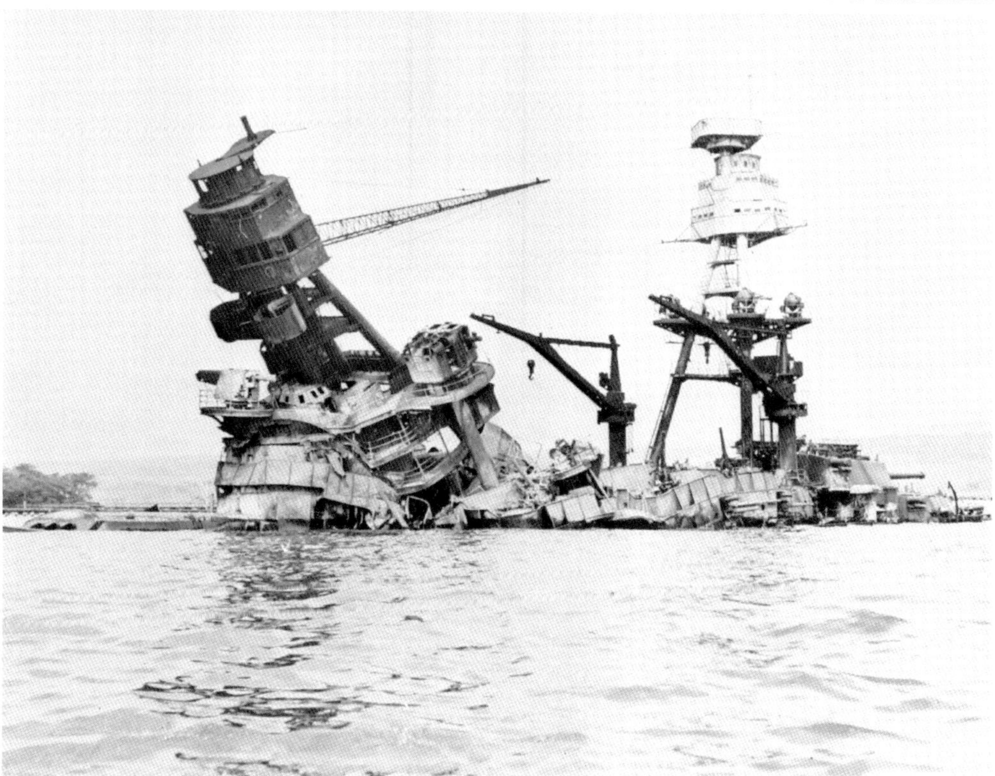

Prisoner of War

When she signed on the dotted line to join the US Army, nurse Alice Zwicker never figured that her enlistment would include duty in a Japanese prisoner-of-war camp.

After studying nursing at the Eastern Maine General Hospital in Bangor, Zwicker (below, left) joined the Army Nurse Corps as a second lieutenant. Originally from Brownville, she was stationed in the Philippines when Japanese forces attacked on December 8, 1941.

Most American and Filipino troops surrendered at Bataan on April 9, 1942, but a few thousand men held out on nearby Corregidor Island in Manila Bay. Working in horrible conditions, Zwicker and other nurses—53 Americans and 26 Filipinas—cared for the large numbers of wounded men.

Japanese artillery and aircraft pounded the men and women trapped on Corregidor Island. Zwicker foresaw that surrender was inevitable; there was no hope of rescue. "Even all the rumors of what the Japanese may do to all of us and especially the women mean little or nothing to me at the present," she confided to her diary. "Just end this awful destruction and find help for these patients who need the barest essentials so badly."

Zwicker became a prisoner of war of the Japanese in early May 1942. She survived the increasingly hellish conditions at the infamous Santo Tomas prison camp in Manila until the camp's liberation by American troops in early February 1945.

Zwicker soon donned an Army uniform and rejoined the service. Her repatriation was quick; flown to Dow Army Air Base in Bangor, a happy Zwicker smiled and waved as she left the transport plane and reunited with her parents, Mary and James Zwicker of Brownville (opposite page).

The 1945 Eastern Maine General Report noted that "following the liberation of the Philippines we were more than grateful to have one of our nurses, Lt. Alice Zwicker . . . return to us safely and on April 19, a testimonial dinner was given Lt. Zwicker by the trustees, medical staff and personnel staff."

An impressive monument to "The Angels of Bataan and Corregidor" was dedicated on Corregidor on May 6, 2000. Representing Bangor and Maine on the monument is the engraved name of "2nd Lt Alice Zwicker McAlevey." (All, courtesy of Rod Tenney.)

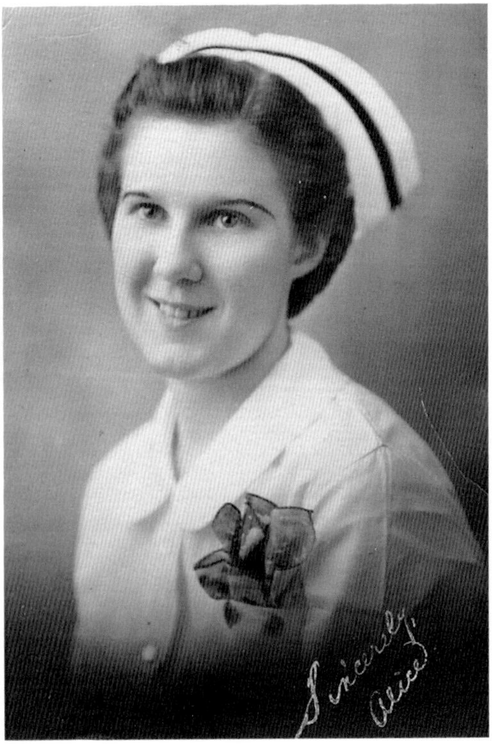

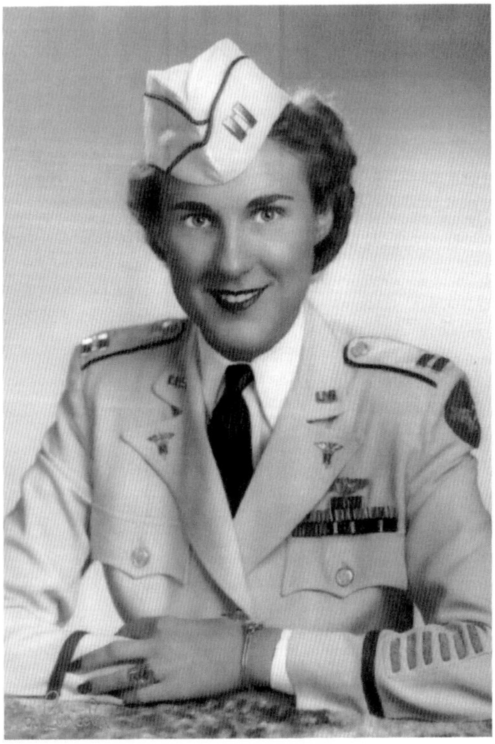

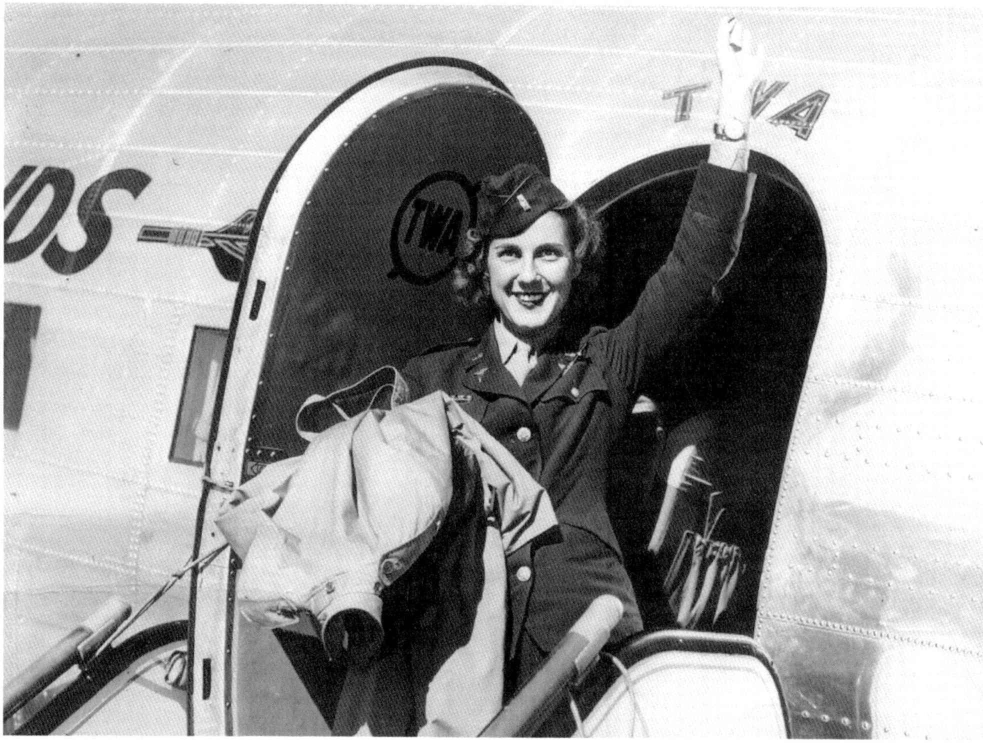
TWA
TWA

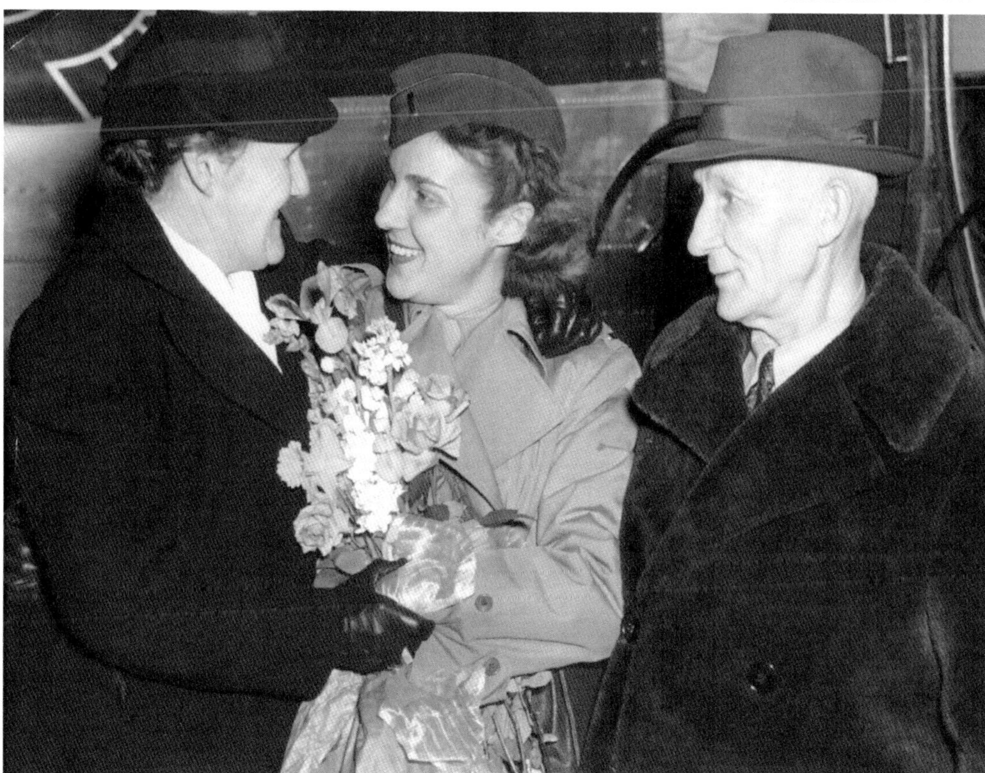

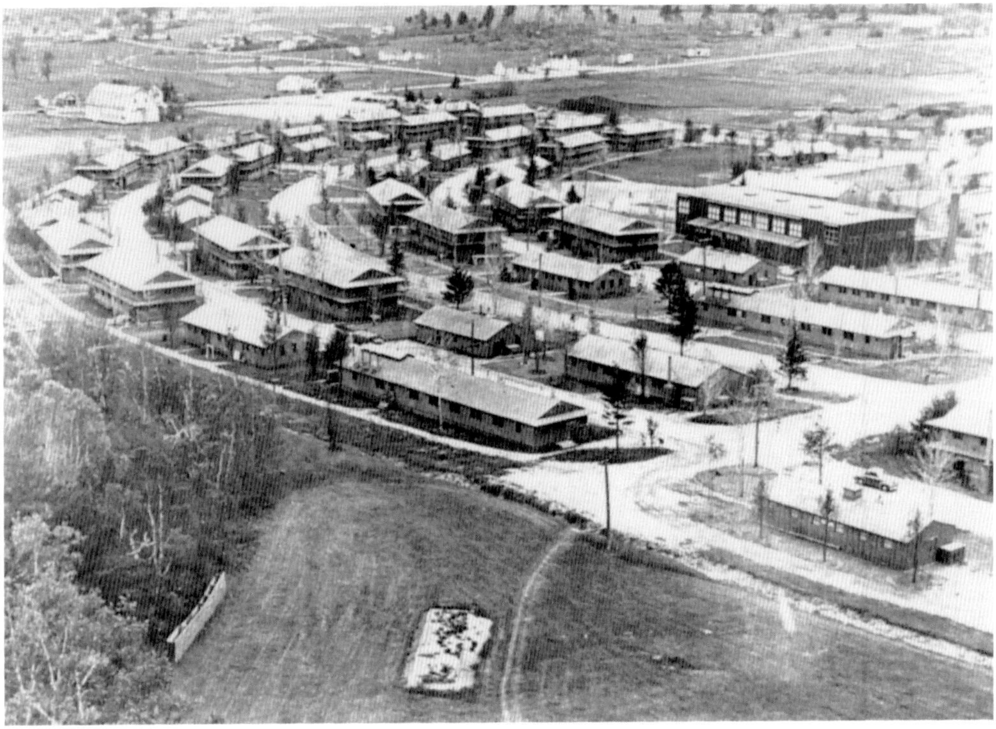

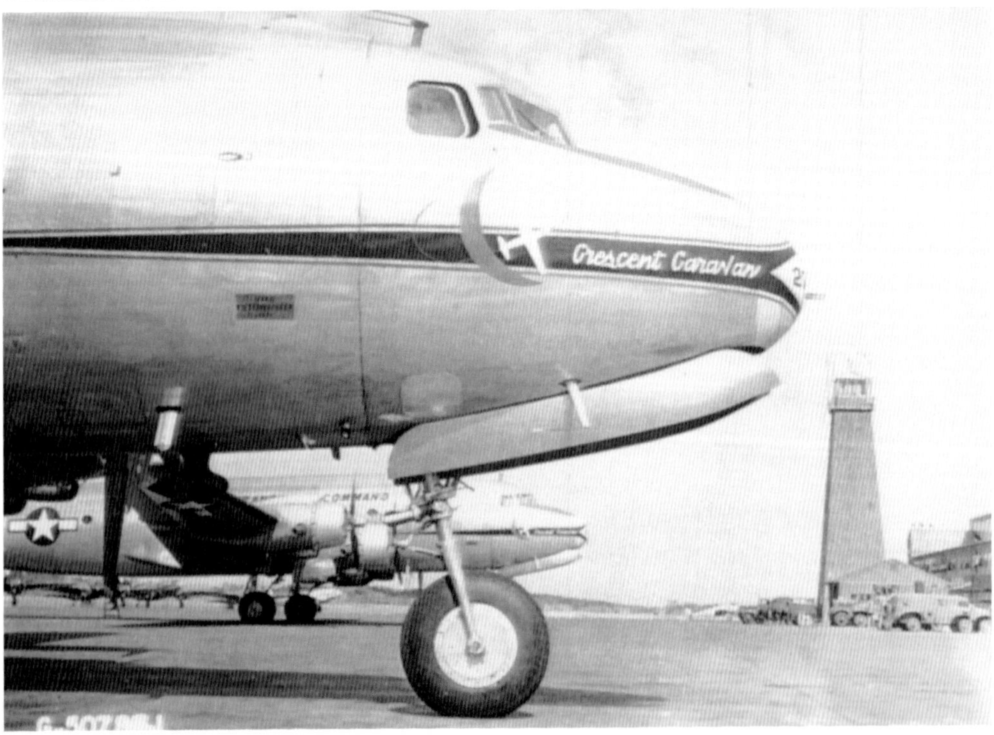
Crescent Caravan
COMMAND

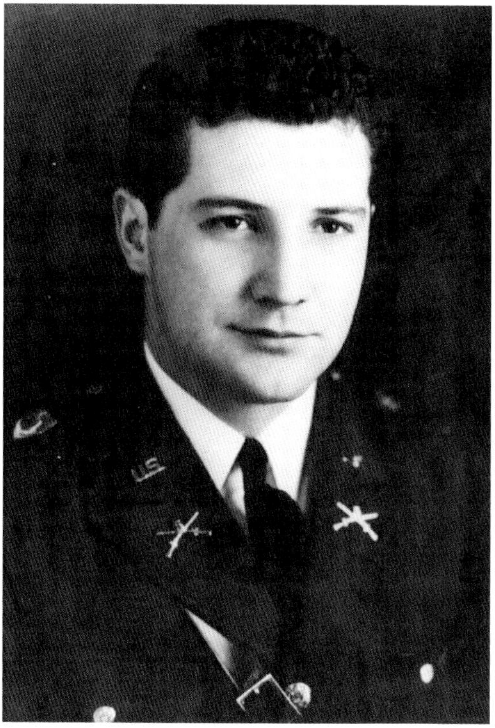

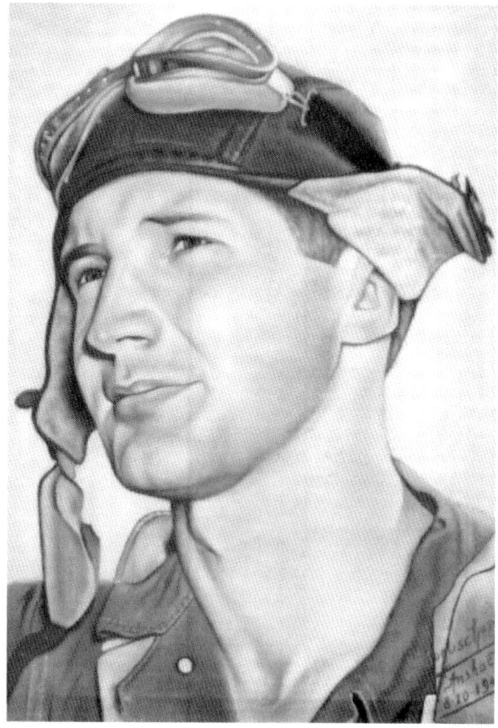

A Love of Flight

James Frederick Dow loved to fly—and his legacy lives on at Bangor International Airport. Hailing from Oakfield, Dow graduated from Houlton High School in the early 1930s and played football at the University of Maine, from which he graduated in 1937. He then learned how to fly via the Civilian Pilot Training Program operated by Parks Air College.

Dow joined the Army Reserve, then completed military flight training at Randolph Field in San Antonio, Texas; there he received his pilot's wings and a commission as a second lieutenant in March 1940.

Unfortunately, while on a training flight over Queens, New York, on Monday, June 17, 1940, the 26-year-old Dow "was flying a B-18 in formation when two of the planes hit each other," recalls Bangor historian David Bergquist. "Both pilots were conscious and able to maneuver their planes so that no houses were hit when they crashed." Dow and nine other aviators were killed.

Early the next year, the Army started building an airstrip at Godfrey Field, the civilian airport that had served Bangor for the last 20 years or so. Known originally as the Bangor Army Cantonment, the fledgling base was redesignated Dow Field in January 1942.

According to Bergquist, Dow Field (opposite page) was a major base for aircraft (especially bombers) and crews staging to Allied bases in Europe. He estimated that some 7,000 aircraft and at least 100,000 air-crew members staged through Bangor during the war.

After abandoning Dow Field postwar, the Air Force reopened the facility as Dow Air Force Base in the late 1940s. Stationing various units—including the 75th Fighter-Interceptor Wing and the 397th Bomb Wing—at Dow, the Air Force rebuilt the World War II–era base and lengthened the runway to 11,100 feet to accommodate B-52G Stratofortress jet bombers.

After the Air Force closed Dow AFB in mid-1968, the City of Bangor acquired the facility and renamed it Bangor International Airport. Today, major airlines use the domestic and international terminals, and the airport is a major departure point for travelers from Maine and the Canadian Maritimes.

The military legacy established by James Dow lives on in the Air and Army National Guard flying units stationed at Bangor International Airport. (Clockwise from top left: courtesy of RRS; courtesy of BPL; courtesy of Bangor International Airport; courtesy of RRS.)

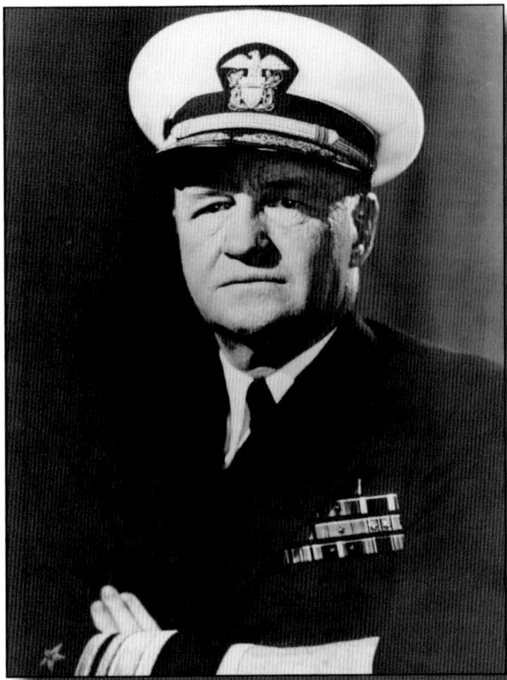

Blue-Water Sailor

The Imperial Japanese Navy made an enemy by bombing Cmdr. Carl Frederick Holden at Pearl Harbor on December 7, 1941.

A native of Bangor, Holden served on destroyers after graduating from the Naval Academy in 1917. He first commanded the USS *Mason* in 1920 and pursued his naval career during the following decades.

Holden was serving as executive officer aboard the USS *Pennsylvania*, a battleship, when the Japanese attacked Pearl Harbor. His ship was damaged during the battle, and Holden survived to fill several vital positions during the next four years. Named captain of the new battleship USS *New Jersey* (below) in 1943, Holden was promoted to rear admiral in 1945 and was placed in charge of Cruiser Division Pacific. He watched the Japanese surrender ceremonies at Tokyo in 1945. (Left, courtesy of BPL; below, courtesy of US Navy.)

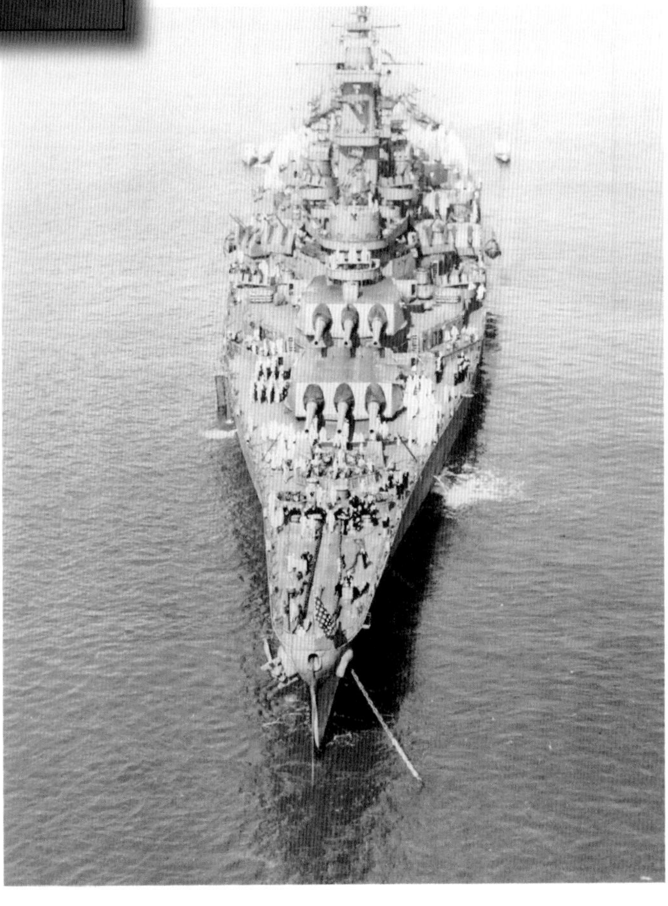

CHAPTER THREE

Household Names

Almost 250 years have passed since the first settler built a log cabin and called Bangor "home." Countless families have done so since then, and their memories live on as legendary household names in the Queen City.

The stylishly clad gentleman strolling with his cane in hand on Kenduskeag Mall in downtown Bangor represents one such name. An attorney and a US senator long before Abraham Lincoln selected him as a vice presidential running mate in 1860, Hannibal Hamlin was the scion of a famous clan that populated Bangor for two generations. He and his two wives—and there lies an interesting tale in itself—had a total of seven children, some of whom lived in Bangor for many years. Today, the Hannibal Hamlin statue on the mall recalls the Hamlin family.

Everyone growing up in Bangor from the 1920s through the early 1980s will remember Freese's, the six-story department store that towered above Main Street and Pickering Square. A. Langdon Freese started the family-owned store in the late 19th century; although apartments and a children's museum now occupy the former store, older Bangoreans still refer to it as "the Freese's building."

Gen. Sam Veazie, a 19th-century wheeler-dealer in railroads, lumber, banks, and sawmills, took umbrage at the taxes that Bangor levied against his personal property. The affronted "General" literally took himself and a few thousand disaffected Bangoreans across a new town line by lopping off part of Bangor and naming it "Veazie."

The memory of Mabel Wadsworth, an early and vocal (and successful) advocate for women's health issues, lives on in a clinic on Mount Hope Avenue. A school built on Broadway in 1927 and still in use today honors Mary Snow, a Bangor School Department legend.

Although some folks might associate his surname with a Bangor college, Flavius Beal was a hard-charging entrepreneur who turned the failing Bangor House into a profitable operation and served Bangor as mayor in the 19th century.

And speaking of Beal College, higher-education proponent Mary Beal established the private college in 1891.

Some household names loom above people visiting downtown Bangor. Joseph Wheelwright was a co-owner of a new, four-story "stone" building erected next to West Market Square in 1859; today, that building houses a popular fashion store. The surname of Charles Stetson—Bangor judge and mayor, among other accomplishments—lives on with Central Street's Stetson Block.

Native son William Cohen literally walked his way to winning his first election to Congress and launching a successful political career that spanned several presidential administrations. Francis "Skip" Rist prepared and served sandwiches that made his East Side eatery a "must-stop" destination for hungry diners.

And other Bangor legends live on as household names.

Freese's

A major landmark on Main Street in Bangor, Freese's Department Store was literally the tallest such store in Bangor in the first three-quarters of the 20th century.

In March 1954, the store's employees gathered at the Lucerne Inn in Dedham for the company's annual banquet (opposite page). Seated at the head table were, from left to right, Mrs. William Freese, William Freese, Mrs. F.D. Freese, F.D. Freese, and Mrs. Stanley Cunningham, Mr. Cunningham, Mrs. P.W. Freese, and P.W. Freese.

A. Langdon Freese started his men's clothing store in 1892. After surviving a 1922 fire, the store expanded and, as Maine's physically largest department store (opposite page), featured six floors of diverse merchandise, elevator operators, a lunch counter, and the only two escalators north of Portland.

Freese's was a top retail destination for Christmas shoppers, including thousands of people who annually trekked from Aroostook County and Down East Maine to browse for gifts in Bangor, the retail hub of central, northern, and eastern Maine. The store often featured colorful displays, such as a 1947 assortment of Valentine's Day candies (below) being sold by clerks Velma Russell (left) and Nola King (right).

Freese's opened a second store at the Airport Mall in the late 1960s. Suburban retail competition led to the closure of both stores in the mid-1980s. (Clockwise from top right, courtesy of BDN; courtesy of RRS; courtesy of Maureen Walsh.)

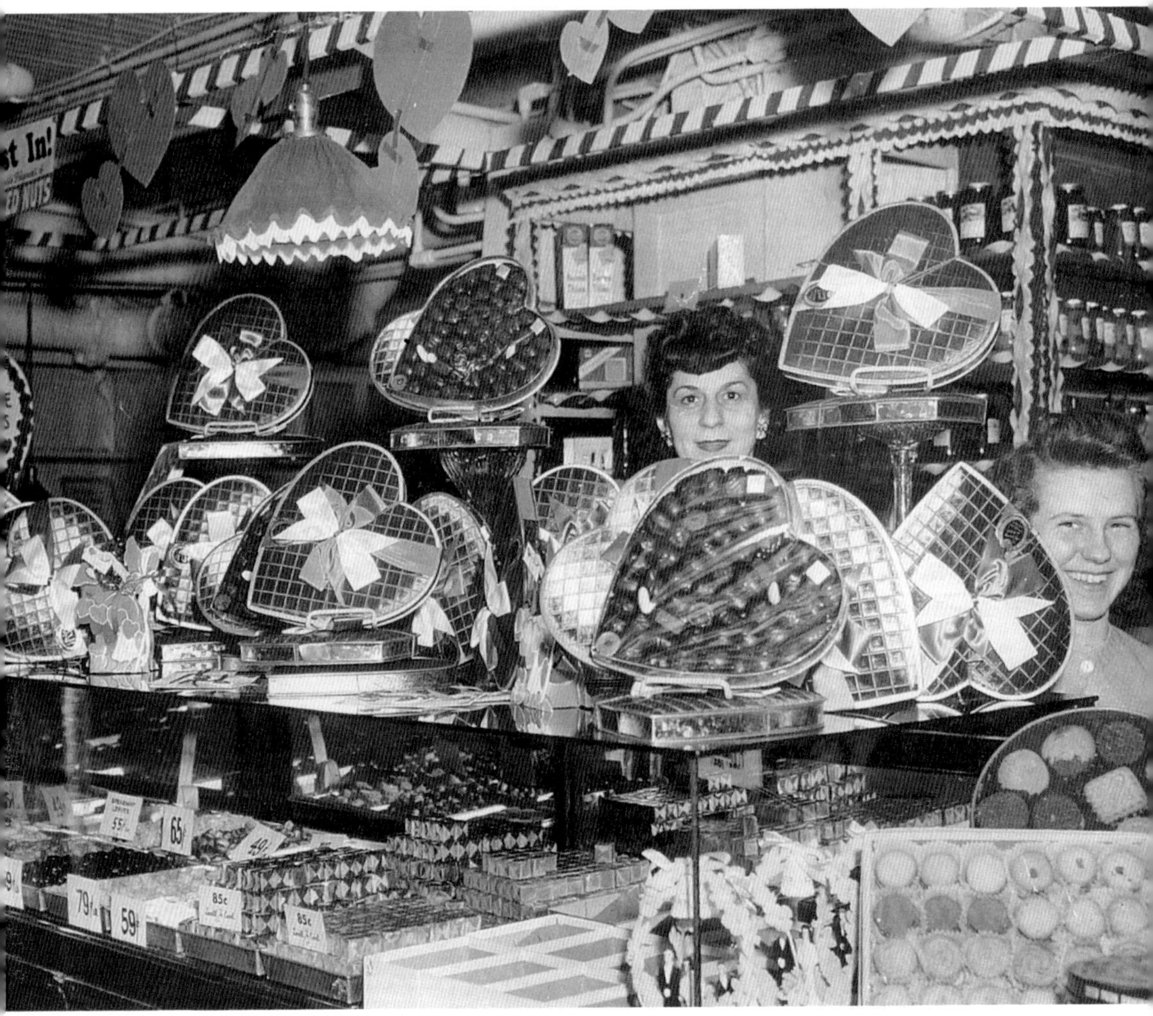

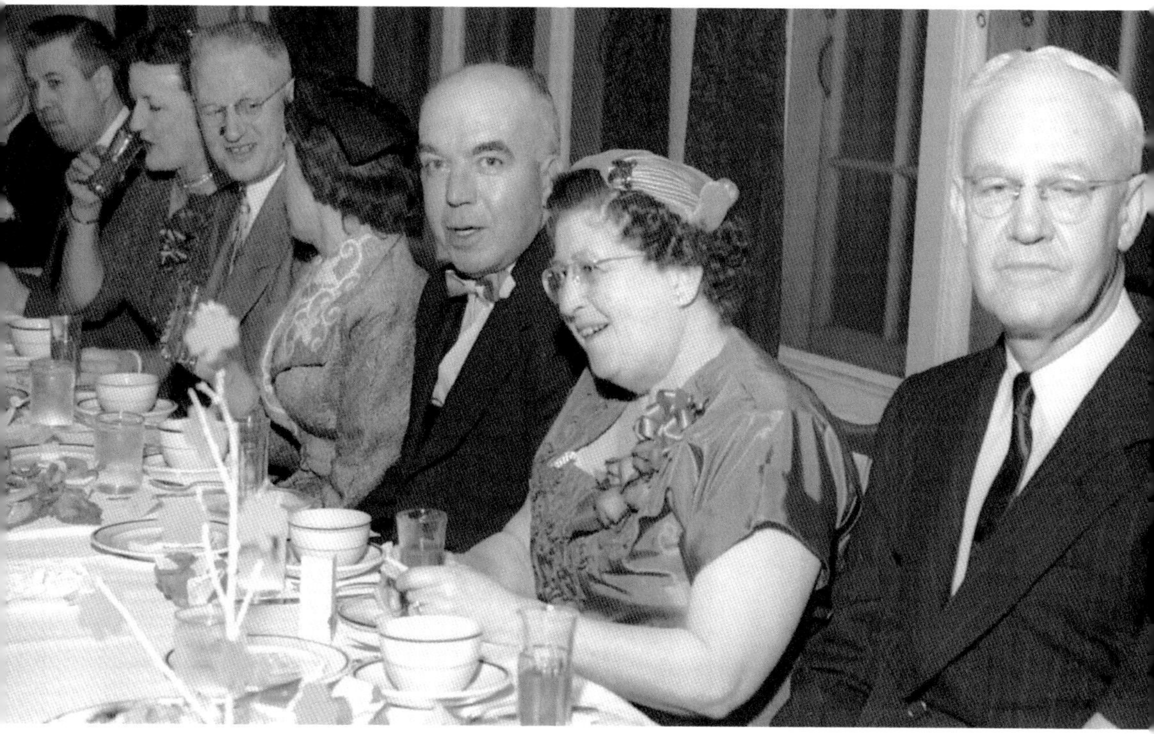

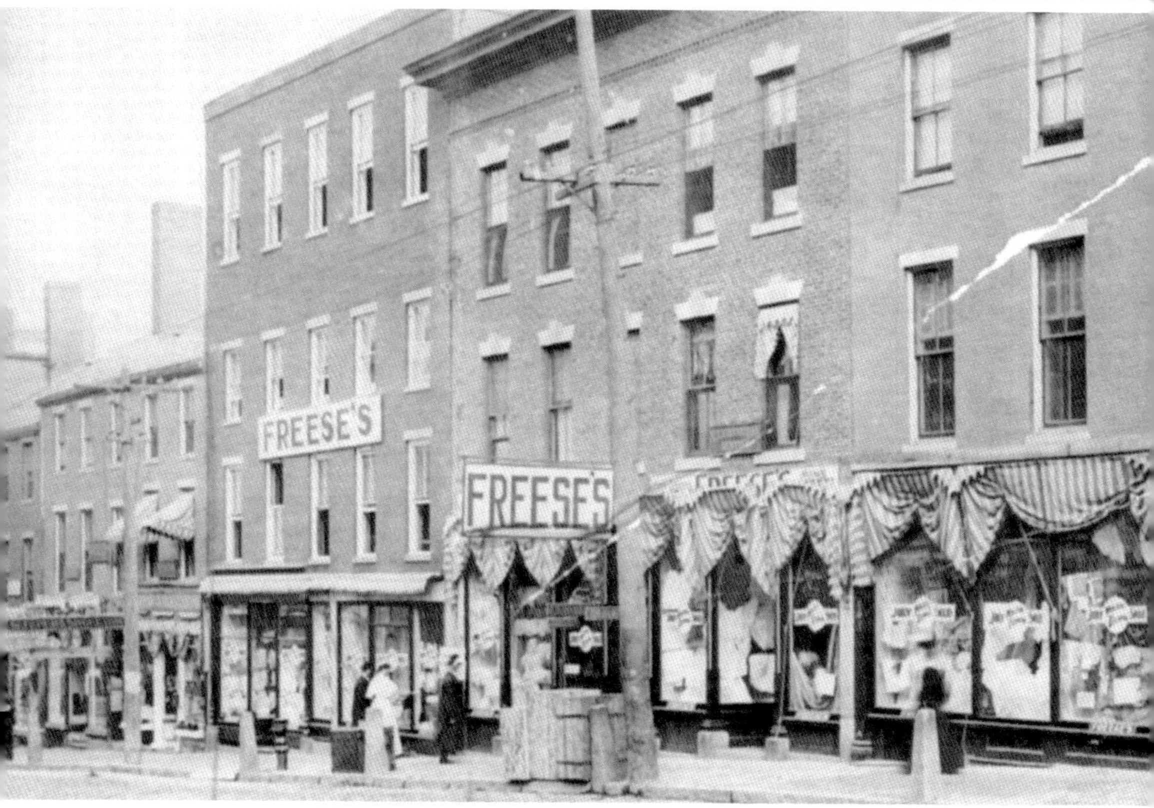
FREESE'S
FREESE'S

Bangor's Prominent Separatist

Fed up with Bangor taxes, Gen. Sam Veazie decided to move—and he took a chunk of the Queen City with him. Already a successful businessman when he arrived in Old Town in 1826, Veazie purchased sawmills along the Penobscot River and produced lumber that shipped from the port at Bangor.

Six years later, he moved downriver to the Queen City and gradually acquired ownership of the profitable business activity known as the "Penobscot Boom." Stretching along the Bangor shore upriver from the confluence of the Kenduskeag Stream and the Penobscot River, the "Boom" was where logs were gathered and sorted for processing in local sawmills. No one could move their logs through the Penobscot Boom unless General Sam received his cut. As for his generalship, Veazie traced it to his status as a high-ranking Maine militia officer during the War of 1812.

In time, Veazie bought 20 sawmills in North Bangor and 13 sawmills in Orono. He ventured into the world of high (and uncertain) mid-19th-century finance by buying majority ownership in the Bank of Bangor, soon renamed the Veazie Bank. General Sam operated the bank profitably; his reliable reputation spilled over into bank operations, and when Ellsworth's two banks failed, he opened a Veazie Bank branch there.

In the mid-1800s, a rickety railroad was carved through the woods and marshlands from Bangor to the Penobscot River shore in Old Town. Suing when the railroad crossed his Old Town property, Veazie won a $17,000 judgment.

Realizing that the railroad could easily carry lumber to Bangor, Veazie soon bought the line, which would be forever known as the Veazie Railroad. Frequented year-round by outdoor recreationists, its abandoned bed remains accessible today.

Always looking for ways to reduce his expenditures and thereby raise his income, Veazie decided that he was paying too much in personal property taxes in Bangor. In 1853, people living in North Bangor had split from Bangor and named their town "Veazie" after the good general, who certainly had done nothing to prevent the separation from Bangor.

Returning the honor bestowed upon him by Veazie residents, General Sam moved into a new house in Veazie in 1854. This house apparently was the general's summer home; *The History of Penobscot County, Maine* notes that Veazie "died in Bangor, in his winter home," on March 12, 1868. (Courtesy of BPL.)

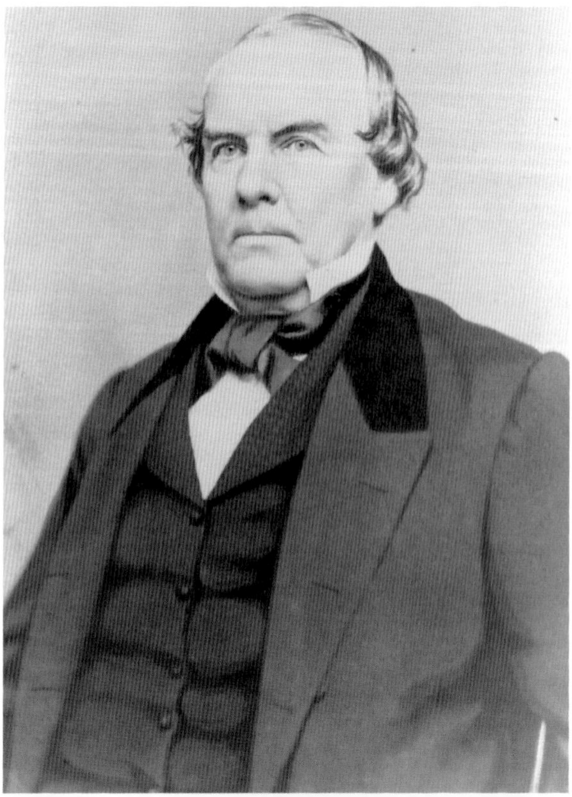

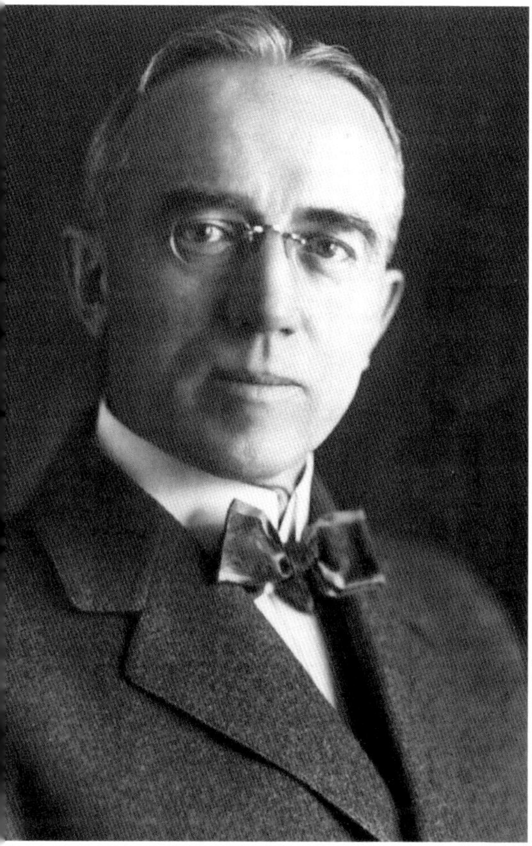

A Short-Lived Governorship

Stranger than fiction was the 25-day governorship of Frederic Hale Parkhurst. Elected Maine's chief executive on January 5, 1921, by a remarkable 65 percent of the vote, the Republican fell ill on his first day in office and died of pneumonia on January 31. The former Bangor attorney, businessman, city council president, state representative, and state senator is buried in his city's Mount Hope Cemetery. (Courtesy of BHS.)

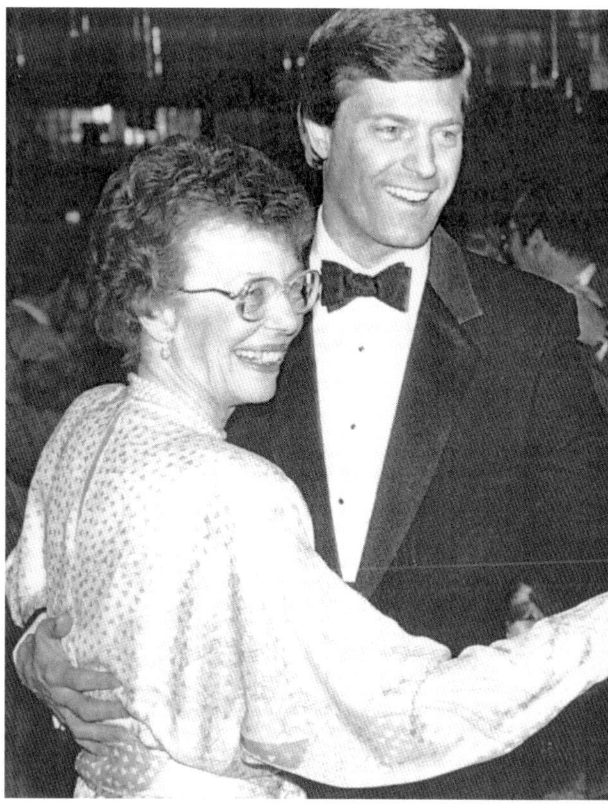

Congressman and Governor

Well known as a two-term Maine governor, John "Jock" McKernan Jr. once served his state as a member of the Maine Army National Guard. The son of John McKernan Sr. and Barbara Guild McKernan (photograph), he graduated from Bangor High School, Dartmouth College, and the University of Maine School of Law. A former congressman, McKernan is married to former Maine senator Olympia Snowe. (Courtesy of BDN.)

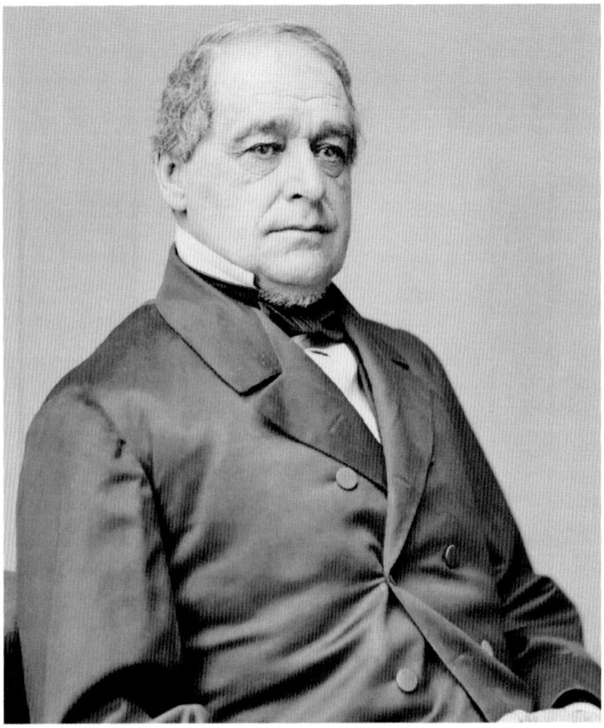

The Vice President Shoulders a Rifle

The only Mainer ever elected on a national ticket might have assumed the presidency, except for Abraham Lincoln seeking to secure the electoral votes of a Southern state that had rejoined the Union.

Born in Paris, Maine, in August 1809, Hannibal Hamlin (above) studied law intermittently until finally being admitted to the Maine bar in 1833. A year later, he opened a law office in Hampden, and in 1836, Hamlin won election to the Maine House as a Democrat. His constituents returned him to Augusta the next four years, and Democrat legislators elected Hamlin speaker of the House in 1837, 1839, and, 1840.

Later a congressman and then a senator, Hamlin spoke out against slavery; this viewpoint led him to join the Republican Party in June 1856. Reappointed to the Senate, Hamlin had expressed little interest in national politics when Republicans nominated him as Lincoln's vice presidential candidate in 1860.

After Lincoln won election, Hamlin remained in the Senate. Moving to Bangor in 1862, he seldom spent time in Washington, DC, except when the Senate was in session—and unlike most American vice presidents, Hamlin wore a uniform and shouldered a firearm during wartime.

When Bangor's existing militia companies went to war in April, the state created a few replacement companies. Hamlin joined one such company and, when duty called, marched as a private. He was among the uniformed honor guards for the funeral held in Rockland in May 1863 for Maj. Gen. Hiram Berry, killed at Chancellorsville. When his company was mobilized to garrison Fort McClary, the middle-aged Hamlin accompanied his comrades to Kittery and actually worked as a company cook.

Political tradition called for Hamlin to remain on the 1864 Republican ticket. Figuring that Maine was a secure Republican stronghold, however, Lincoln decided that Andrew Johnson, the Democratic governor of Tennessee, should replace Hamlin. After seceding from the Union in 1861, Tennessee had rejoined the United States. Expecting a strong challenge from Democratic nominee George B. McClellan, Lincoln needed Tennessee's electoral votes.

Hamlin later became the American ambassador to Spain. A statue honoring him was later erected on Bangor's Kenduskeag Mall.

After his death in Bangor on July 4, 1891, Hamlin was buried in Mount Hope Cemetery. (Courtesy of BPL.)

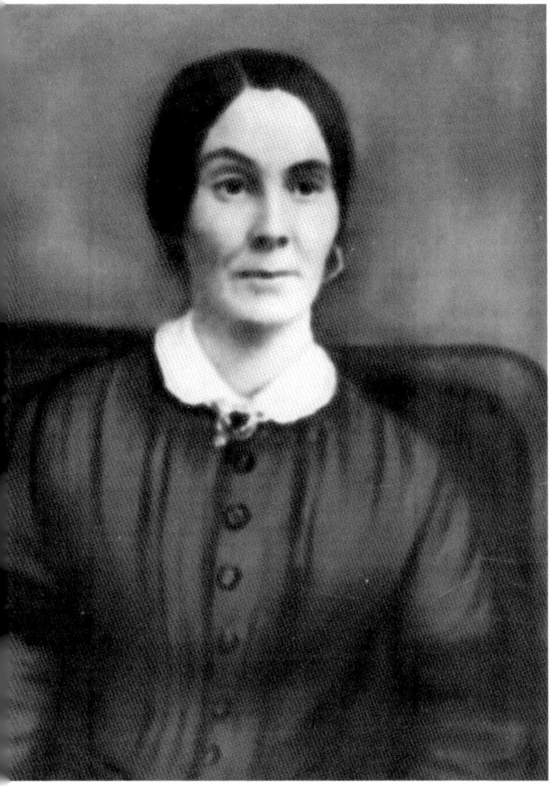

Vice Presidential Relations

Hannibal Hamlin loved two women from the same family.

He married Sarah Jane Emery (left) in Paris, Maine, in 1833; her father was Stephen Emery, a probate judge. The Hamlins' five children (four sons and a daughter) were born after Hannibal and Sarah moved to Hampden in 1834; during the Civil War, two sons became Army generals.

Sarah Jane died of tuberculosis in April 1855. About 17 months later, the lonely Hannibal married her half-sister, Ellen Vesta Emery (below), born to Stephen Emery in 1835. Despite the 26-year gap in their ages, the newlyweds settled into a comfortable marriage.

Ellen bore Hannibal two sons; the youngest, Frank, was the only child of the 15th vice president of the United States to be born in Bangor. (Left, courtesy of Special Collections Department, Fogler Library, University of Maine; below, courtesy of BPL.)

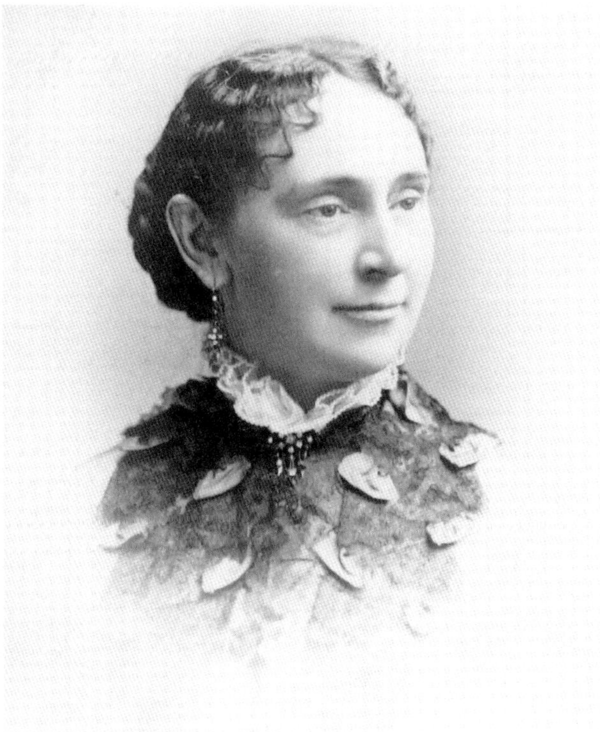

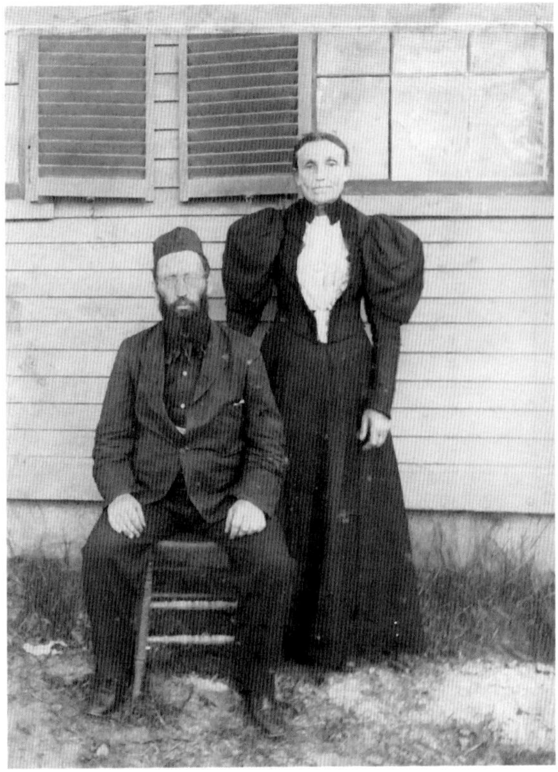

Hardworking Immigrants

Nathan and Rosa Cohen found a better life in Bangor after fleeing Russia's anti-Semitism. Rosa Kramer (born 1840) stood more than six feet, which allowed Nathan (born 1844) to "marry tall." Nathan arrived in Boston in 1882, but after enduring harassment, he moved Rosa and his five children north to Bangor, where he sold clothing and shoes. He helped found the Beth Israel Society. (Courtesy of BPL.)

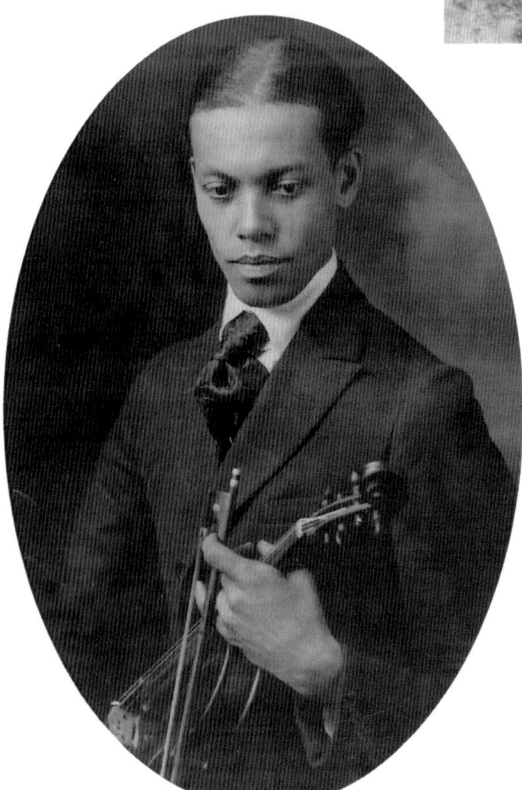

Musician and Merchant

W. Alonzo Johnson was a respected member of Bangor's black middle class. His father, William A. Johnson, a child of the slave era, left Virginia and settled in Bangor in 1870. Alonzo attended the University of Maine and performed in the Bangor Symphony Orchestra. He took over his father's business after his death in 1913, selling costumes, tools, jewelry, and musical instruments. (Courtesy of BHS.)

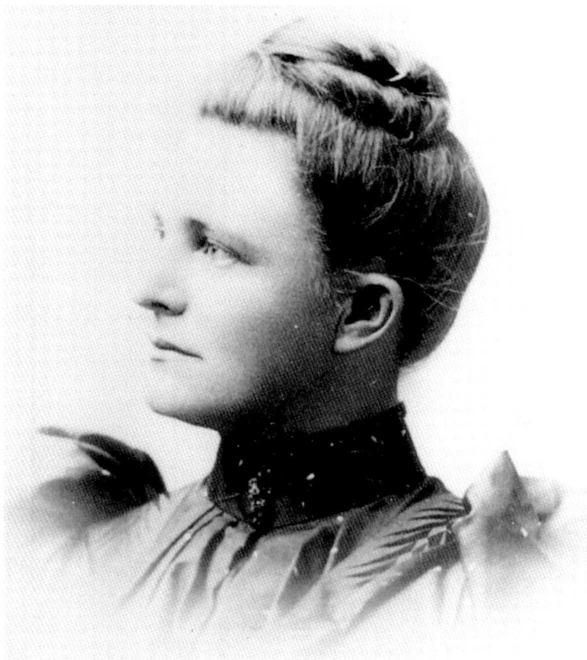

First Woman School Superintendent

An elementary school located on Broadway honors Mary S. Snow, described by the *Bangor Daily News* in November 1926 as "Bangor's most famous daughter."

Born in Bangor in April 1857, Snow attended Queen City schools and, later, taught in them. An avid supporter of the public education system, she was soon elected the first woman president of the Maine Teachers' Association. In time, Snow became the principal at the Hannibal Hamlin School, but after a while, she left the education field to go onto private business with a friend.

Snow won election to the Bangor School Board; she proved herself so capable as an education administrator that the City of Bangor named her its school superintendent. Snow's hiring marked the first time that a woman had held such a position in Maine.

Snow broke ground in other ways during her 11-year tenure in Bangor. To provide well-educated teachers for Bangor schools, she opened a normal training school, the first in Maine. Fledgling teachers studied specific courses and learned the skills of the professional teacher; the training was tough and thorough, and "those teachers who were graduates of [Snow's] Training school found it easy to get positions anywhere in Maine or Massachusetts," the *Bangor Daily News* reported.

The concept of a teachers' school in Bangor soon caught on at the state house; Maine would later establish normal schools in Castine, Farmington, and elsewhere to provide college-level educations for aspiring teachers.

Rather than sit behind a desk, Snow often visited the Bangor schools to see how staff and students were doing. "She was an indefatigable worker," according to the *Bangor Daily News*, "a forceful speaker, ready and resourceful in argument, witty, and sincere."

The New England Superintendents' Association elected Snow as its first woman president. During her years as Bangor's superintendent, Snow spoke to many organizations about the value of a public education. In recognition of her contributions to education, the University of Maine at Orono later awarded Snow with a master's degree in philosophy.

Leaving Bangor, Snow took a supervisory position at the Pratt Institute in Brooklyn and then became the supervisor in household arts in Chicago public schools. Snow died in New York City in March 1924; the City of Bangor named a new school on Broadway after her in 1927.

Snow is buried at Mount Hope Cemetery in Bangor. (Courtesy of RRS.)

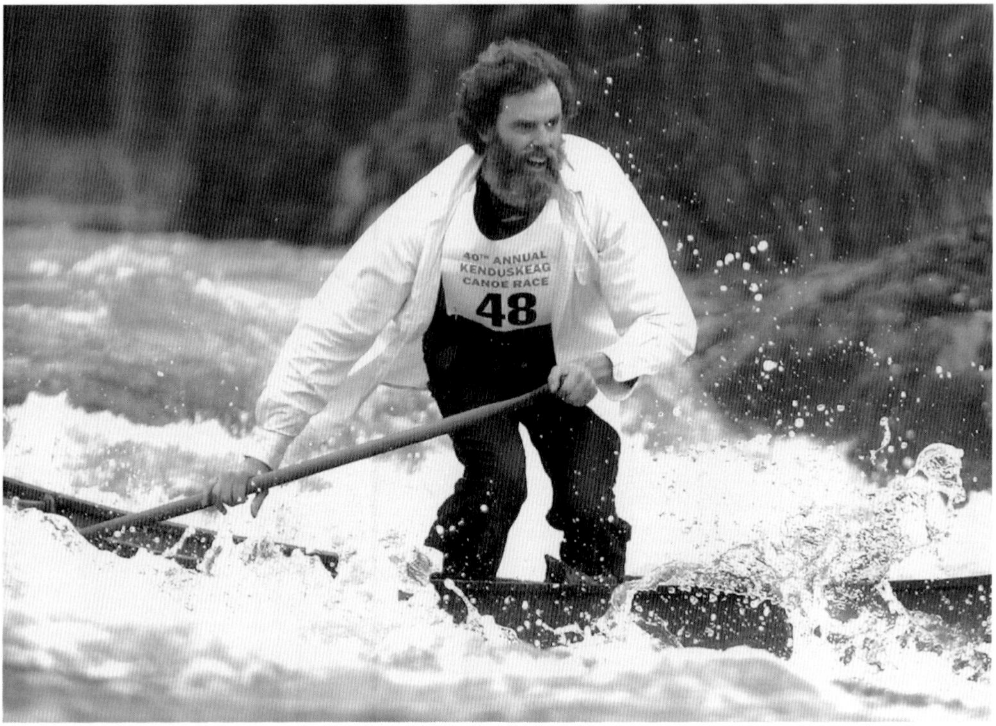

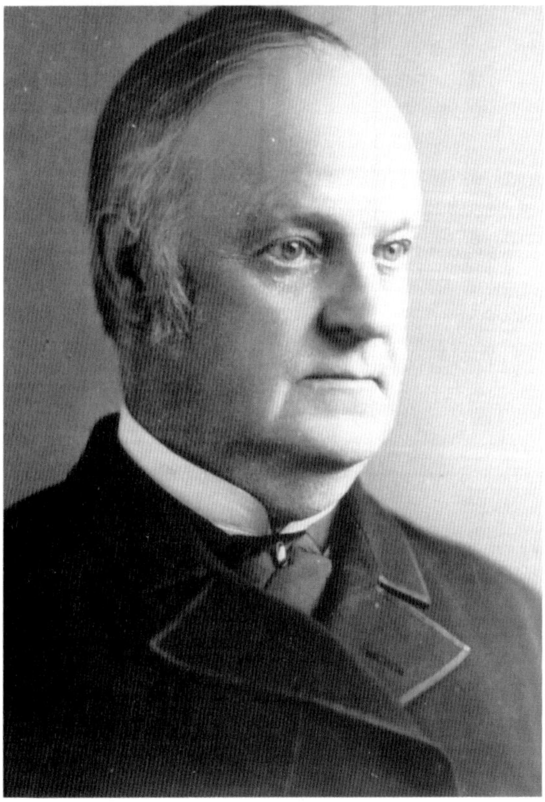

Standup Canoe Master

Nearly every year since 1967, spectators have held their breath as Edward "Zip" Kellogg paddled his canoe, while standing up, in the Kenduskeag Stream Canoe Race. Kellogg grew up in Bangor near the stream, the son of Juliet and Dr. Robert Kellogg. As a child, he was lured by water and boats. A career librarian, he has written extensively about Maine's rivers and streams. (Courtesy of Zip Kellogg.)

Merchant Left His Name on Bangor Building

Joseph Wheelwright, a Bangor clothier since the 1830s, took on J.G. Clark as a business partner in 1850. Their clothing store generated sufficient revenue for Wheelwright, Clark & Company to construct a modern four-story building next to West Market Square in 1859. Among the first "stone" structures in downtown Bangor, the Wheelwright-Clark Block thrives today as home to Mexicali Blues. (Courtesy of BPL.)

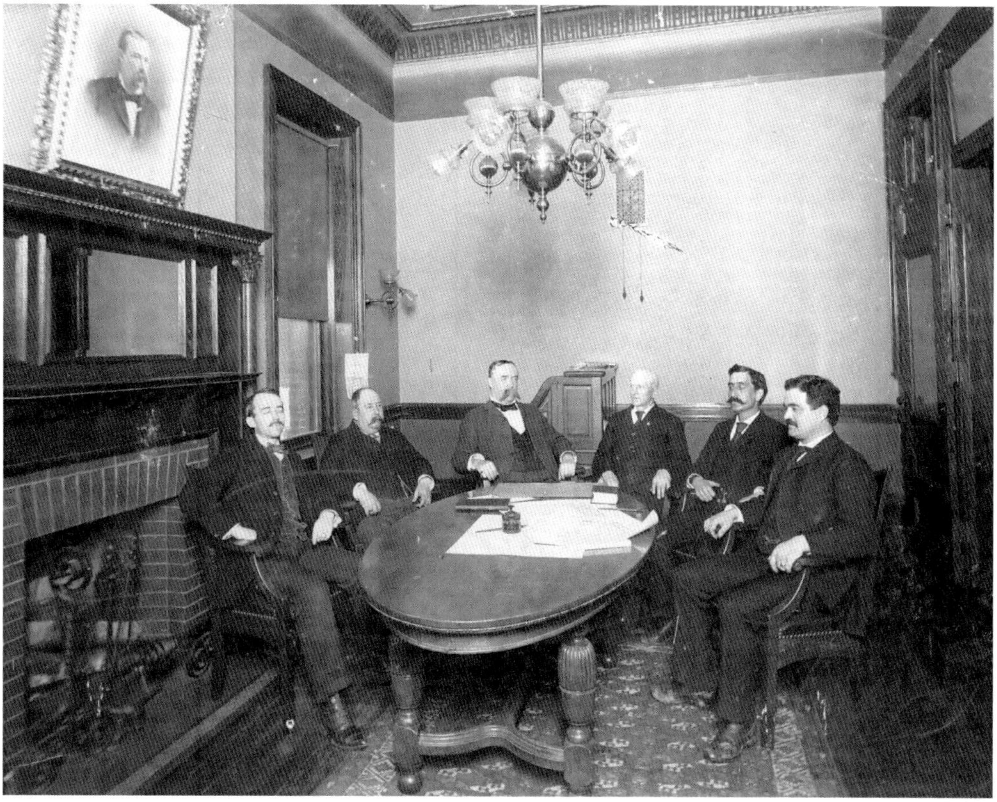

A Mayor of All Trades

Dairy farmer, brush cutter, soldier, railroad conductor, stagecoach operator, and politician, Flavius Orlando Beal was successful at whatever job or profession he pursued.

Originally from Monmouth in Kennebec County, Beal arrived in Bangor in June 1874 and bought the livery (horses and equipment) kept in the Bangor House stables. He launched a Bangor-to-Bar Harbor stage line in 1878.

Leasing the poorly managed Bangor House, Beal made the local landmark profitable.

He later won election for Bangor City Council. His fellow councilors named him mayor, and when they posed with Beal in the council chambers at Bangor City Hall, his photograph hung high on the wall. The six councilors seated at the table were, from left to right, F.H. Parkhurst, J.W. Taney, Flavius O. Beal, H.G. Thompson, W.A. Palmer, and J.F. Angley. (Courtesy of BPL.)

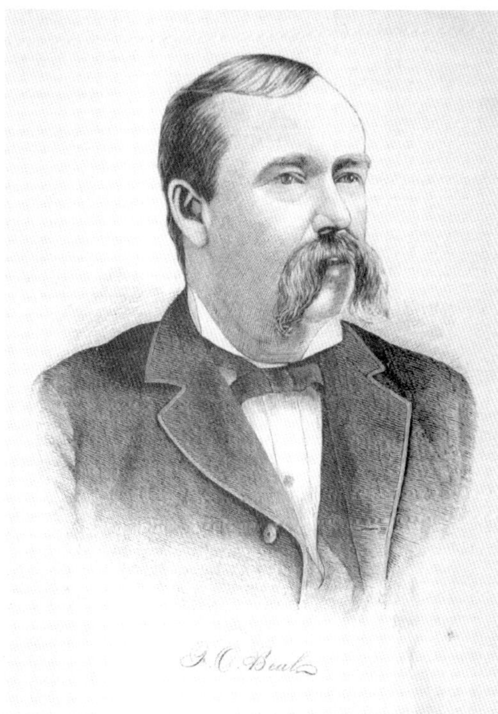

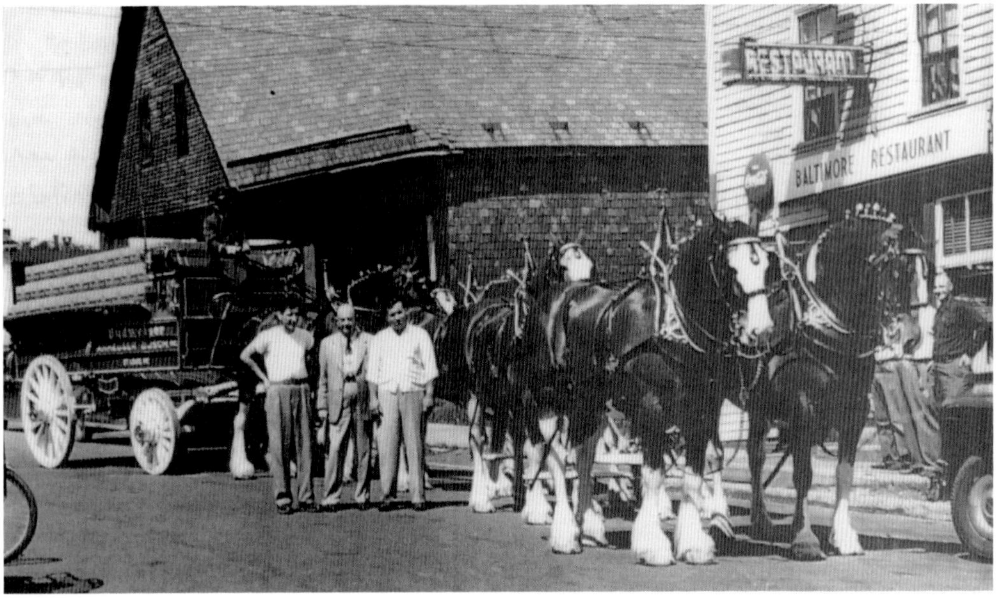

Italian Cuisine Under the Bridge
Hungry diners lined up at the Baltimore Restaurant, located at 15 Union Street "under" the Joshua Chamberlain Bridge. James Caparelli started "The Balty" in the 1930s before the bridge was built. Brothers Robert (left) and Vasco (right) Baldacci ran it into the 1960s. The unidentified man standing between the Baldaccis worked for Anheuser-Busch, Inc., which brought the Clydesdales to Bangor around 1962. (Courtesy of Robert Baldacci Jr.)

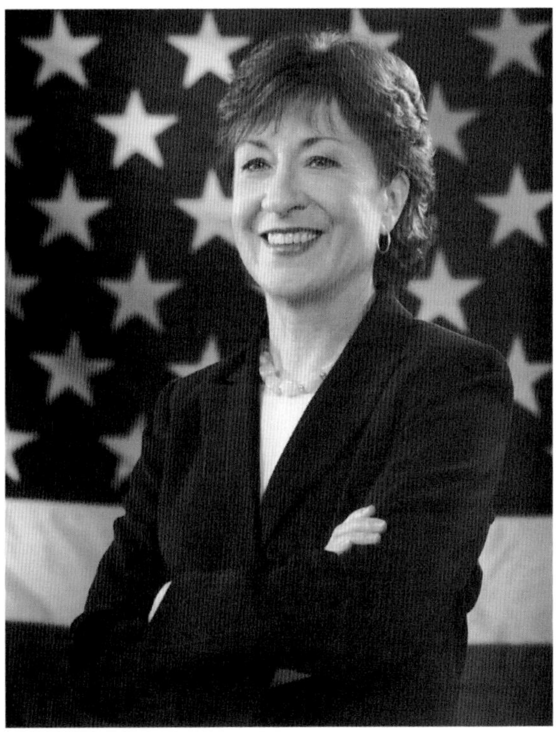

Four-Term Senator
Sen. Susan Collins began her political career in Washington, DC, in 1975 as an aide to US Rep. William Cohen. Running as the Republican candidate for governor, Collins lost the 1994 gubernatorial election. She won the 1996 election for US senator; she was reelected in 2002, 2008, and 2014. Collins and her husband, Thomas Daffron, live in Bangor. (Courtesy of US Senate.)

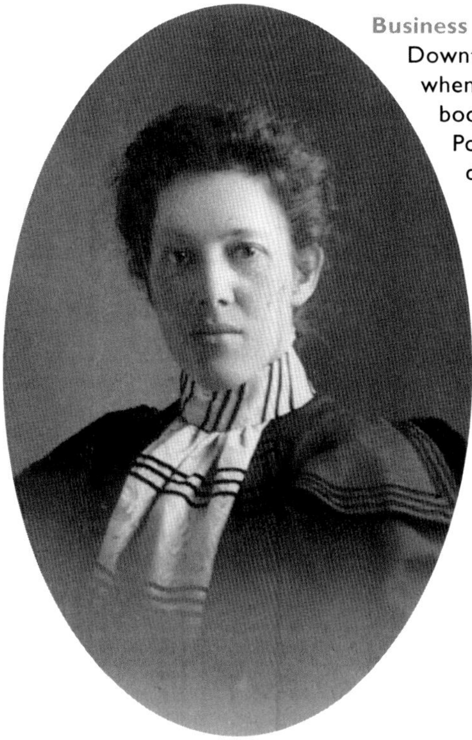

Business College Founder

Downtown business colleges were all the rage in 1891, when Mary Beal started a school for future secretaries, bookkeepers, and accountants. Some had branches in Portland and other cities. Known as Miss Beal to her devoted students, she hired a staff of teachers who knew how to type 70 words a minute and dictate shorthand. Today's modern Beal College is located at 99 Farm Road. (Courtesy of BHS.)

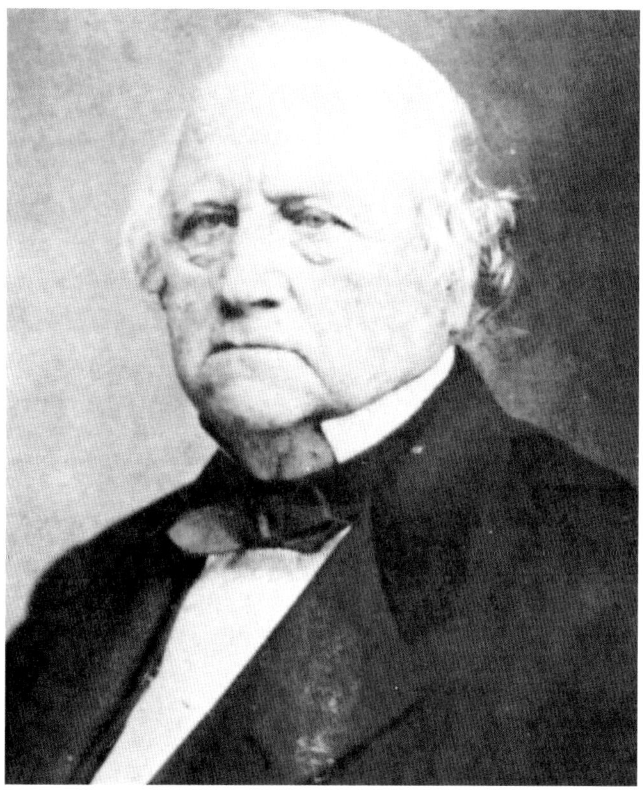

Kent Negotiated for Aroostook

When tempers flared as Maine and Great Britain argued over the border between the Aroostook Territory and New Brunswick, federal officials asked Bangor attorney Edward Kent in 1843 to represent Maine during the proceedings that led to the signing of the Webster-Ashburton Treaty. Thus did Kent, who had been a Maine legislator and governor, help determine the boundaries of Aroostook County. (Courtesy of BPL.)

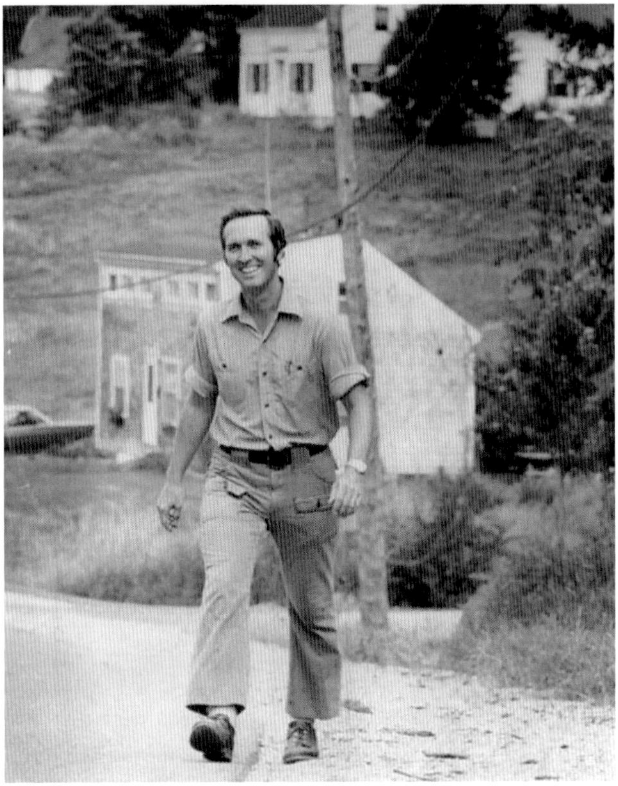

On the Congressional Road

Bangor native William Cohen literally launched his government career step by step in 1972 when he crisscrossed Maine's Second Congressional District on foot (above) while seeking his first term in the House of Representatives. Only 32, he garnered much attention from younger voters and the Maine media.

Elected to office as a Republican that November, Cohen represented Maine in the House and, later, in the Senate.

Born in 1940 to Reuben and Clara Hartley Cohen, William Cohen worked at his parents' Bangor Rye Bread Company on Hancock Street for some years. He starred in varsity basketball at Bangor High School and at Bowdoin College, from which he graduated before earning a law degree at the Boston University School of Law.

Cohen initially pursued a typical legal career in Bangor, where he was a law-firm partner and assistant district attorney for Penobscot County; the latter position particularly placed his name before the public. Cohen won election to the Bangor City Council and served a one-year term as the city's mayor.

Setting his eyes on Congress, Cohen walked his way into office in 1972. In Washington, DC, he served on the House Judiciary Committee—a natural fit for his legal skills and, ironically, a committee assignment that thrust him into the limelight. The House Judiciary Committee investigated the Watergate break-in; it revealed that Cohen was not a straight party-line politician. He voted to impeach President Richard Nixon, who later resigned from office.

Winning election to the Senate in 1978, 1984, and 1990, Cohen represented Maine during the Carter, Reagan, George H.W. Bush, and Clinton administrations. Pres. William Clinton tapped Cohen as secretary of defense in 1997; he is among a select group of elected politicians who served presidents of the opposing political party.

Cohen married author Janet Langhart on Valentine's Day 1996. Cohen later wrote such books as the novel *Dragon Fire* and, in joint authorship with his wife, *Love in Black and White*. (Courtesy of Fogler Library, University of Maine.)

Keeper of the Blue Hotel

The wooden house at the corner of Harlow and Cumberland Streets held many secrets. Separate outside doors invited a clientele of woods-weary loggers with money in hand. Young Nancy Jones, formerly of West Brooksville, purchased the property for $4,000 in 1867. For the next 50 years, she operated it as Bangor's most infamous brothel. Stewart Holbrook's 1938 book, *Holy Old Mackinaw*, spun a yarn of "Fancy Fan" painting her chimney blue to attract river workers. Jones, seen in this c. 1870 portrait, had a common-law husband, John Thomas, and enjoyed carriage rides to Pushaw Pond, pictured below around 1880. When Jones died of tuberculosis in 1917, she was 87 years old and a fading memory on Harlow Street. Her property, which had barely escaped destruction in the great fire of 1911, by then was more of a boarding home for single men. When the home was demolished in 1950, a local newspaper recounted its lurid past. Today, the space is a parking lot. (Right, courtesy of RRS; below, courtesy of BHS.)

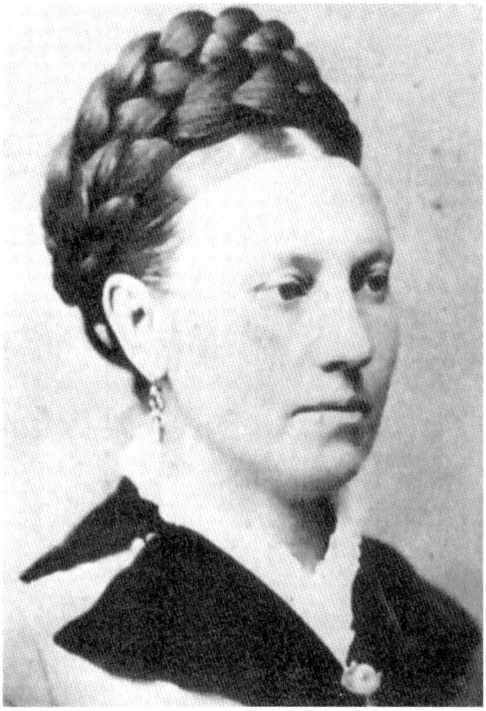

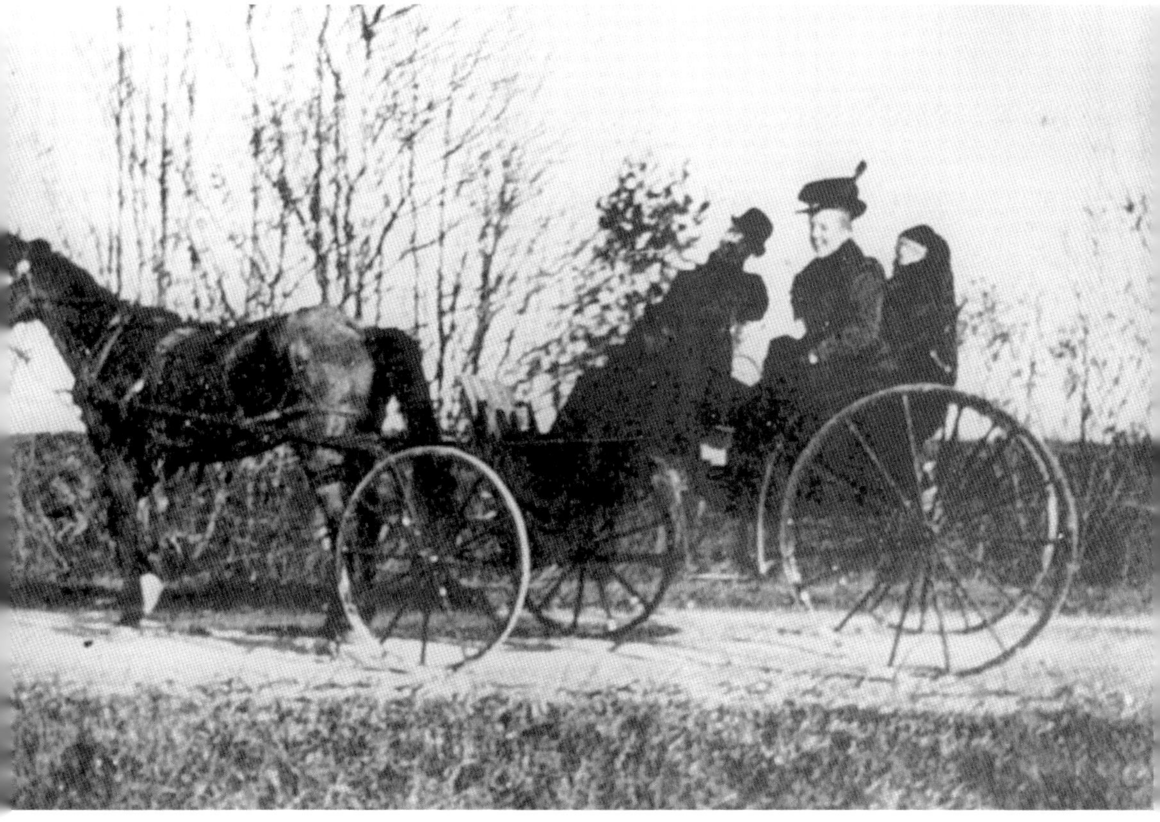

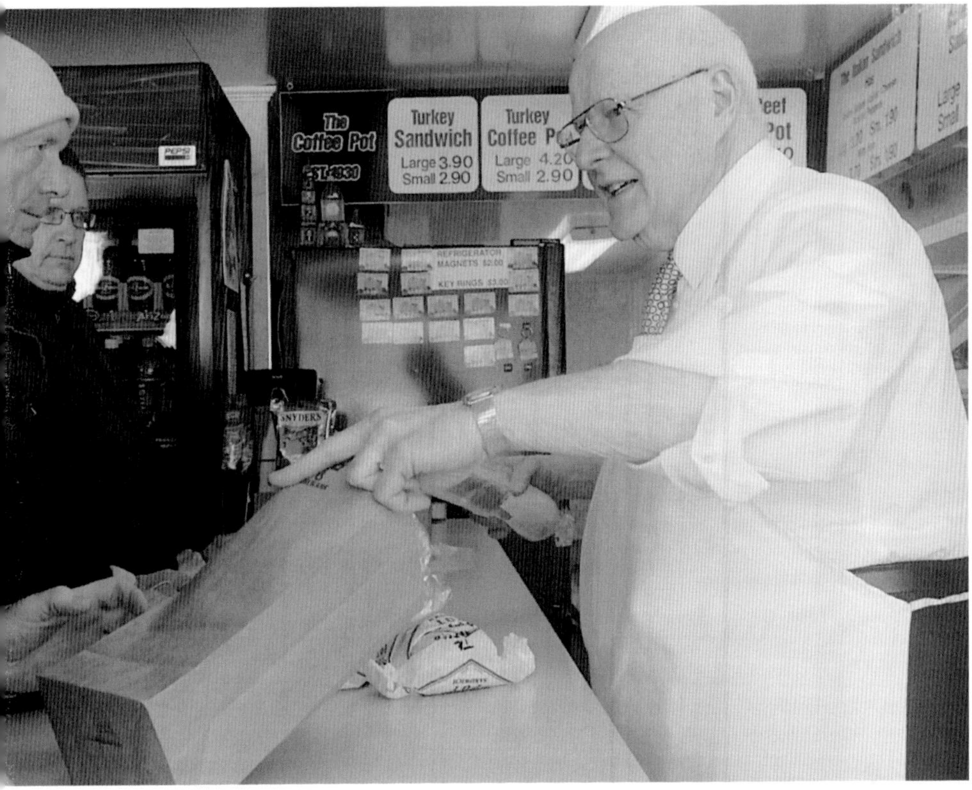
The Coffee Pot
Turkey Sandwich
Large 3.90
Small 2.90
Turkey Coffee Pot
Large 4.20
Small 2.90
REFRIGERATOR MAGNETS $2.00
KEY RINGS $3.00

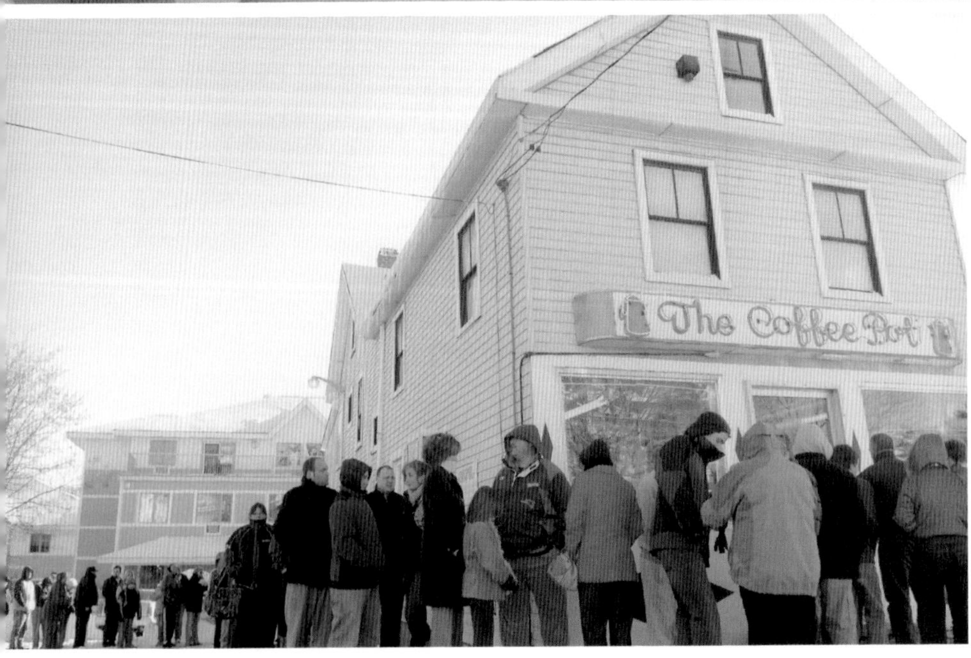
The Coffee Pot

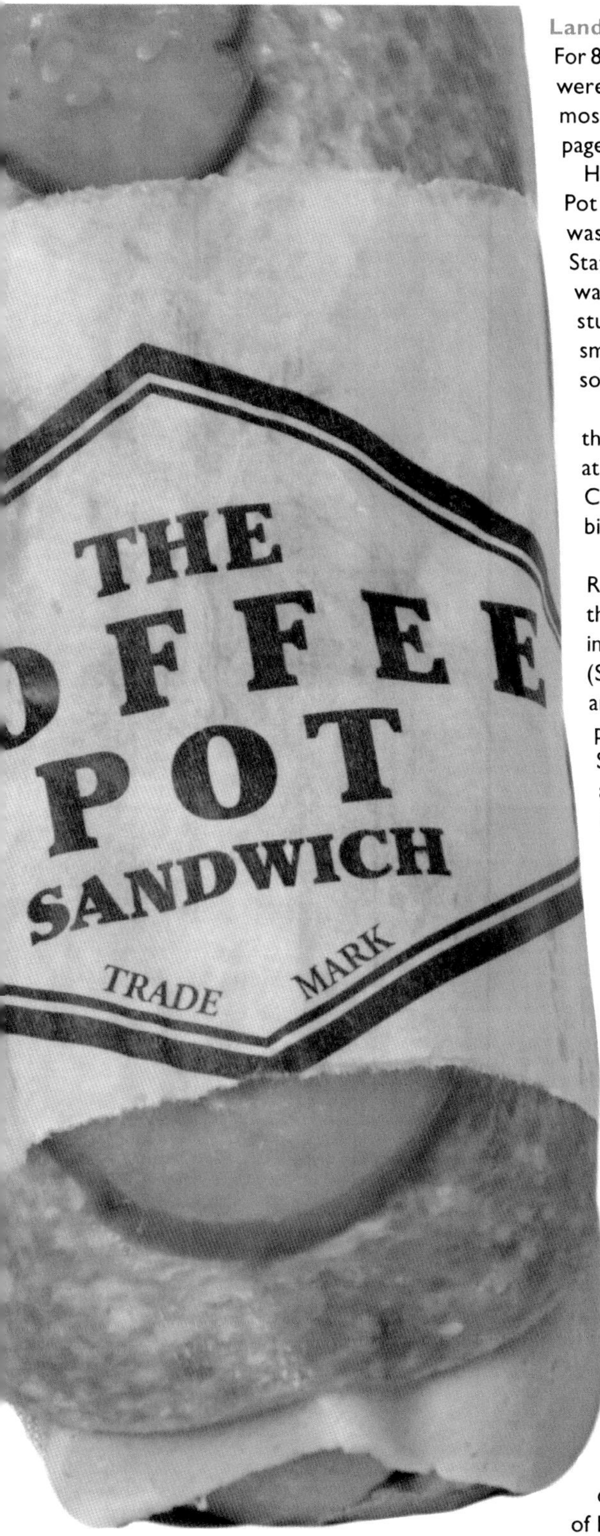

Landmark Sandwiches

For 80 years, the Coffee Pot and delicious sandwiches were synonymous on Bangor's East Side, and for most of that time, Francis "Skip" Rist (opposite page) was synonymous with the Coffee Pot.

His father, Richard Grover Rist, started the Coffee Pot on Hancock Street in 1930. "Grover," as he was known, relocated his sandwich shop to 173 State Street in 1937, the year that his son, Skip, was born. "He sold sandwiches and hot soup and stuff like that," Skip said. "My father, he was a smart man" and created each style of sandwich sold at The Coffee Pot.

The eatery was open seven days a week back then. Grover Rist bought his food each morning at the mom-and-pop First National next to the Coffee Pot; "every night he'd go over to pay his bill," Skip said.

All the Rist children, Skip, Richard "Dick" Jr., Rosemary, Robina, and Mary Lou, worked at the Coffee Pot to serve a growing clientele that included people traveling into Bangor on Route 2 (State Street) from northern Penobscot County and Aroostook County. "We were the fast-food place on the East Side. There was no McDonald's," Skip said. "We used to have buses stop. We had a lot of Aroostook County customers, [people from] Calais, Machias [in Washington County], more from Bangor north," he recalled. "We were always hoping the northern [Maine] or Down East teams had won" at the basketball tournament in Bangor.

As for the eatery's popular sandwiches, "everything was a play on 'Coffee Pot,'" such as Deluxe Coffee Pot, Skip said. When Grover died in 1960, his children ran the eatery. Dick Jr. died in 1970, and Skip, Rosemary, and Mary Lou kept their customers happy with help from the Coffee Pot's pretty loyal employees, Skip said.

He continued the eatery after his sisters retired in 1990. "I worked all my life" there "up until I was 72. That's when it became time to retire." When the landmark closed on January 1, 2010, customers queued out the door (opposite page) to buy the last sandwiches that Rist and his talented staff would ever make. "I enjoyed the customers," Skip said. "We had some of the nicest customers." (Clockwise from top left: courtesy of BDN; courtesy of RRS; courtesy of BDN.)

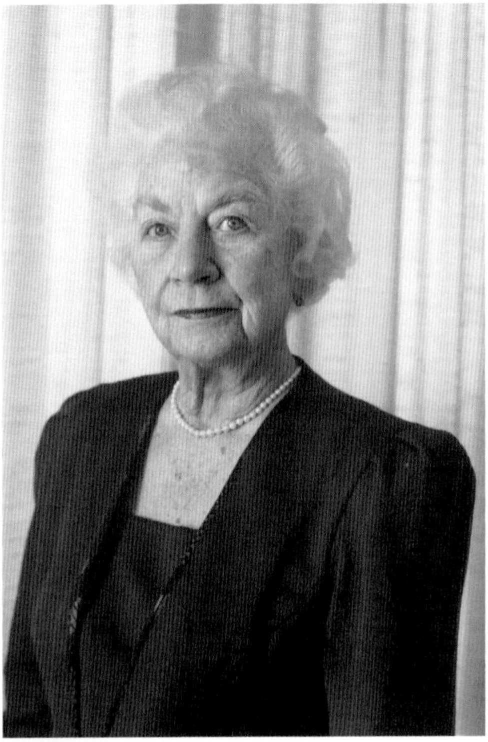

Health Center Pioneer
Its cofounder and namesake died in 2006, but the Mabel Wadsworth Women's Health Center, located at 700 Mount Hope Avenue, lives on. Established in 1984, the center carries out her vision of reproductive justice through health services, advocacy, and education. Wadsworth moved to Bangor in 1946 after graduating from the University of Rochester, where she received a nursing degree. (Courtesy of BDN.)

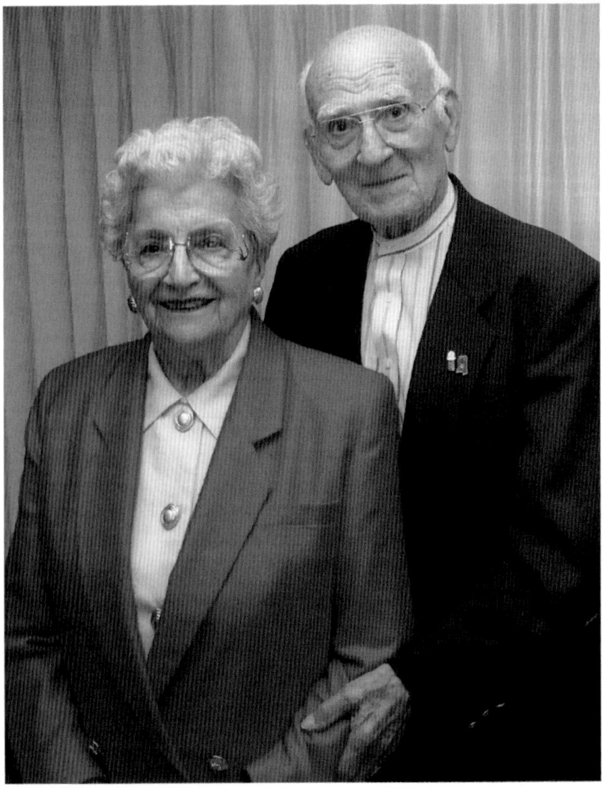

Mr. and Mrs. Miller Drug
Customers stopping by Miller Drug at 210 State Street could always find the owners in the store. In the 1950s, Abe and Frieda Miller, joined by their son Bill, converted the onetime store and luncheonette to a full-service pharmacy that offered home deliveries. Miller Square at Harlow, a downtown senior citizen residence, is named in honor of the Millers' commitment to elder care. (Courtesy of BDN.)

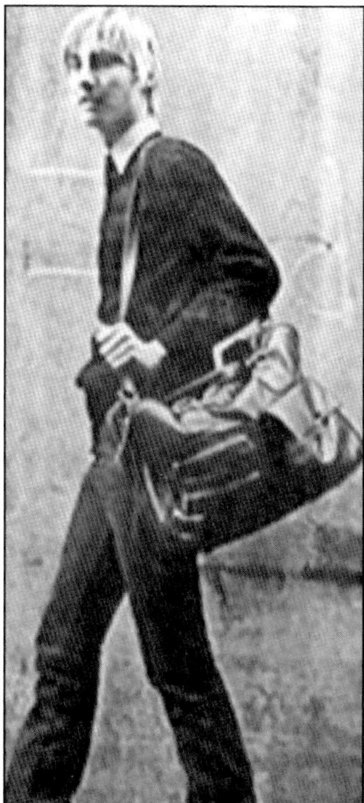

Turning Tragedy into Action

Charlie Howard is a household name for tragic reasons. On the night of July 7, 1984, the 23-year-old was accosted by three teenagers for being gay. The youth chased Howard and a companion, beating Howard and throwing him over a bridge into the Kenduskeag Stream. Asthmatic and a nonswimmer, Howard drowned. His body was discovered by rescue crews later that evening.

The event spread throughout the nation and put Bangor on the map. The three youths were tried as juveniles and sent to the Maine Youth Center.

As an adult, Jim Baines, one of the three former youths, shared his story in a book, *Penitence: A True Story*, by Edward Armstrong. Howard's life and death have been recounted in books such as *Us and Them: A History of Intolerance in America*, by Jim Carnes. Bette Greene's novel *The Drowning of Stephan Jones* also deals with the tragedy.

Every July, the Unitarian Universalist church sponsors a walk to the State Street Bridge, where Howard died. Participants toss flowers into the stream and gather by a monument erected by the Charles O. Howard Memorial Foundation. (Left, courtesy of Unitarian Universalist Society of Bangor; below, courtesy of BFS.)

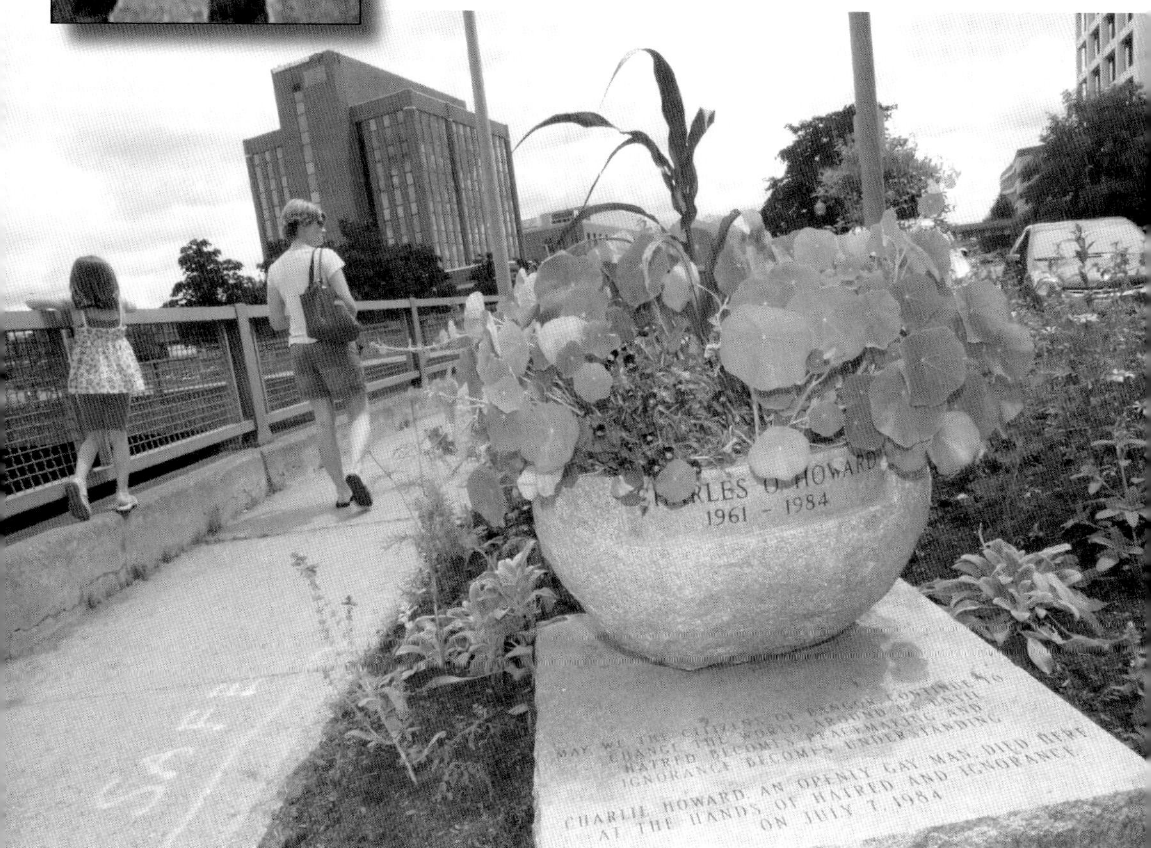

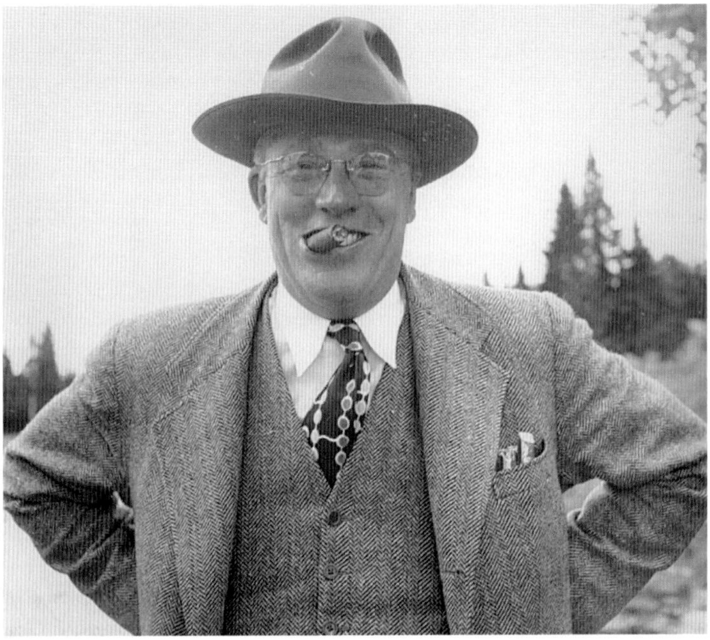

Five-Day Governor

When he was not busy presiding over the Bangor-Hydro Electric (BHE) Company, Robert N. Haskell (above) was presiding over the Maine State Senate and, for five days in 1959, the state.

Haskell earned an engineering degree at the University of Maine and hired on with BHE as an engineer. The "Hydro" expanded its service area substantially in the 1930s and 1940s, and for a long time, it operated an electric trolley line that connected Bangor with surrounding towns (below).

Haskell served in the Maine House of Representatives and Maine State Senate before being named BHE president in 1958. Gov. Edmund Muskie resigned on January 2, 1959, to fill a US Senate vacancy; as senate president, Haskell was sworn in as governor and held that position for five days until the inauguration of Gov. Clinton Clauson. (Above, courtesy of BHS; below, courtesy of BDN.)

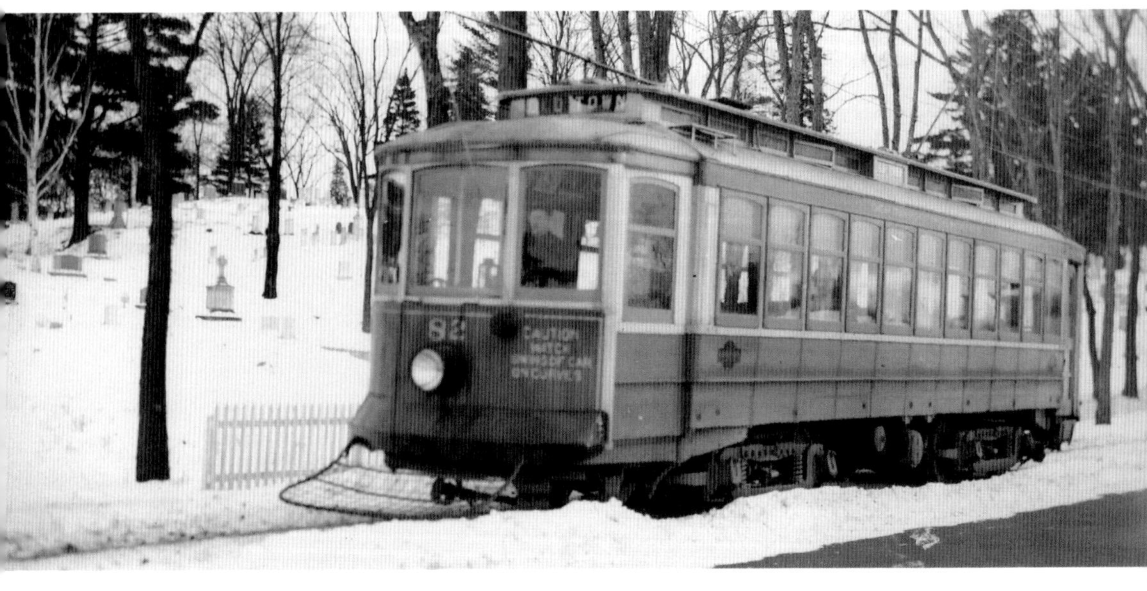

CHAPTER FOUR

Writers and Artists

For a small city on the edge of Maine's great forests, Bangor has always provided fertile soil for aspiring writers and artists. Journalists and newspaper publishers started "spreading the news" among Bangoreans in the early 19th century and continue to do so today; artists discovered the beauty of central Maine and its residents by the mid-1850s.

And as for sculptures, more than one Bangor monument was designed and cast by a miracle worker in bronze or iron.

Continuing a decades-old tradition of journalism in the lower Penobscot Valley, Marcellus Emery published an opinionated and decidedly unpopular newspaper that greatly offended certain Bangor residents in the summer of 1861. In the 1920s and 1930s, Lawrence Smyth was the face and voice of the *Bangor Daily News*, still the newspaper-of-record in central and northern Maine.

Daughter of a prominent late-19th-century couple, Mary Adele Hopkins grew up in Bangor before honing her journalistic skills in New York City in the early 20th century. Her scathing expose of a disastrous factory fire launched Hopkins on a career that even took her to war-torn Europe in late 1915.

In 1827, a successful Bangor businessman hired Jeremiah Pearson Hardy to paint a portrait. His first check—and the favorable attention received by the portrait—convinced Hardy that he could make a living as an artist.

He did so for a quarter century, and today his paintings adorn public buildings in downtown Bangor. Sprinkling sculptures and statues here, there, and everywhere in the Queen City, sculptor Charles Tefft created art that graces Bangor into the 21st century. His highly detailed bronze statue of Vice Pres. Hannibal Hamlin stands in the center of Kenduskeag Mall, a pleasant walkway connecting Central and State Streets in downtown Bangor.

Wilfred Mansur was also a designer, but of buildings, not monuments and statues. A well-known local architect in the late 19th century, he rose to prominence after the 1911 fire that devastated downtown Bangor (ironically, two Mansur-designed buildings did survive the deadly blaze). Hardly had the ashes cooled when Mansur started designing buildings that arose on specific empty lots; among his post-1911 buildings still in use today is the Stetson Block (see page 20).

A high school English teacher by trade and an astute central Maine historian by desire, James Vickery collected thousands of photographs and hundreds of stories from the region's past. His books revealed the people and tales of yesteryear in Bangor, Brewer, and elsewhere.

Countless readers worldwide discovered the world of horror through the stores of Stephen King, Bangor's most famous writer. He and his wife, author Tabitha King, established their home on the West Side; although not open to the public, the house and its bat- and spider-adorned wrought-iron fence remain a favorite "must-photograph" destination for King fans.

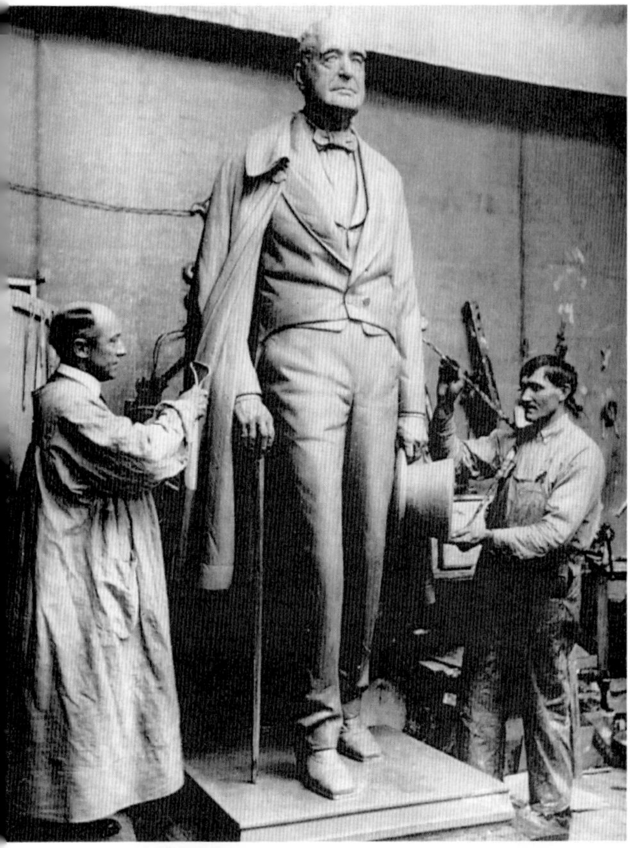

He Sculpted Bangor

The art of sculptor Charles Eugene Tefft graces Bangor.

Born in Brewer in October 1874, Tefft sculpted a bust of Gen. Joshua L. Chamberlain when 17. Tefft studied sculpture at the Artist-Artisan Institute in New York City and apprenticed with John Quincy Adams Ward.

The talented Tefft was commissioned to create sculptures at various American venues, but his works are quite evident in Bangor. He designed the Spanish-American War Memorial on Main Street and the Hannibal Hamlin statue (left) on Kenduskeag Mall.

When the descendants of Bangor lumber baron Luther H. Peirce funded a memorial in his honor, Tefft sculpted a statue of three river drivers in 1925. This memorial stands next to the Bangor Public Library (below).

Tefft sculpted the Lady Victory statue on Norumbega Parkway. (Left, courtesy of RRS; below, courtesy of BFS.)

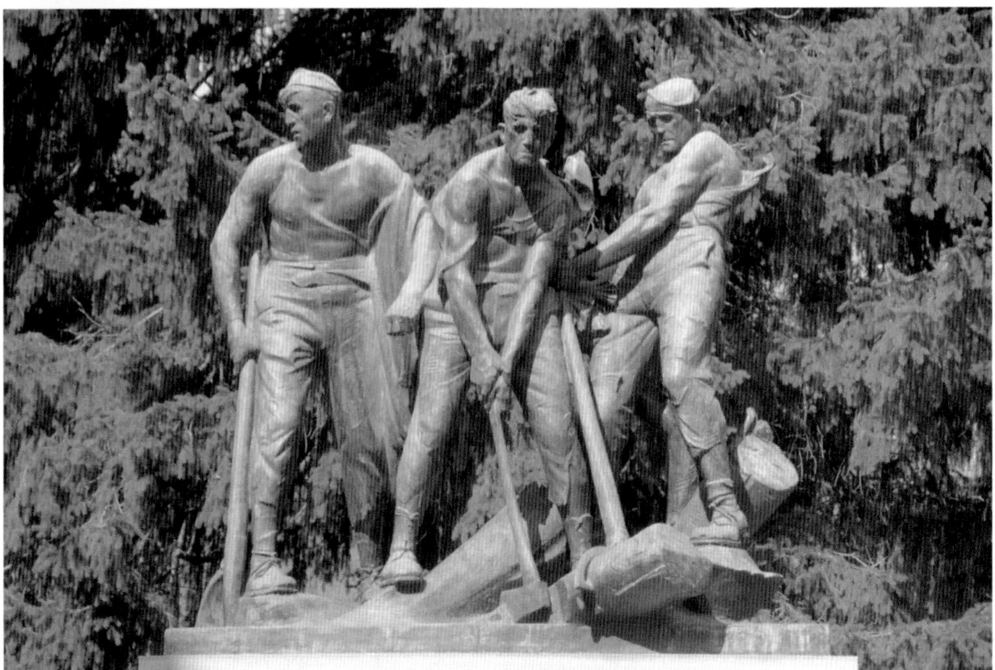

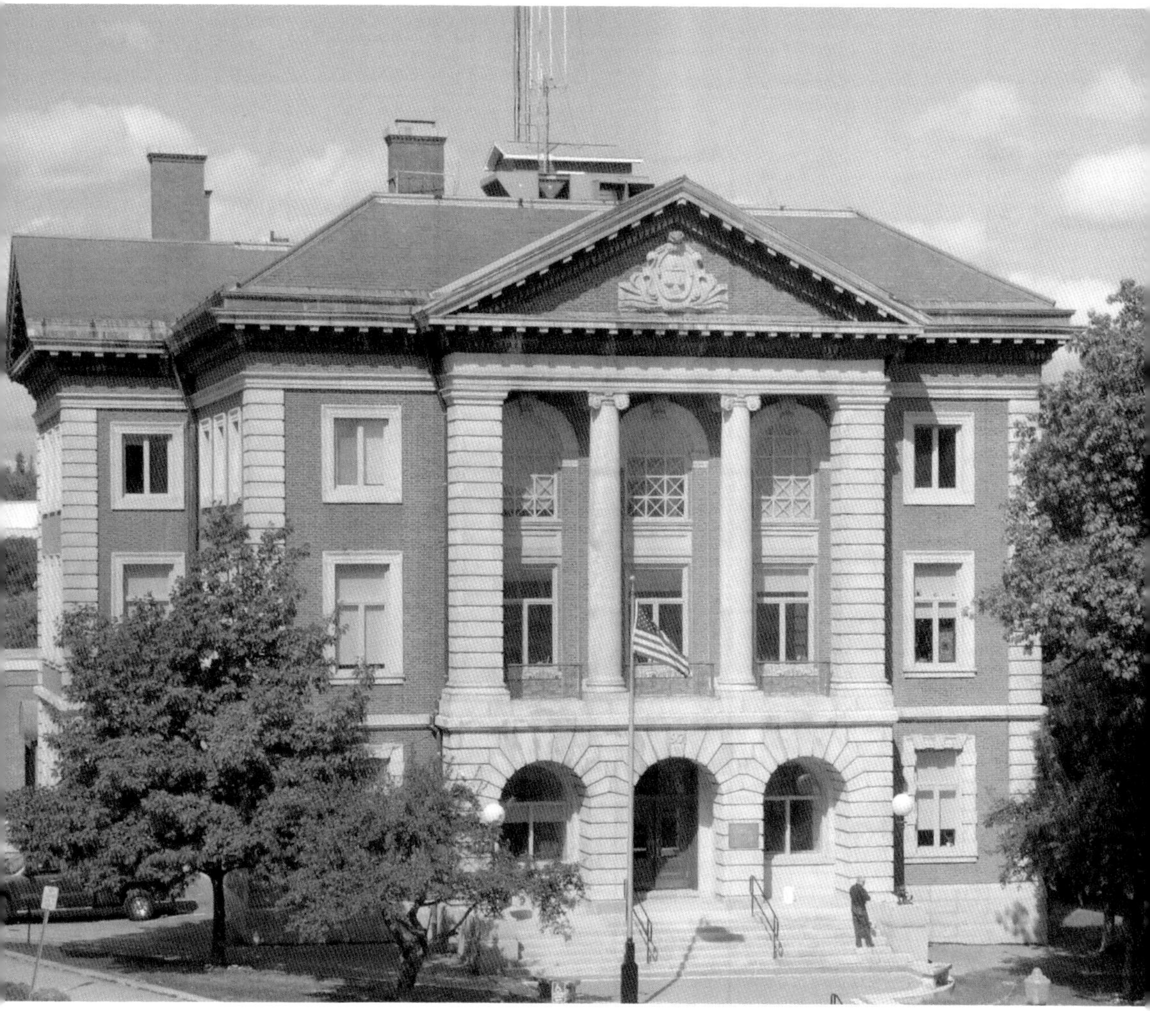

He Designed Bangor

Much historic Bangor architecture owes its creation to Wilfred Mansur, born in Bangor in 1855. A prominent architect, he designed buildings lost to the 1911 fire and buildings that rose from its ashes.

Mansur often designed buildings built in brick or stone; among them were the Penobscot County Courthouse (above) and the Bangor YMCA, once located across Court Street. Surviving from 1892 are the Columbia Building at Columbia and Hammond Streets and the Nichols Block on Exchange Street.

After the 1911 fire, Mansur designed the Stetson Block on Central Street, the Hall and Stearns Blocks on Exchange Street, and the Graham Building at Harlow and Central Streets.

Among other distinctive buildings attributable to Mansur are two former Bangor fire stations, No. 5 on State Street and No. 6 near St. Joseph Hospital on Center Street. (Courtesy of BFS.)

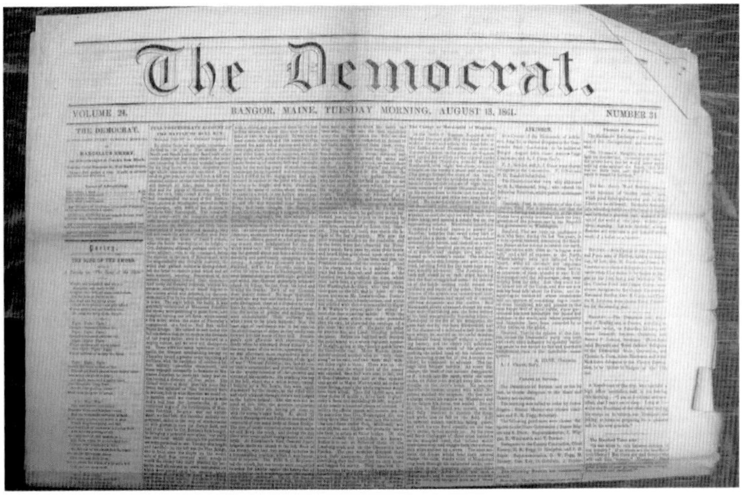
The Democrat.

VOLUME 28. BANGOR, MAINE, TUESDAY MORNING, AUGUST 13, 1861. NUMBER 31

THE DEMOCRAT.

The First Amendment Takes Flight

The First Amendment rights of newspaper publisher Marcellus Emery flew out a window on Monday, August 12, 1861.

Emery editorialized against the Civil War in his newspaper, the *Democrat*, printed on the fourth floor of the Wheelwright-Clark Block, overlooking West Market Square in downtown Bangor (below). Incensed after Emery published Jefferson Davis's account of the Battle of Bull Run in July, pro-Union Bangoreans sacked his newspaper office on August 12.

The mob busted his press and tossed its pieces and his files and furniture out the window onto a bonfire down below. Rioters later physically threatened Emery. He did publish one more issue of the *Democrat* (above).

In 1866, Emery sued 14 suspected mob ringleaders for $30,000 in damages. He was awarded $916.66. (Both, courtesy of BFS.)

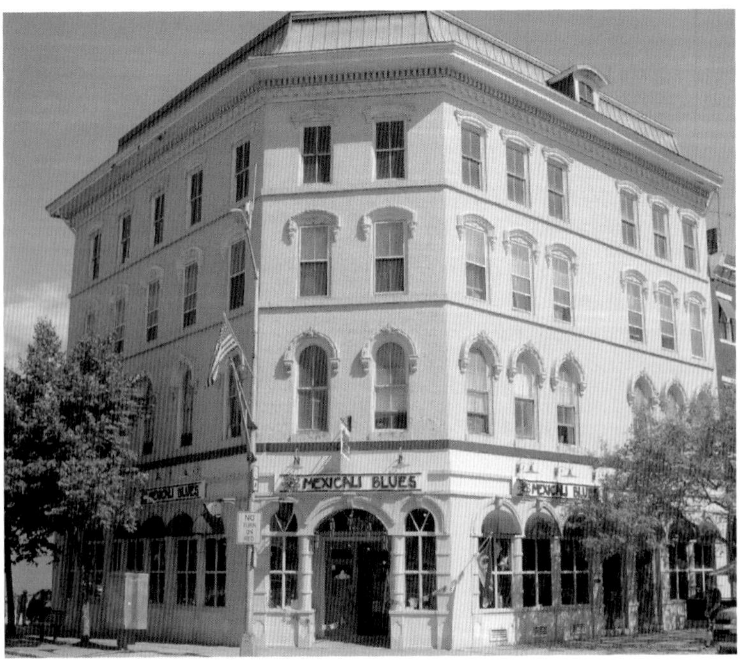

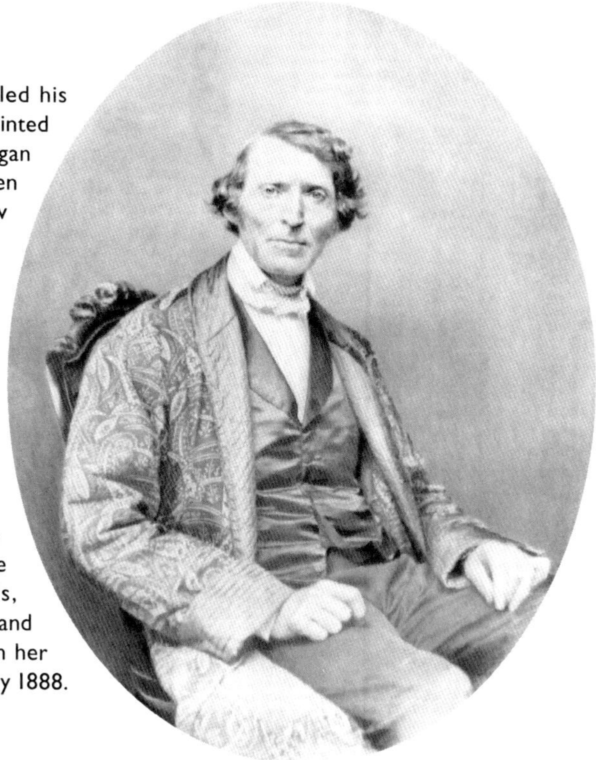

Portrait Artist

Jeremiah Pearson Hardy (right) revealed his artistic propensity at age 15, when he painted a biblical scene. Seven years later, he began his professional training in Boston and then studied painting for a short time in New York before returning home to Hampden in summer 1827.

That year, some Bangor businessmen commissioned Hardy to paint the first portrait for which he received payment. In 1830, he opened a studio in Bangor, and his career took off from there.

During the next 22 years, Hardy became a well-known artist specializing in striking portraiture of Bangor's leading citizens and their relatives. In 1840, he painted Lt. John Hodsdon of the Maine militia (below). Hardy's son, Francis, opened a photography studio in Bangor, and his daughter, Annie, became a painter in her own right. Jeremiah Hardy died in February 1888. (Both, courtesy of BPL.)

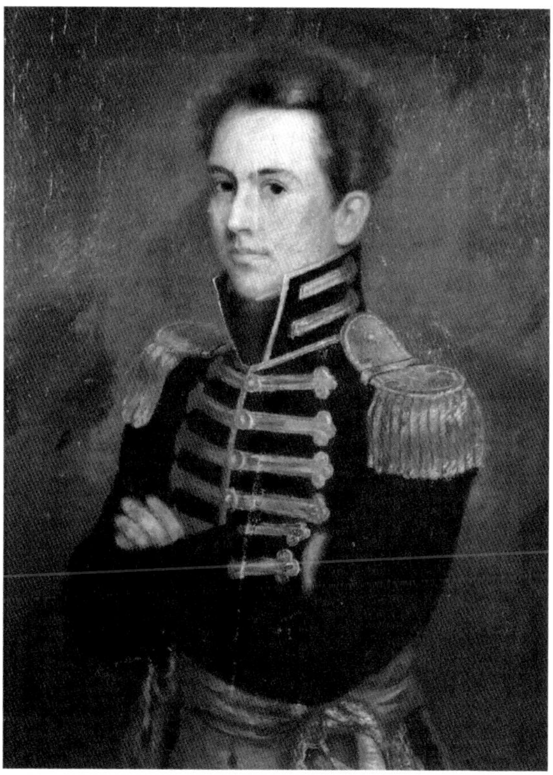

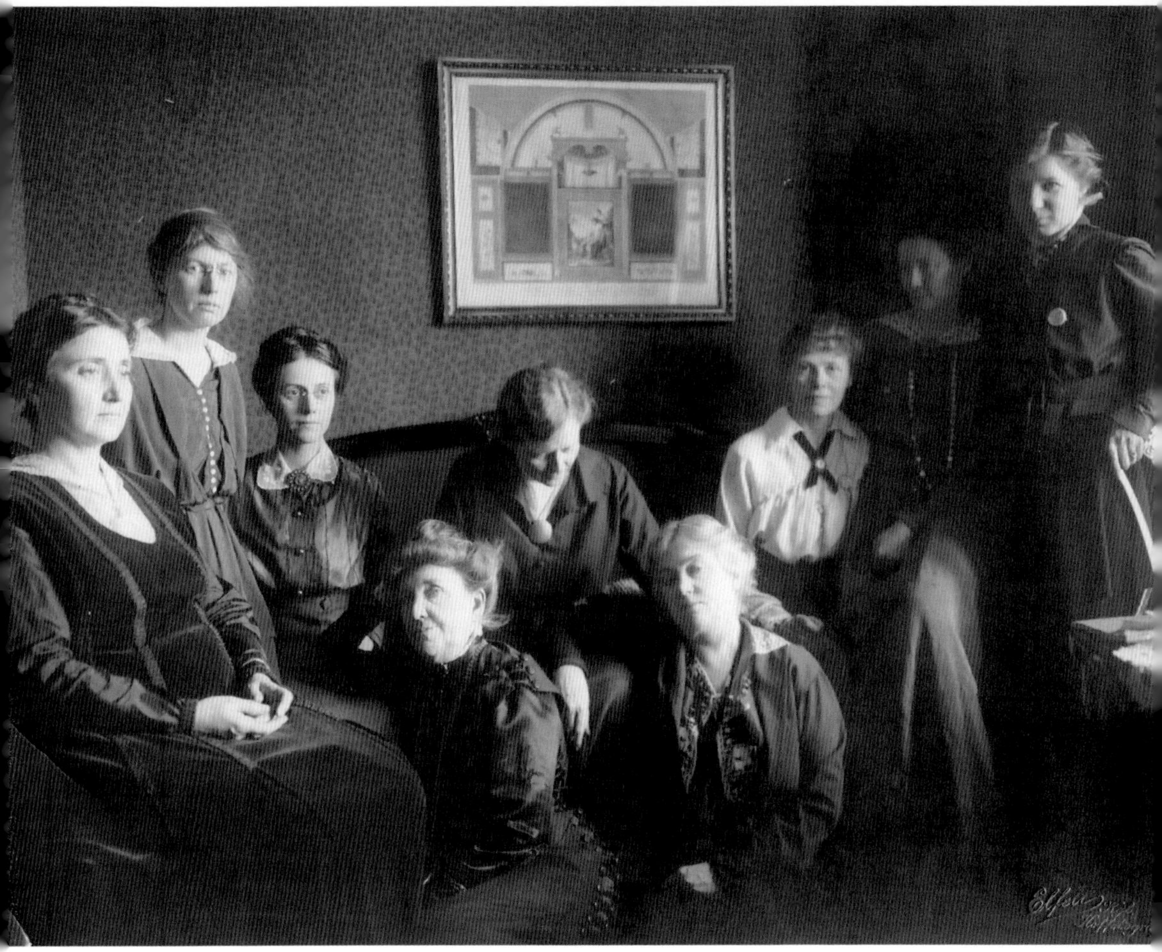

A Scathing Expose

A desire to write lured feminist and suffragette Mary Adele Hopkins from Bangor to Manhattan. She painstakingly investigated a November 1910 fire that killed 25 women working in a substandard Newark, New Jersey, factory. In April 1911, *McClure's Magazine* published her scathing expose excoriating the building's owners and negligent state officials. That article launched Hopkins's literary career.

Hopkins participated in the Henry Ford Peace Expedition to Europe in winter 1915–1916. Among the women involved with that expedition were, from left to right, Lola Bross Lloyd, Winnetka, Illinois; Mary Adele Hopkins, New York City; Julia Grace Wales, professor at University of Wisconsin; Florence Holbrook, Chicago; Dr. Naima Solpbom, Sweden; Katherine Leckie, New York City; Baroness Ellen Palmotierna, Sweden; and Elizabeth Watson, New York City. (Courtesy of Henry Ford Peace Expedition Collection, Rare Book & Manuscript Library, Columbia University in the City of New York.)

Reporter Broke Glass Ceiling
Presidents, aviators, and sports figures met their match when tiny Nelle Penley began an interview. From the 1930s to the 1960s, when women were often called "society editors," Penley did a man's job at the *Bangor Daily News.* Among her best-known subjects were Amelia Earhart, John F. Kennedy, and gutsy World War II bomber crews like the one pictured at Dow Air Force Base. (Courtesy of BPL.)

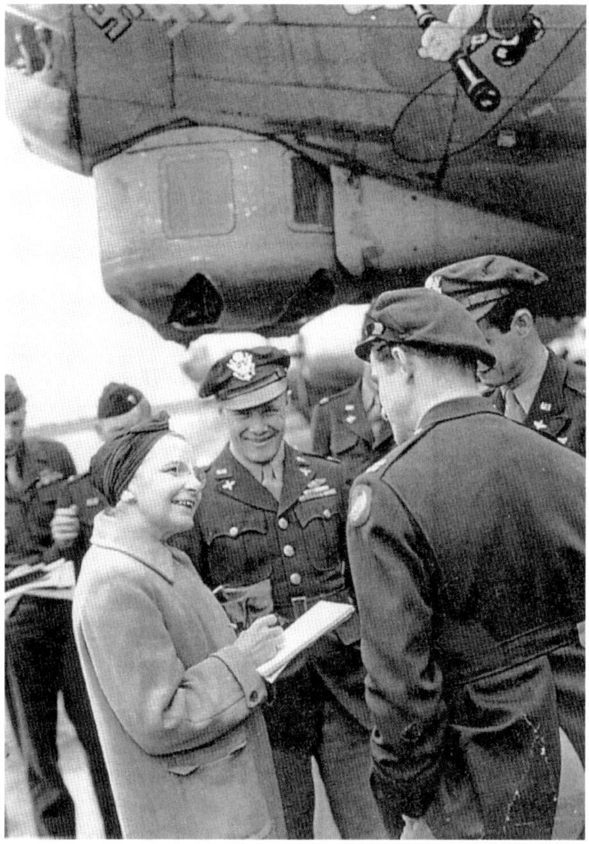

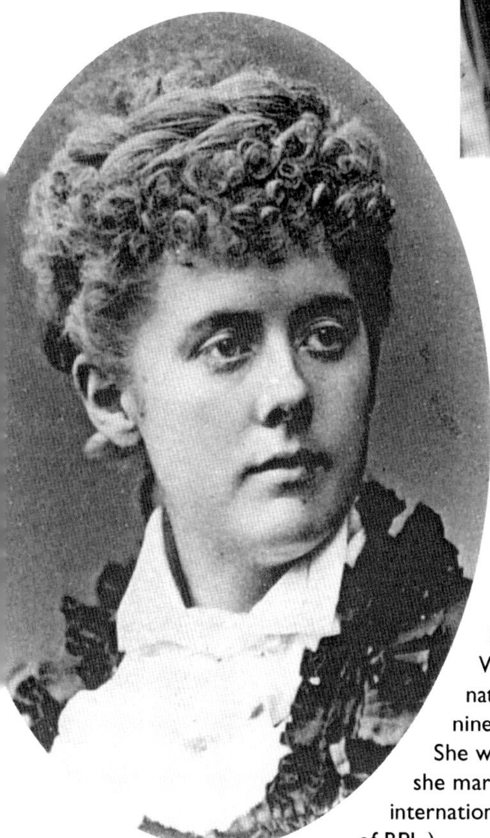

Best-Selling Novelist
Danielle Steel has nothing on the prolific writer Blanche Willis Howard, who escaped the "close confinement" of her native Bangor for the openness of Germany, where she penned nine novels, a travelogue, numerous short stories, and poems. She was a gifted pianist and friend of Richard Wagner. In 1890, she married Baron von Teufel, thereby becoming a baroness. An international reading audience mourned her death in 1898. (Courtesy of BPL.)

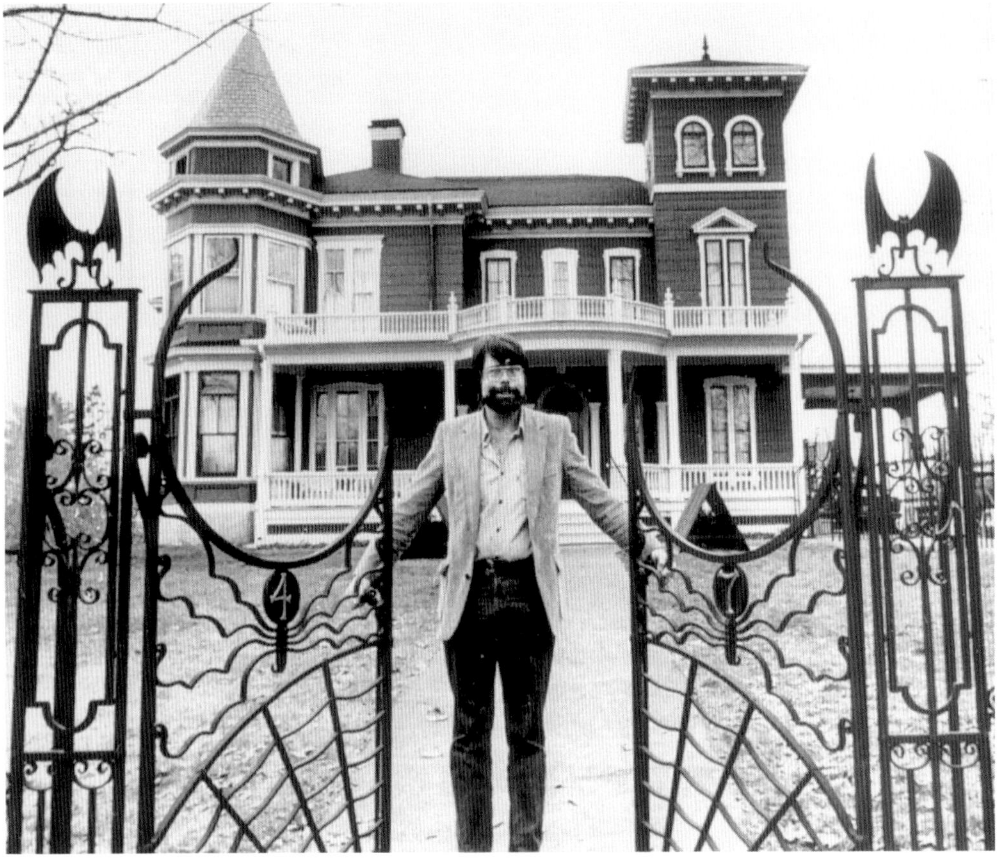

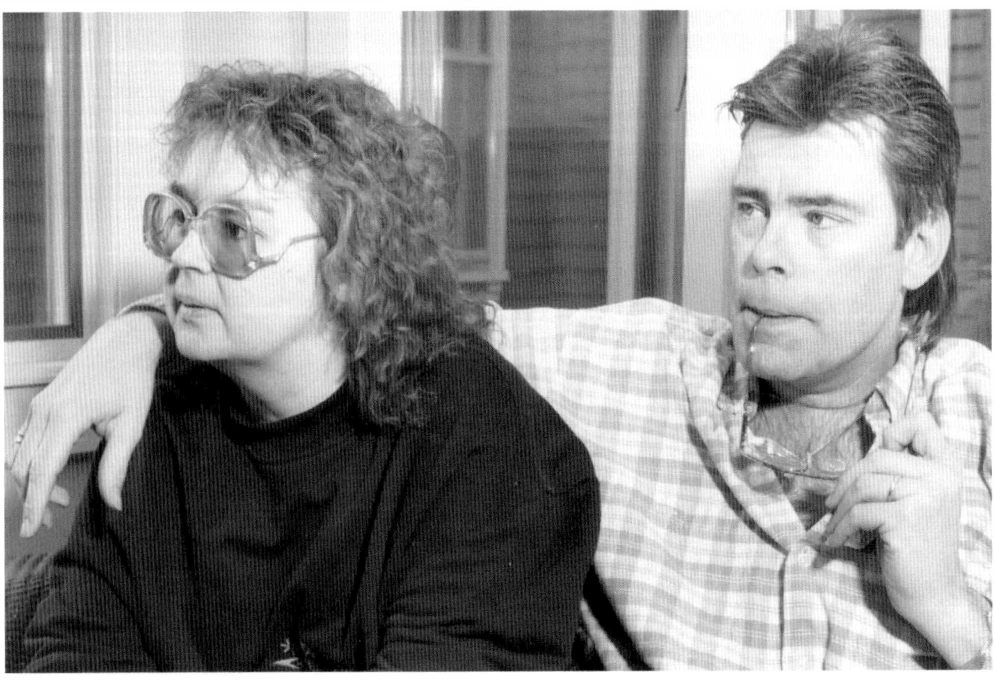

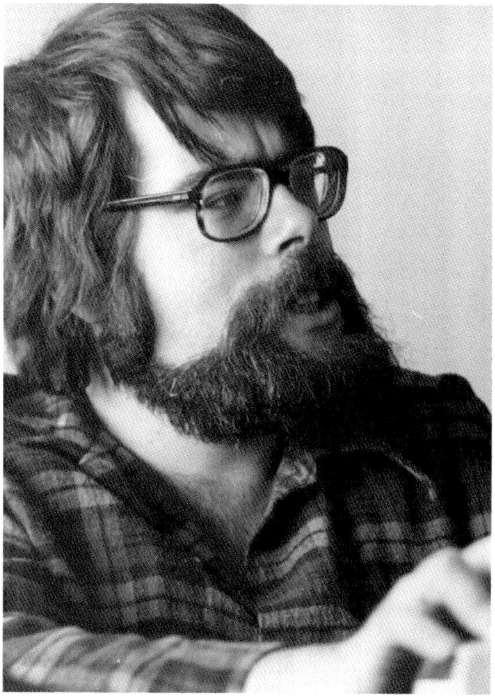

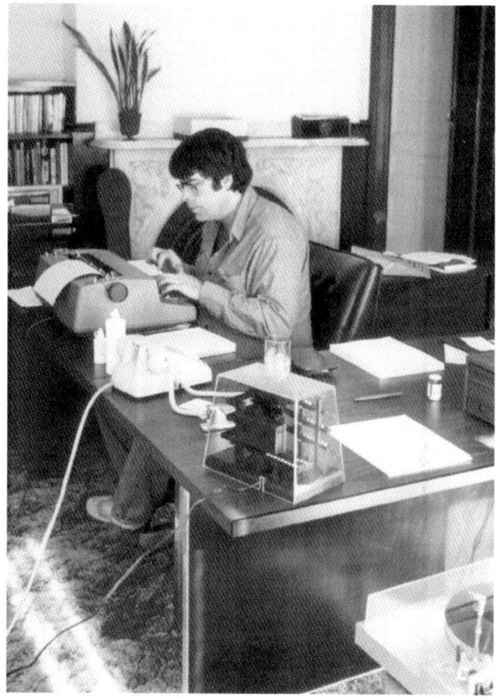

Bangor's Beneficent Horror Kings

Along with the Paul Bunyan statue and the Thomas Hill Standpipe, Stephen and Tabitha King's red Victorian home at 47 West Broadway is a tourist attraction. Nearly every day, die-hard fans and photographers crowd around the bat- and spider-adorned fence to perhaps glimpse one of history's best-selling authors.

The West Side residence is closed to the public, and the chances of seeing the King family are slim. But that does not stop Stu Tinker, operator of SK Tours, from bringing tourists by for a look. Tinker explains that King purchased the home in early 1978, having moved to the area from southern Maine to attend the University of Maine, later teaching English at Hampden Academy.

While a teacher, he penned his first novel, *Carrie*. After King tossed the manuscript into the trash, believing it to be just that, it was retrieved by Tabitha and submitted to a publisher in 1973. Scores of books, plays, and screenplays later, he is still writing.

Among the list of sites associated with King's many novels, especially the opus *It*, are the Standpipe, which is rolled into the river; Central Street, the scene of a gangster gun battle; and the State Street Bridge, where a young gay man died. A scene from *Pet Sematary* was filmed at Mount Hope Cemetery. George Beahm's illustrated *Stephen King Country* documents many of these locales.

The Kings' philanthropy is evident in some of their favorite projects, including the enlargement of the Bangor Public Library and the building of the Beth Pancoe Municipal Aquatic Center and the Shawn T. Mansfield Stadium, home to the Senior League World Series.

"The fun of writing novels isn't in the finished product, which I don't care about that much," he said in a 2014 *Bangor Daily News* interview. "To me, those [books on the shelves] are like dead skin. They're things that are done. But I love the process."

Tabitha King has published eight novels and two nonfiction works. She married Stephen King, whom she met while working at the University of Maine library, on January 7, 1971. They have three children; Naomi Rachel King, a Unitarian-Universalist minister; and authors Joseph Hillstrom King and Owen Phillip King.

Author Joyce Carol Oates may have summed up King's legacy best while introducing him at a public talk at Princeton University in 1997: "His fellow writers admire him for his commitment to the craft of fiction and the generosity of his involvement in the literary community." (All, courtesy of BDN.)

Bangor's Prolific Architect

Eaton Tarbell left his mark on Eastern Maine. From the angular roof of the Bangor Auditorium, demolished in 2013, to the round Peakes Auditorium at Bangor High School, the architect worked for decades. A former student of Frank Lloyd Wright, Tarbell designed homes in the 1950s and 1960s that reflected Wright's style. By the time of his death in 1992, Tarbell had designed 2,500 Maine buildings. (Courtesy of BDN.)

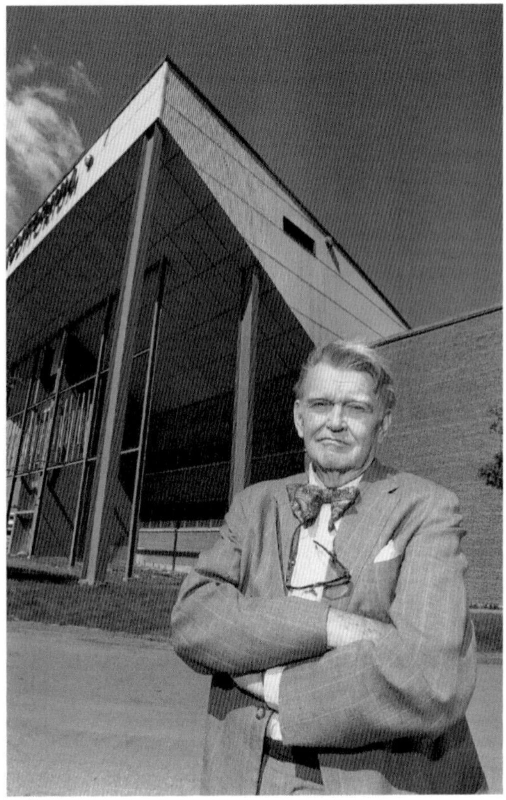

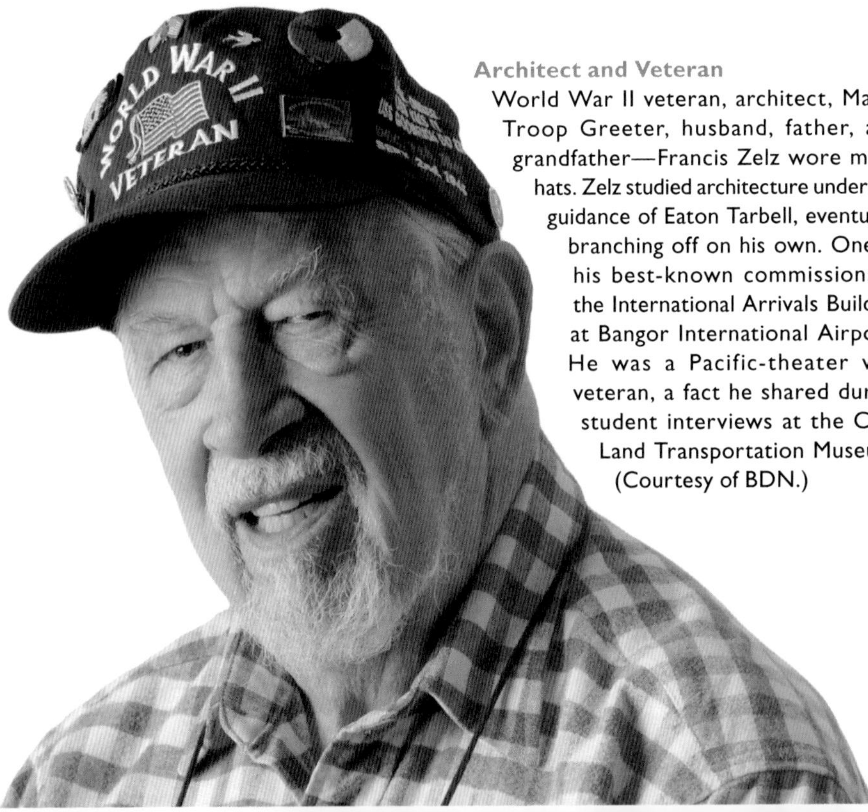

Architect and Veteran

World War II veteran, architect, Maine Troop Greeter, husband, father, and grandfather—Francis Zelz wore many hats. Zelz studied architecture under the guidance of Eaton Tarbell, eventually branching off on his own. One of his best-known commissions is the International Arrivals Building at Bangor International Airport. He was a Pacific-theater war veteran, a fact he shared during student interviews at the Cole Land Transportation Museum. (Courtesy of BDN.)

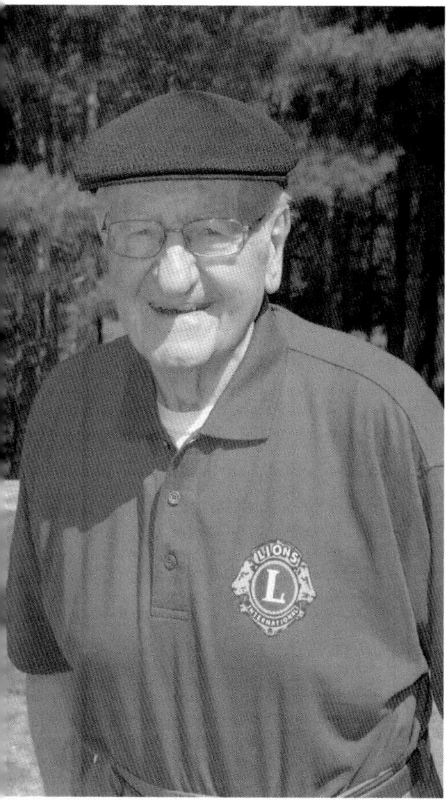

Paul Bunyan Designer

The Paul Bunyan statue on Main Street in Bangor is the "biggest" project with which J. Normand Martin (left) was involved during his career as a graphic artist.

Martin hails from Madawaska, where he started drawing as a child. Completing a three-year course at the School of Practical Art in Boston, he later worked for Hampden-based Tom Kane Advertising. Martin created many detailed drawings of well-known Maine personages. He designed and crafted a 12-car Bangor & Aroostook Railroad model train displayed at the 1967 World Expo in Montreal.

Martin designed the Paul Bunyan statue, which was dedicated in February 1959 to celebrate Bangor's sesquicentennial as a city. Dressed up as Bunyan (right), Martin later posed for a photograph by the statue. He did not design the statue after himself, he stresses. (Left, courtesy of BFS; below, courtesy of J. Normand Martin.)

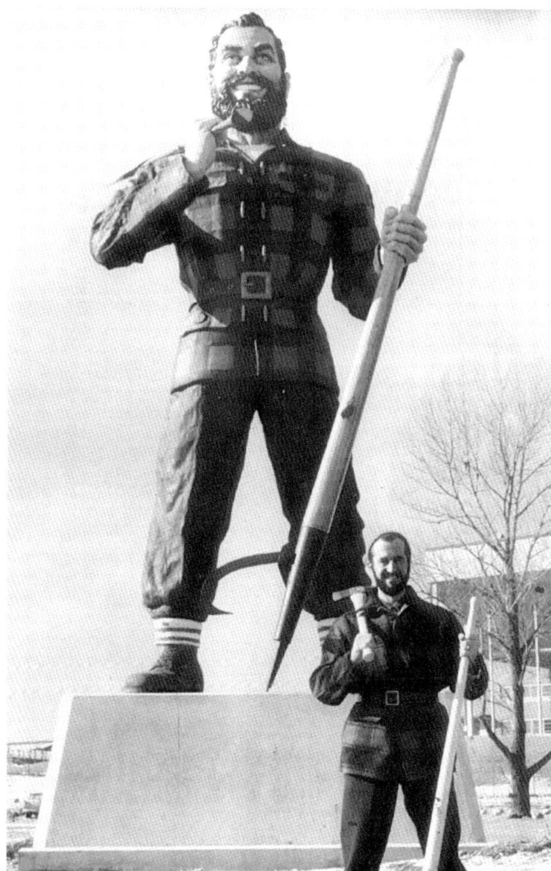

A Dedicated Bangor Newspaperman

Many interesting people have worked behind the scenes at Bangor newspapers since Peter Edes published the first local newspaper in 1815. Among the city's 20th-century journalism stalwarts was Lawrence T. Smyth, who finished his 45th year with the *Bangor Daily News* on August 17, 1937.

Smyth was a natural in the journalism profession. At 13, he left Bangor schools to work for the Bangor harbormaster and then joined the *Bangor Commercial*, a daily newspaper that competed with the *Bangor Daily News*. Later, Smyth honed his writing skills for a New York newspaper; after a brief return to the *Bangor Commercial*, he left Bangor in 1886 to work for such larger newspapers as the *New York Evening Star*, *Boston Post*, and *Commercial Bulletin*.

In 1892, Smyth joined the *Bangor Daily News*. He soon rose to city editor, managing the reporters responsible for covering Bangor. Posting their stories without bylines, reporters wrote in descriptive prose about every possible topic from international stars gracing the Bangor Opera House to police raids on illegal bars to, in time, the advent of automobiles, electricity, and telephones.

On the job, "there were two things he would not tolerate—hypocrisy in any form, and careless or slovenly writing," the *Bangor Daily News* noted.

Over the years, Smyth's staff wrote about many events with consequences far beyond Bangor. The 1911 fire that almost wiped out the Queen City may have been Smyth's shining moment as a city editor; encompassing print and photography, the coverage captured the disaster as it unfolded. Later, Smyth and his staff detailed Bangor's rise from the ashes.

Smyth became the editorial writer in 1930. During his long career at the *Bangor Daily News*, then located on Exchange Street, the newspaper increased its circulation and political clout. Other newspapers, including a large daily in St. Louis, offered Smyth upper-management positions.

He declined because, according to the *Bangor Daily News*, "he had a theory, a philosophy . . . that a relatively small city is the finest and cleanest place in all the world in which to live and bring up a family."

Smyth "believed that being editor on the morning paper of such a city would in the end pay larger dividends, in contentment and even in worth-while accomplishments" than working for "some great city publication," the *Bangor Daily News* extolled Smyth on his 45th anniversary with the newspaper. (Courtesy of RRS.)

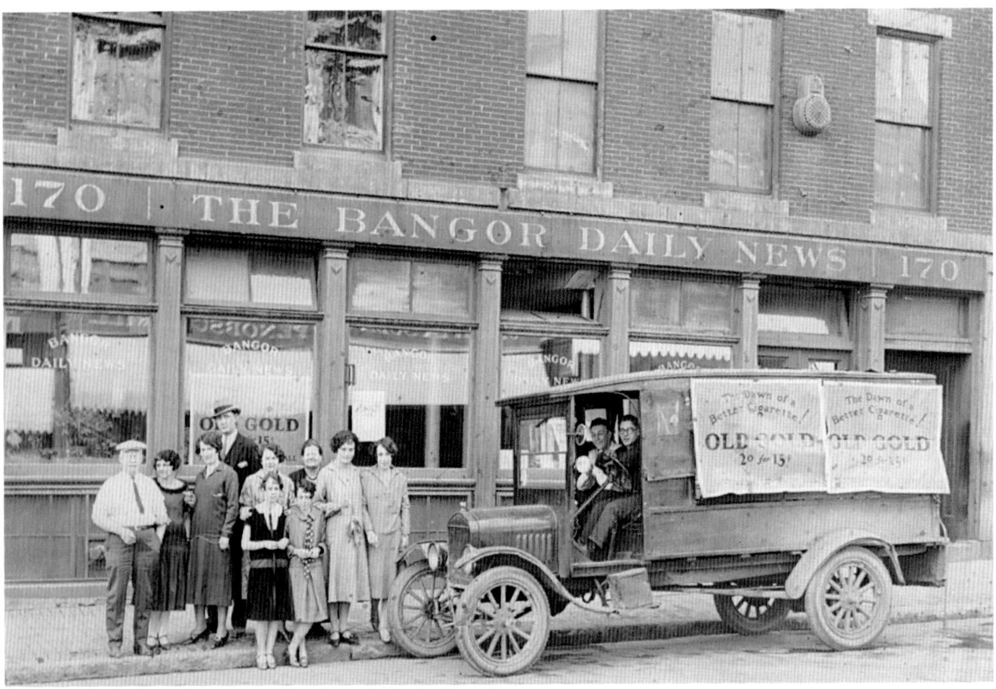

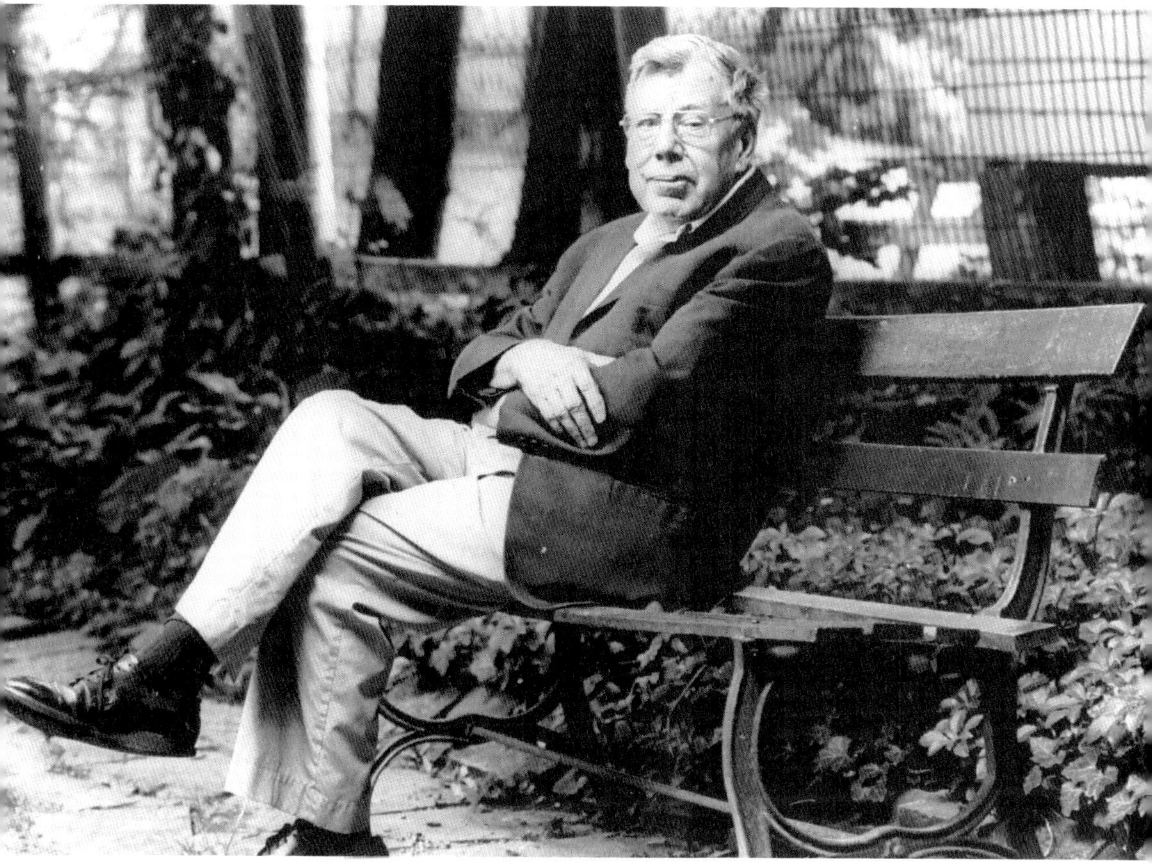

Queen City's Eminent Historian

The late James B. Vickery was a veteran English teacher, completing decades in the classroom at Brewer High School. But it was his passion for history—Bangor history, in particular—that endeared him to anyone who came into his presence. The Unity, Maine, native (born in 1917) taught throughout the state, but the day he moved to Bangor was in itself historic. At first, he lived in a classic brick apartment house on Broadway that reminded him of Boston's Beacon Hill. Finally, he occupied an apartment in the former high school building next to the public library, his second home. Years of library research produced a 1969 illustrated history of Bangor, various booklets, annotations, and other papers. Earlier he wrote a history of Unity that is still in use today. Jim Vickery's daily routine would be to spend the morning in the library, then walk downtown for lunch at a restaurant, return to the library, and then back to his apartment for dinner, TV news, and bed. Among his hobbies were Harley-Davidsons and cowboy scenes. His ancestors migrated west to Montana, a state that he and a cousin visited and enjoyed to the fullest. Following his death in 1997, his extensive collection of books and documents was divided among the Bangor Public Library, Fogler Library, and other institutions. (Courtesy of BDN.)

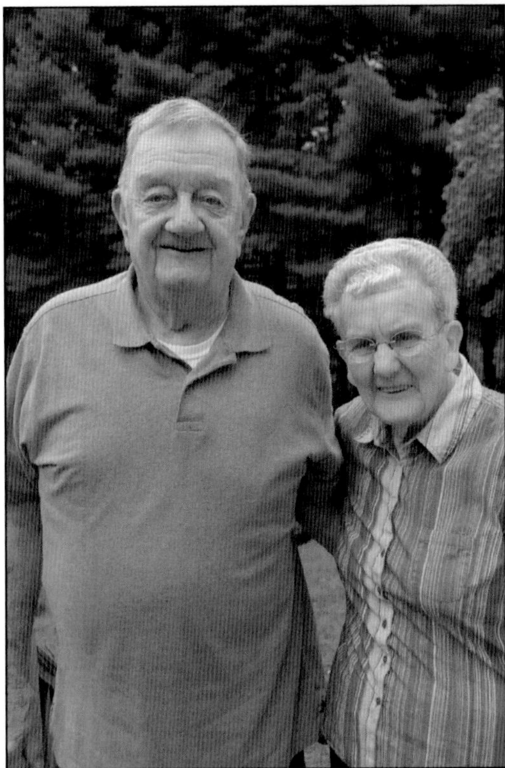

Bangor Model

Years ago, Charles "Bill" Tuck of Bangor and his brothers—Warren Young and Richard Tuck—"met together every Saturday to do things." They decided to build a scale-model Thomas Hill Standpipe (below). Warren and Richard built the frame and wired its lights; Bill glued on the tiny cedar shingles "one by one." The brothers painted the model, displayed it at their family church (Columbia Street Baptist), and presented it to the Bangor Water District.

Today, the model standpipe is displayed at Bangor International Airport's domestic terminal.

Bill also designed and handcrafted a scale-model Noah's Ark to biblical dimensions. Made from white pine, the 4.5-foot ark had three floors. Bill and his wife, Ethel (left), traveled throughout New England, the Maritimes, and even to Florida to talk about the ark before more than 500 groups. (Courtesy of BFS.)

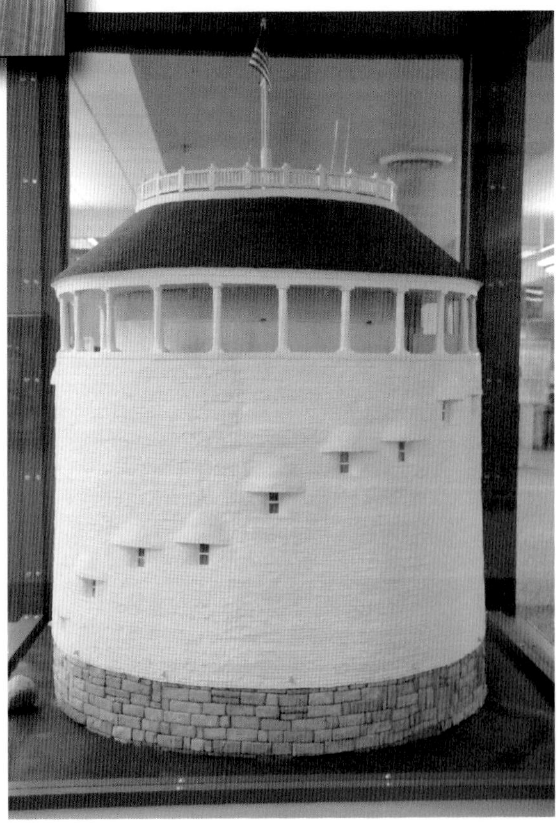

CHAPTER FIVE

Entertainment and Sports

Living as they did so far from Boston—the heart of New England–based entertainment and sports—Bangor residents learned to "make do" by the mid-19th century. Famous actors, actresses, and musicians appeared for decades at such local venues as the Bangor Opera House (the modern home of a busy and talented theater group).

Established before the Civil War, the Bangor Band remains active more than 150 years later. Since its founding in 1896, the Bangor Symphony Orchestra (BSO) has staged incredible concerts that rival the best concerts to be heard in Boston or New York. The BSO has attracted talented conductors like Horace Mann Pullen and Werner Torkanowsky.

The advent of recorded music, radio, and TV created new opportunities for talented Bangoreans. Dick Curless and "Yodeling" Slim Clark brought country music to Bangor and America with their often Maine-based songs; Curless's 1965 hit, "A Tombstone Every Mile," popularized the travails of truck drivers hauling freight along Route 2 in northern Maine and made Curless famous. In the 1950s and the 1960s, Clark appeared frequently on programs produced at Bangor-based WABI-TV.

George Hale was a young broadcaster at another WABI, an AM radio station in Bangor. For decades, he provided the live play-by-play for local high school basketball games and the popular Eastern Maine Basketball Tournament. Hale is still at the microphone on a local FM radio station.

Over at rival WLBZ-TV, the brilliantly innovative Eddie Driscoll charmed almost two generations of Maine children (and often their parents) while appearing on locally produced programs. At WVII-TV, local businessman Dick Stacey started sponsoring the *Country Jamboree* in the mid-1970s, and he soon became a household legend in Maine and Atlantic Canada.

Bangoreans took an early liking to sports, as evidenced by the often informal leagues created by local baseball and basketball aficionados. Local high school and college athletes excelled in various varsity sports (and often in more than one), and some Bangor boys went on to play baseball and other sports at the professional level.

Leroy Patterson was a star athlete in four varsity sports at Bangor High. Local baseball star Matt Kinney was drafted by the Boston Red Sox and pitched for four major-league teams. Matthew Stairs hit the game-winning home run for the Philadelphia Phillies in the 2008 National League Championship Series.

A longtime Bangor resident, John Winkin coached the University of Maine Black Bears' baseball team to regional championships and six trips to the College World Series. He later coached the Husson University Eagles' baseball team.

As a child, Bangor native Bob Cimbollek developed a lifetime passion for basketball; he went on to break high school and collegiate scoring records and to coach tournament winning high school basketball teams.

Bangor sports fans liked their boxing then and now, as evidenced by the popularity of boxers Michael Daley and Marcus Davis. Known as the "Irish Hand Grenade," Davis became a successful mixed martial arts fighter with the Ultimate Fighting Championship in the 21st century.

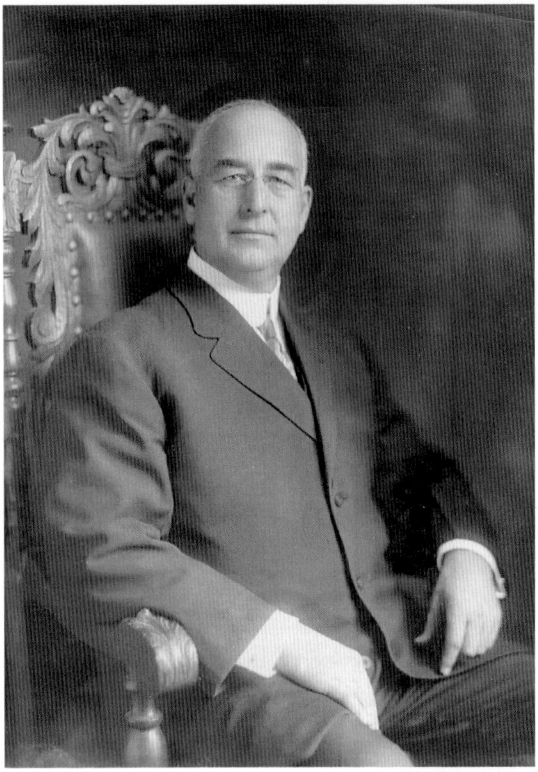

Baton in Hand, Music in Heart
Horace Mann Pullen operated a dancing school in 1896, but it was his orchestra that wowed audiences. That year, with help from piano teacher Abbie Garland, Pullen became the Bangor Symphony Orchestra's first conductor. At its premier concert at city hall on November 2, the 16-member group performed Schubert's Unfinished Symphony. Ten conductors later, the BSO is one of the nation's oldest continuously operating orchestras. (Courtesy of BHS.)

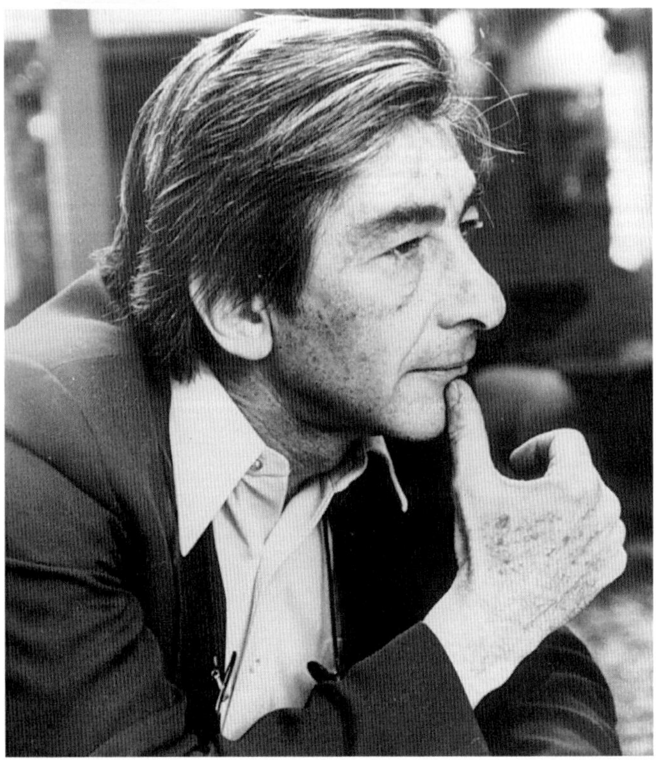

World-Class Symphony Conductor
Born in Berlin, Germany, and raised on a kibbutz in Israel, Werner Torkanowsky transformed Bangor's community symphony into a world-class orchestra. After immigrating to the United States in 1948, he studied conducting under Pierre Monteux, who operated a school in Hancock, Maine. Capping a career of opera and symphony conducting, he was music director of the Bangor Symphony Orchestra from 1981 until his death in 1992. (Courtesy of BHS.)

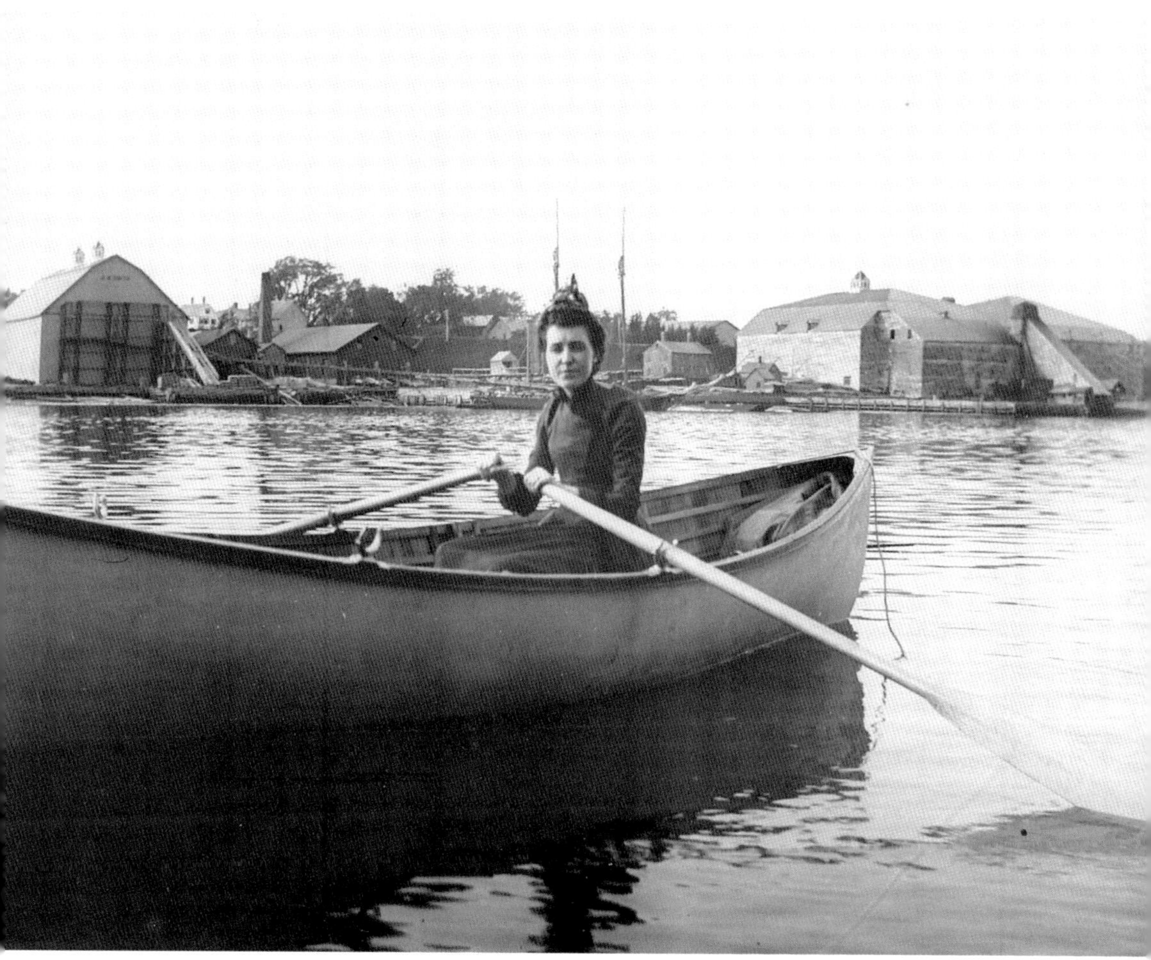

Salmon-Catching Jennie Sullivan

Dressed in a long black dress with feathers in her hair, Jennie Sullivan was an unforgettable character during spring salmon fishing season. Pictured above in 1892 paddling a pea pod–shaped fishing boat opposite the East Hampden icehouses, Sullivan relished being seen on the male-dominated Penobscot River. On March 30, 1902, the *New York Times* reported, "Hundreds of fish are taken with the fly at the Bangor pool every season, but the . . . first fish at the Bangor pool was taken by a young girl [actually a young woman], Jennie Sullivan of Bangor." Two years earlier, Sullivan was the only woman to take two fish in one day. In 1916, four years after the tradition began of sending the first salmon caught to the White House, the angler recorded as Jeanette Sullivan had the honor. Pres. Woodrow Wilson may not have known her name, but he certainly remembered the fish. She took fishing very seriously, escaping to a little shack in North Brewer near what is now the Penobscot County Conservation Association's clubhouse. She lived at 377 Hancock Street, near the banks of the river she loved. (Courtesy of RRS.)

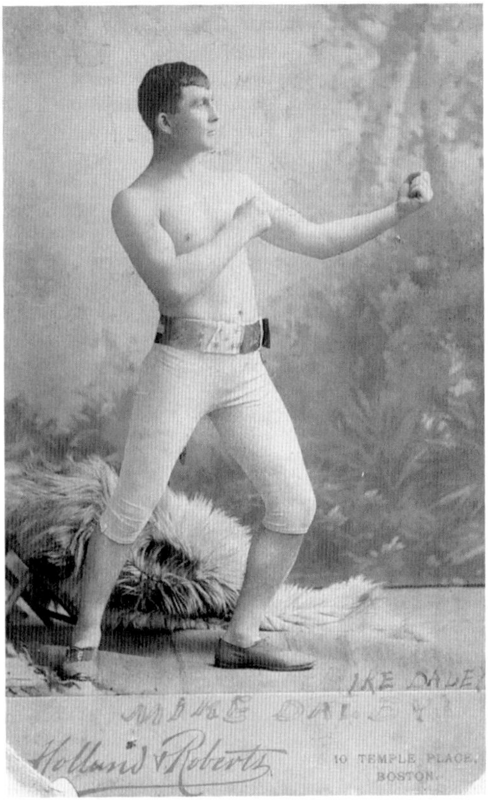

Lightweight Boxer's Tragic Fall

Born in Bangor in 1865 to what the *New York Times* called a "highly respectable" family, Michael Daley won the New England lightweight boxing championship in the late 19th century. While fighting Austin Gibbons for the national championship in 1893, Daley was knocked out in the 31st round. He returned to Bangor, where, in 1910, following criminal convictions, he died in a jail cell at age 45. (Courtesy of Gary W. Woolson.)

Football Coach

Gerry Hodge played football for the Bangor High Rams before joining the University of Maine Black Bears on the gridiron from 1950 to 1952. Hodge then coached the Mexico High School squads to a 30-4-2 record before taking over the helm at Bangor in 1957. The Rams accumulated a 116-50-2 record and won three Class A state championships during his 18-year tenure. Hodge died in June 2014. (Courtesy of BDN.)

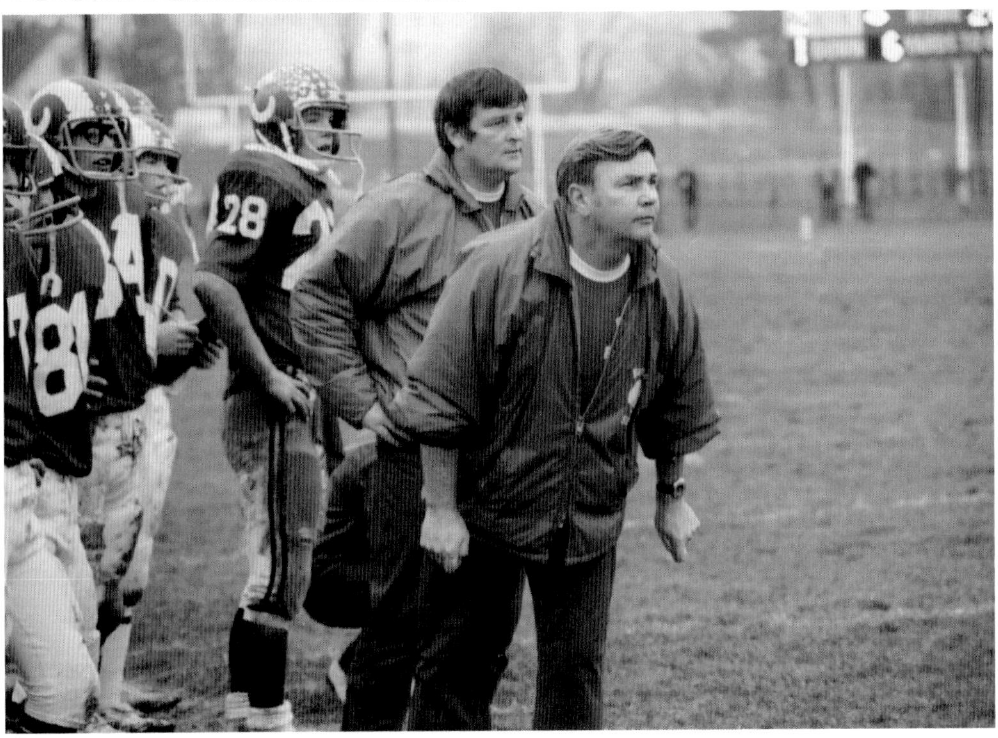

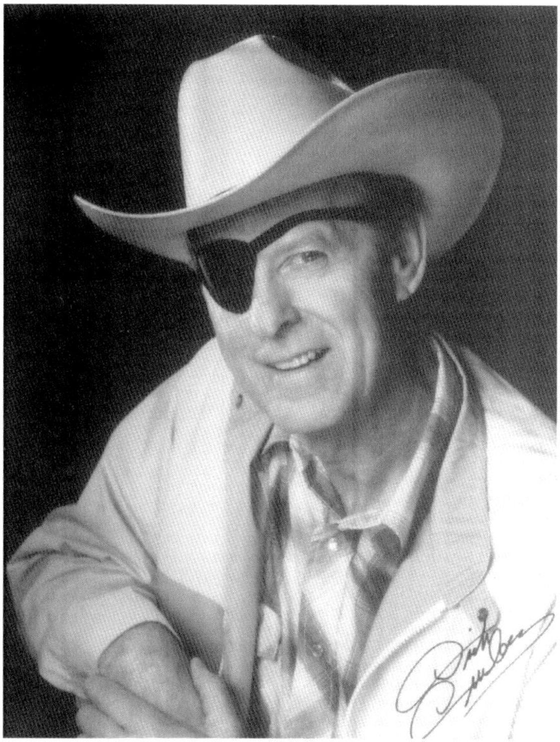

The Baron of Country Music

The eye patch–wearing Richard William Curless sang with a rich baritone voice. Born in Fort Fairfield in 1932, Dick Curless was catapulted to fame in 1965 when his record, "A Tombstone Every Mile," became a Billboard hit. He toured with Buck Owens's All-American Show before moving to Bangor, where a train he had placed beside his home became a curiosity. He died in 1995. (Courtesy of BDN.)

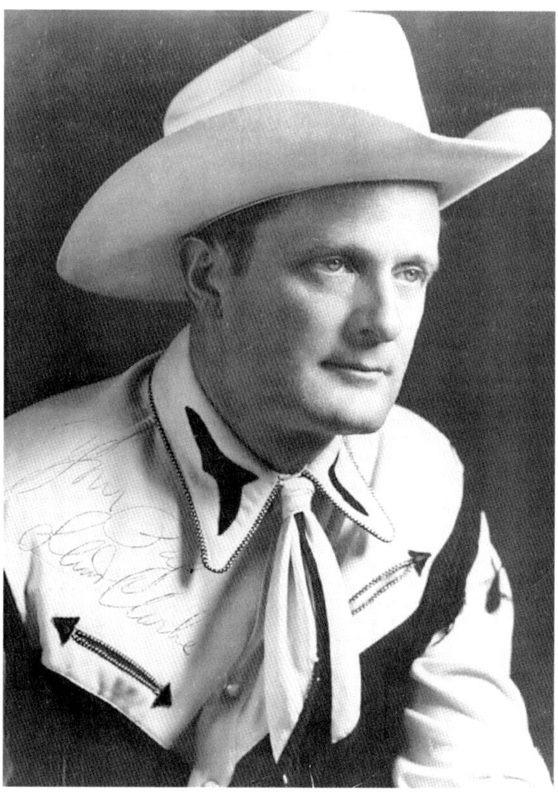

Everyone's Favorite Yodeler

No one could yodel like Raymond LeRoy Clark. For nearly 70 years, the singer known as Slim Clark worked on stage, radio, television, and at festivals where he performed cowboy, Western, and folk music. Born in 1917 in Springfield, Massachusetts, he found a dedicated audience in Maine, where his *RFD Dinnerbell* program on WABI radio was a favorite. Clark, who died in 2000, also painted wildlife scenes. (Courtesy of RRS.)

Dick Stacey and the Jamboree

Although the popular local TV show *Stacey's Country Jamboree* caused many fans to associate Dick Stacey with Brewer, he is actually from Bangor.

His career has included six years' service in the Maine Air National Guard, three summers working as a Bangor park director, and some years working for the Cole family. After buying a gas station at 428 Wilson Street in Brewer in the late 1960s, Chesley Cole replaced the building with a modern Chevron service station. Stacey, who was Cole's business manager, ran the station until 1970, when he leased it as "Stacey's Fuel Mart"; he later owned similar stations in Ellsworth and Harrington.

"I became the biggest tire dealer for Atlas Tires from Maine to Maryland," Stacey recalled. "I was the first dealer to order 1,000 tires at one time."

In 1974, he became the primary sponsor of the *Country Jamboree*, which had been produced live by the ABC-TV affiliate in Bangor since the late 1960s. A station representative "came in to sell me an ad" for Stacey's Fuel Mart, Stacey recalled. "I had never gone to the show, but it was popular."

Television stations in the Canadian Maritimes "picked up [the] ABC [station] out of Bangor" so viewers could watch *Monday Night Football*, and "they got *Stacey's Country Jamboree*," Stacey recalled. "The Canadians loved it."

After buying a motel at 429 Wilson Street in Brewer in 1976, Stacey taped the show in the motel's lounge. "The Canadians came in droves to see it," he said.

Stacey even took the *Jamboree* to Canada, where fans packed the seats to listen to such talented performers as Jennie Shontell. She recorded "Wings of a Snow White Dove," which became a big hit on both sides of the international border.

Stacey's Country Jamboree ran until 1985 and made Dick Stacey a household name in the greater Bangor area and the Maritimes. Dick and his wife, Sue, retired in 1998 and moved to Florida. They spend summers at their fifth wheel in a Bangor-area campground. Married for 42 years, they have six children and 13 grandchildren. (Courtesy of BFS.)

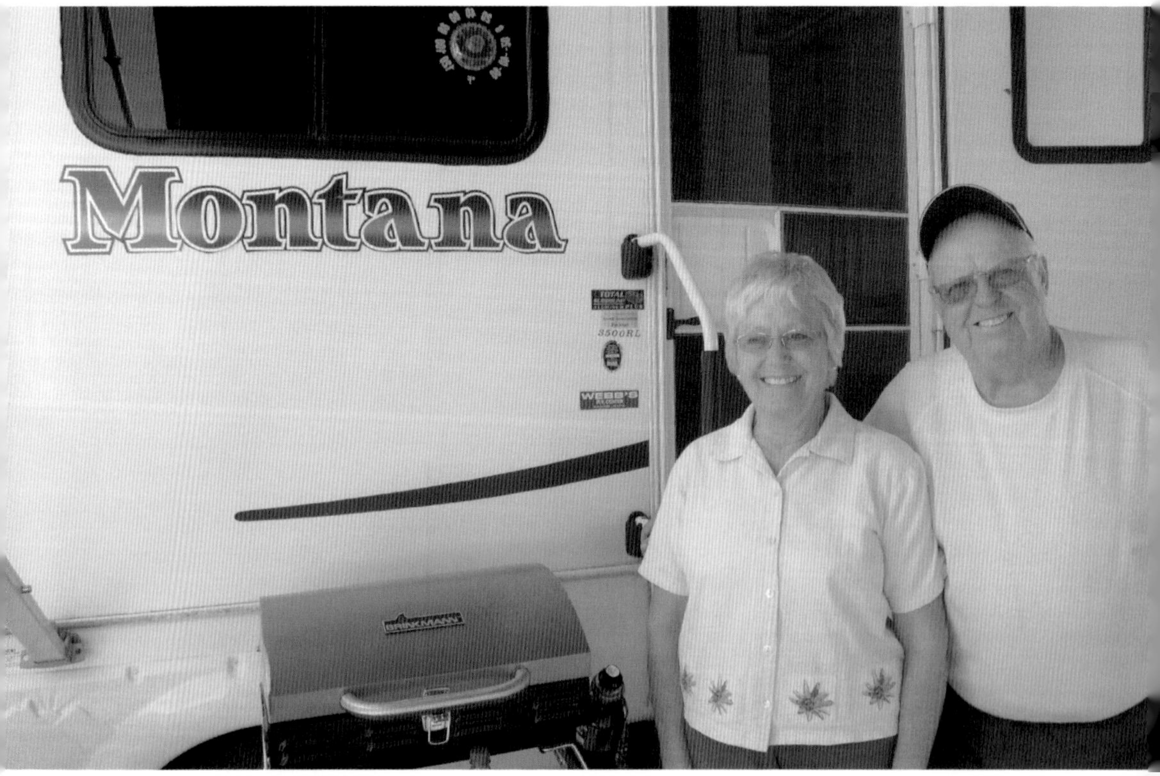

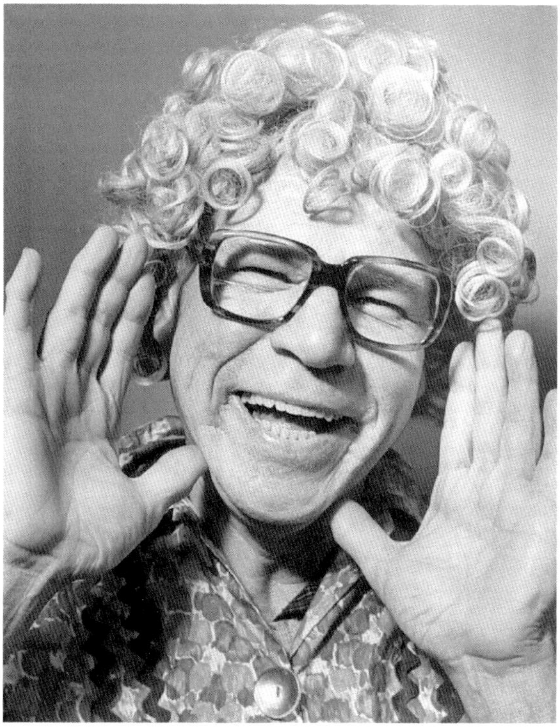

Television's Clown Prince

Stephen King likes to say that Eddie Driscoll warped his childhood. Thousands of other baby boomers also had their childhoods warped in a happy way by the clown prince of local television.

From 1954 until his retirement in 1987, Driscoll had viewers of WTWO, now called WLBZ, in stitches. His zany alter egos included Hadley the Horrible, Zog the Robot, Lance Fleazy, Bruce Budworm, and Aunt Margaret (pictured). For his show *Weird*, on which King appeared, Driscoll played the space alien, Krandel.

When Driscoll died of Alzheimer's disease in 2006, his daughter Amanda Vieira told the Associated Press, "I think he was a cross between Milton Berle and Jackie Gleason."

His programs included *Dialing for Dollars*, *Mason Mutt*, *The Great Money Movie*, and *The Supper-Time Super Show*.

Edgar L. Driscoll Jr. grew up in Brewer and served in the Navy until 1948. He later met and married his wife, Ruby, and went to work at Eastern Fine Paper Company. A fan of movies and vaudeville, he landed his first broadcasting job after answering an advertisement for a WTWO-TV announcer. Unable to find employment at Bangor's first TV station, WABI, he went to work at the other Bangor station in 1954, the same day it began broadcasting.

Driscoll turned down offers from Boston outlets because he loved Bangor. The station's homey atmosphere was a good fit for the surprisingly shy comic. Ruby Driscoll said, "He was quiet at home, but when the red light came on he was ready to perform."

Sometimes the clown needed a censor, as he lampooned local civic leaders. "Unless you really got on top of him, he could be a little naughty," recalled colleague Margo Cobb. Bill Green, a onetime Driscoll show camera man, remembered the double entendres.

Few Driscoll programs were recorded, but his impact lives on in websites such as Gilleymedia.com. Fan Chad Gilley wrote of the clown, "Eddie's personal legacy will be his two daughters, but [he] has left his fans with a lifetime of memories and laughter, and the genius of his talent has created a common appreciation, a bond of community that all of us who fell under his spell, especially those of us who were children at the time, can share and cherish for years to come." (Courtesy of BDN.)

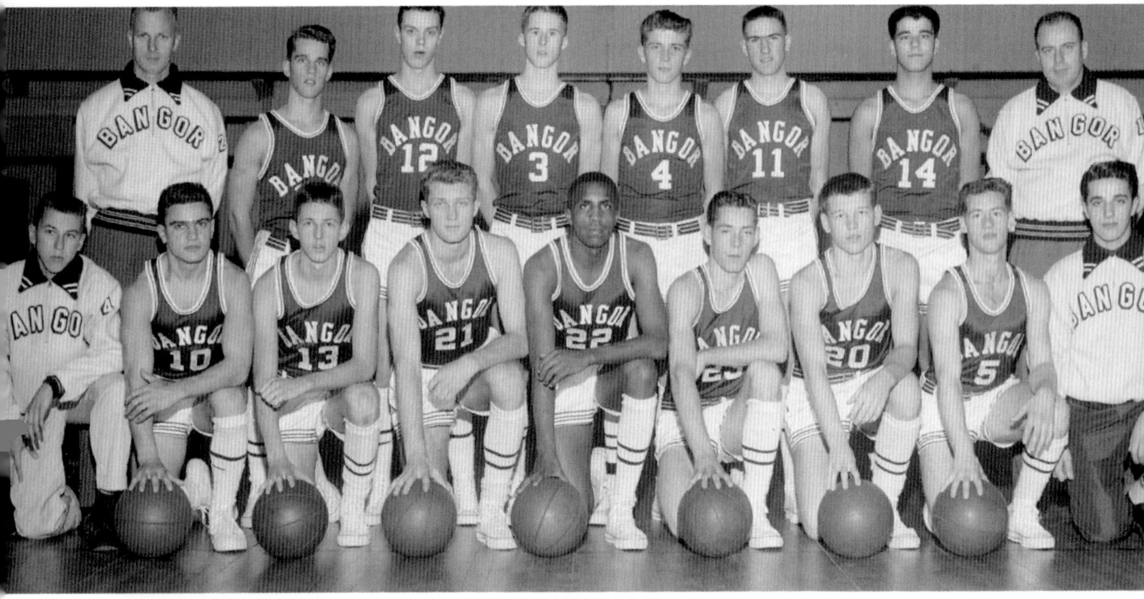

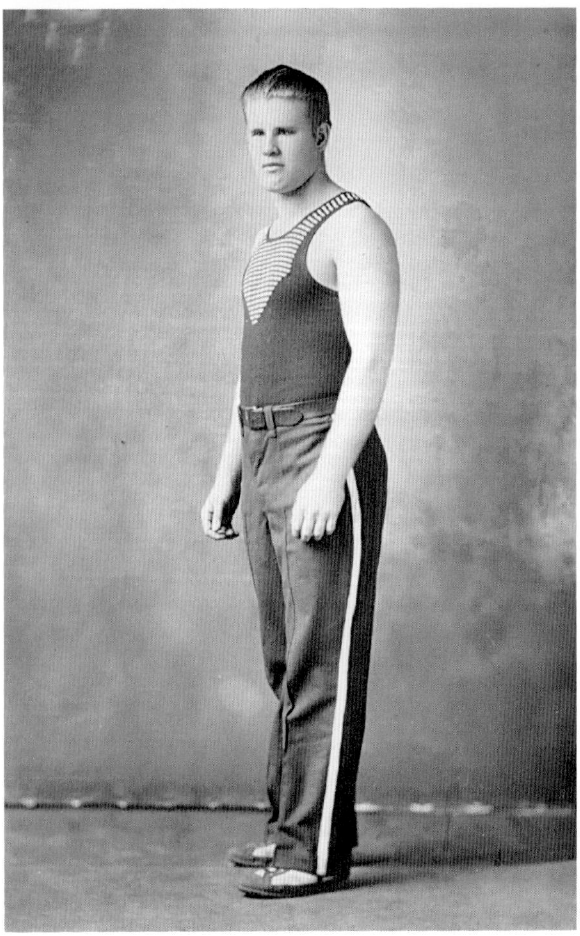

Star Athlete

Leroy Patterson (kneeling, fifth from left) was a stand-out athlete at Bangor High School, where he played baseball, basketball, football, and tennis. He attended the University of Cincinnati on a football scholarship and was named Most Valuable Player of that school's freshman football team. An official at local sports games, Patterson spent 33 years with the University of Maine Police Department before retiring in 2010. He died in 2012. (Courtesy of BDN.)

A Life of Recreation

When Lawrence "Pete" Furrow died in 1967, the parks and recreation department closed the city's playgrounds for two hours out of respect for the veteran recreational enthusiast. An outstanding high school athlete, Furrow also was a professional wrestler and did play-by-play sports broadcasts. He worked with senior citizens up until his death at age 56. (Courtesy of Tim Furrow.)

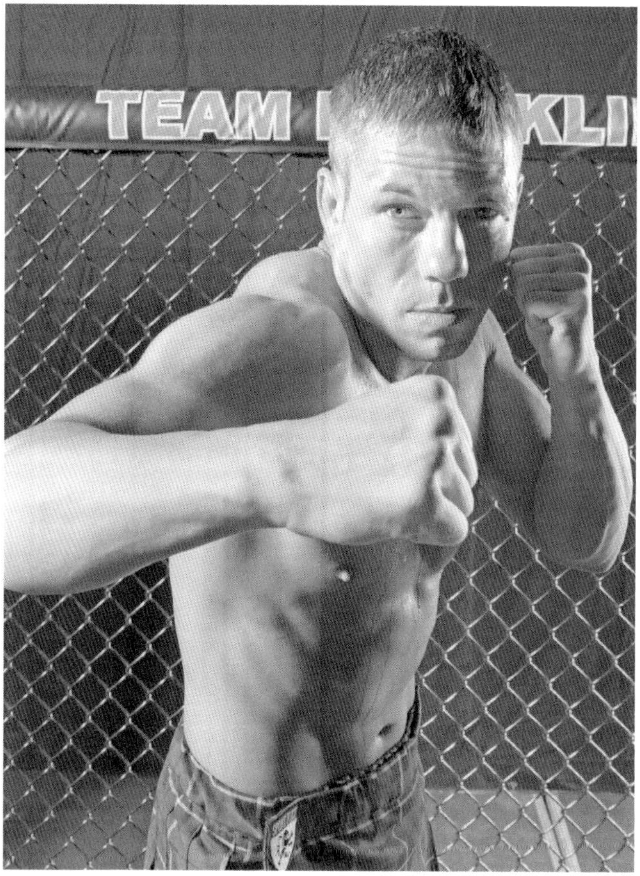

A Bangor Fighter

Recently retired from his successful careers as a professional boxer and mixed martial arts (MMA) fighter, Marcus Davis recalls, "I always wanted to be a fighter. My mother says I was punching before I was walking."

Davis took up amateur boxing in 1986, turned pro in 1994, and won his first two fights in Bangor boxing matches. Going 17-1 as a professional boxer, he defeated several Golden Gloves' champions.

Then, Davis became an MMA fighter with the Ultimate Fighting Championship. Known as "The Irish Hand Grenade," he fought "mostly on their overseas' cards. I was kind of the bad guy," facing local champions "on their ground."

His fighting career took off when Davis defeated British "Cage Rage" champion Paul Taylor in London in 2007. "We were just brawling in the fight," Davis recalls. Altogether, he fought 15 times in the UFC, which he left in 2010.

Spanning "about 200 fights," his career has taken Davis to 10 countries. He recently spent three weeks touring in Europe, where he spoke and taught at locations in Germany, Belgium, France, and Great Britain.

Reflecting his family's ethnicity—his Scottish ancestors settled in Ireland and lived there many years before emigrating to Nova Scotia and then moving to Bangor—Davis has developed a special affinity for Ireland, to which he has traveled multiple times.

Davis owns two Brewer businesses, 207 Athletes and the Team Irish MMA Fitness Academy and the Team Irish Performance Training Center in Westbrook. A 1992 graduate of Bangor High School, he lives in Bangor with his wife and their daughters; Davis has a son and a daughter by a previous marriage.

"I'm a huge family guy," he says. "My wife and I are best friends." (Courtesy of Marcus Davis.)

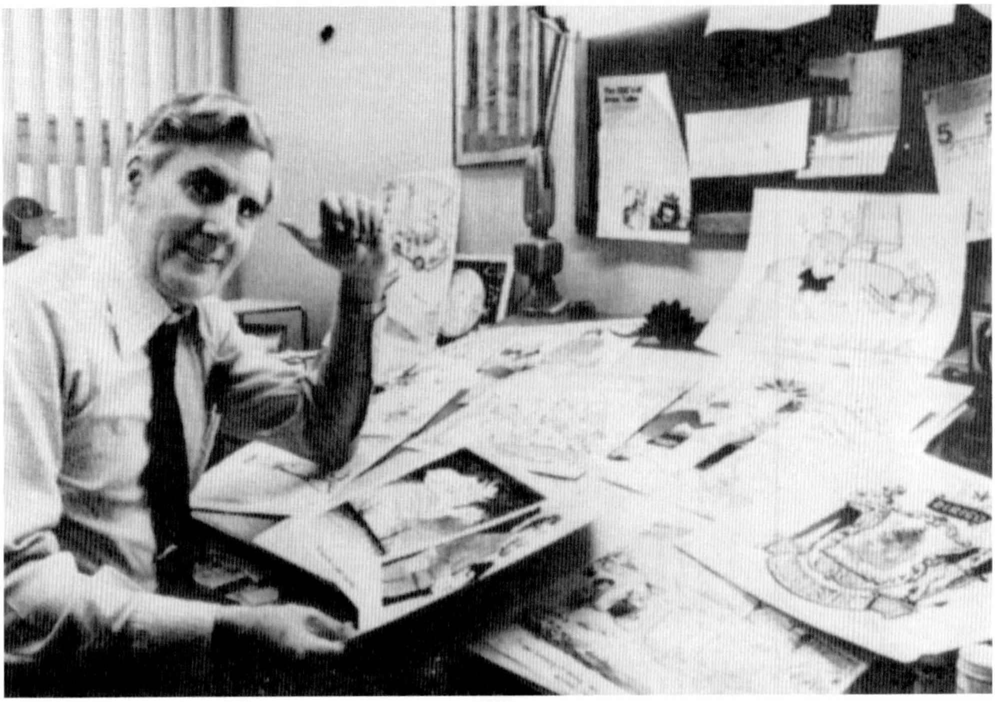

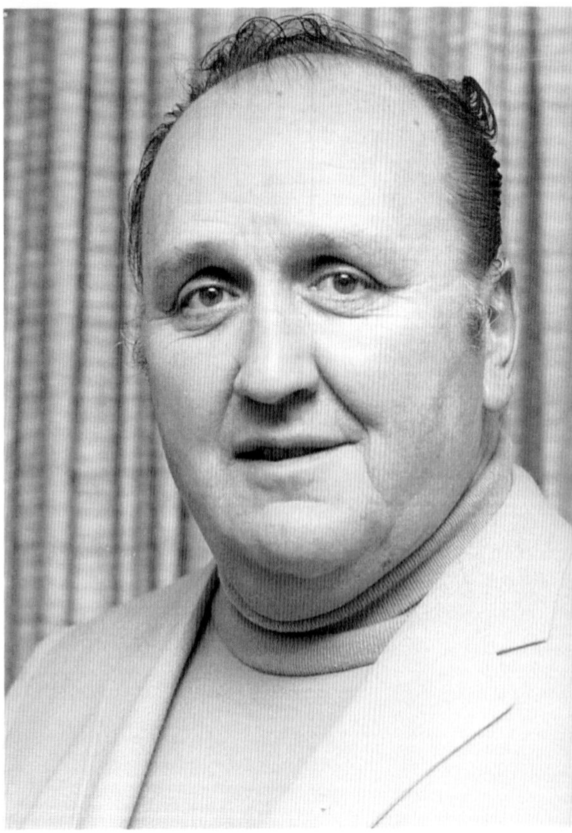

Father of the Bow-Tie Cat

Inside the lanky body of Vic Runtz beat the heart of a feline-loving child. The *Bangor Daily News*' first staff cartoonist moved to Bangor from Prince Edward Island in 1957 and slipped his cat mascot into every political artwork until his retirement in 1982. He sent his friends hand-drawn cards such as the one showing the award-winning artist making the best of his seventies. (Courtesy of Vic Runtz.)

Maine's Happy Wanderer

Ralph "Bud" Leavitt, born in Old Town, Maine, in 1917, was a colorful sportswriter and executive sports editor of the *Bangor Daily News*. He also hosted a Saturday night program on WABI-TV that attracted a range of viewers, many of whom neither hunted nor fished. Columnist Roy Blount Jr. wrote of Leavitt that he "fishes with Ted Williams and Red Smith—or rather, they trout-fish with him." (Courtesy of BDN.)

Passion for Basketball

Bob Cimbollek has been hooked on basketball since, as a second grader, he "watched the fifth and sixth graders play" the sport. "The game intrigued me; I could practice at it alone."

His father erected a two-hoop court at the family's Birch Street home in Bangor. Cimbollek and his friends practiced there, and he played in Bangor's elementary school league and for Bangor middle and high school teams.

Cimbollek set school records while playing for Husson College. Basketball fans remember him most for the years he coached at high schools in Fort Fairfield, Orono, and Bangor, including eight seasons at Bangor High and 14 seasons at John Bapst. His teams achieved a 446-161 record.

"I went into coaching to teach life skills you can't teach in the classroom," Cimbollek said. (Right, courtesy of BFS; below, both courtesy of Bob Cimbollek.)

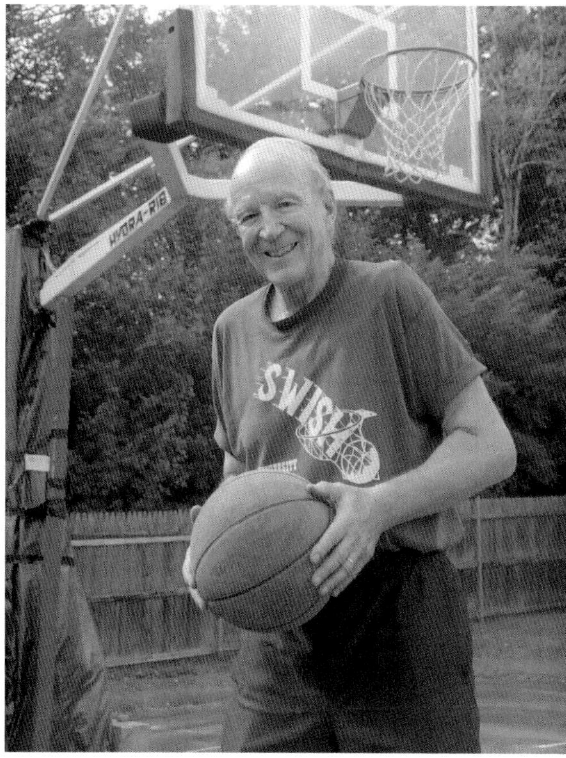

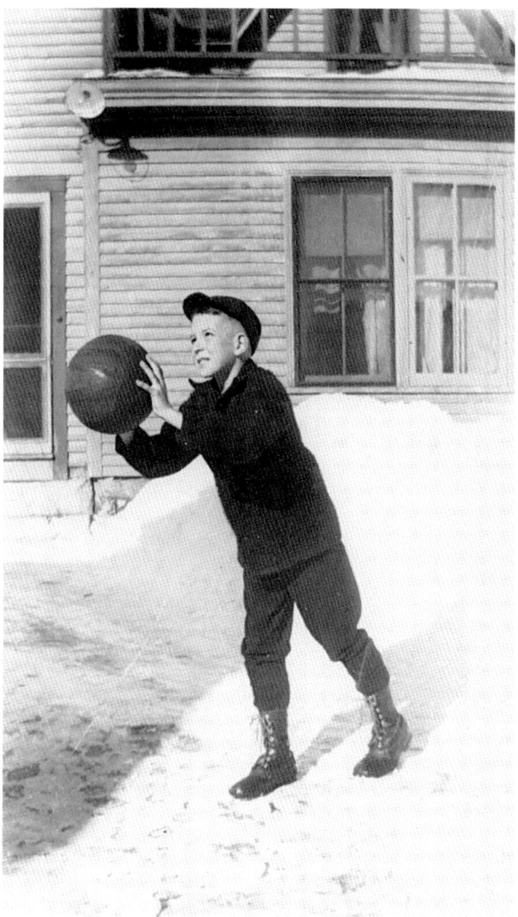

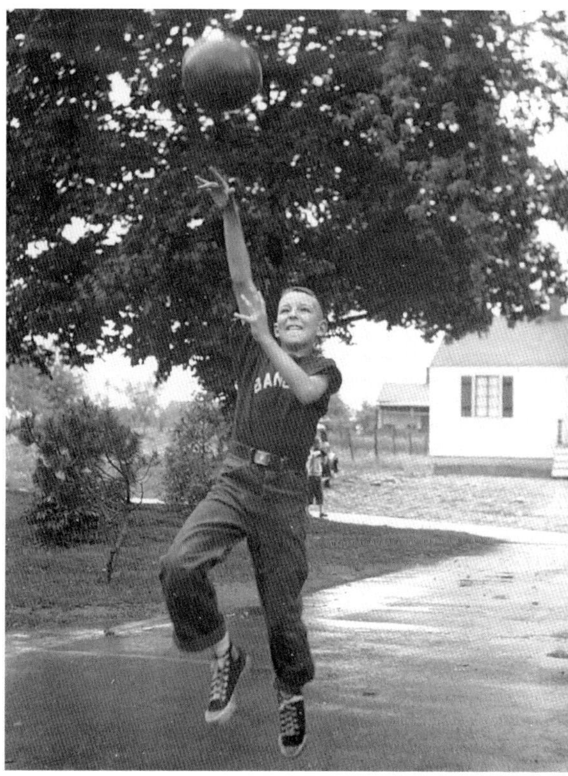

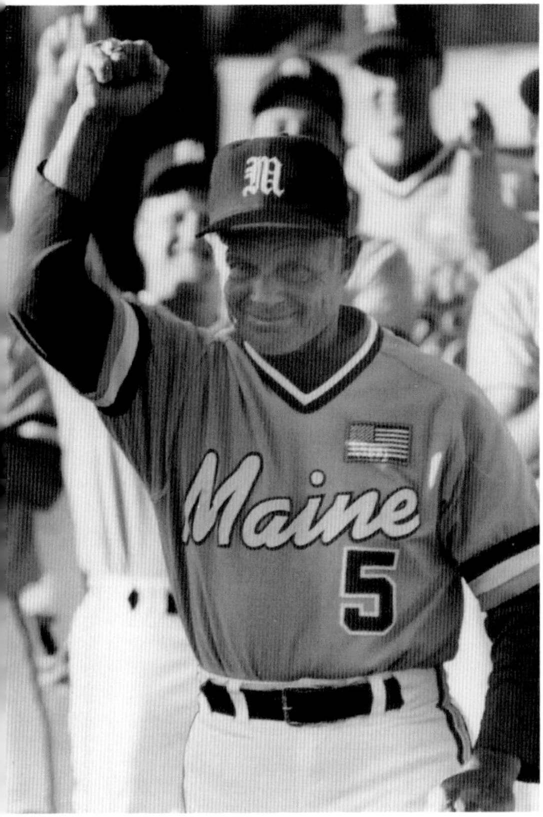

Mr. Baseball

Synonymous with University of Maine baseball for almost a quarter century, John Winkin and his teams made history at Mahaney Diamond at Orono.

And then he brought his coaching skills to Husson University in Bangor.

A New Jersey native and collegiate baseball star, Winkin became the Colby College baseball coach in 1954. Twenty-one years later, he took over the basketball helm at UMaine. Honing the collective skills of many excellent players, Winkin took the Black Bears to the College World Series six times; his teams also played eleven times in the NCAA Northeastern Regionals. Winkin left UMaine in 1996 with a 642-430-3 record.

Named to fill a fellowship in sports leadership at Husson that year, Winkin joined Eagles' baseball as an assistant coach. He took over as head coach in 2003. Winkin died in July 2014. (All, courtesy of BDN.)

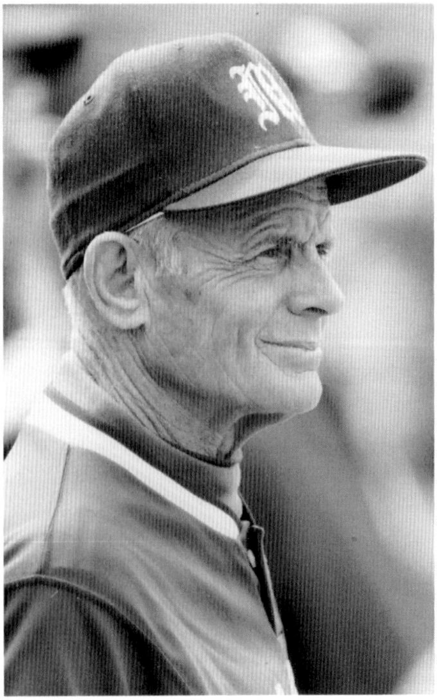

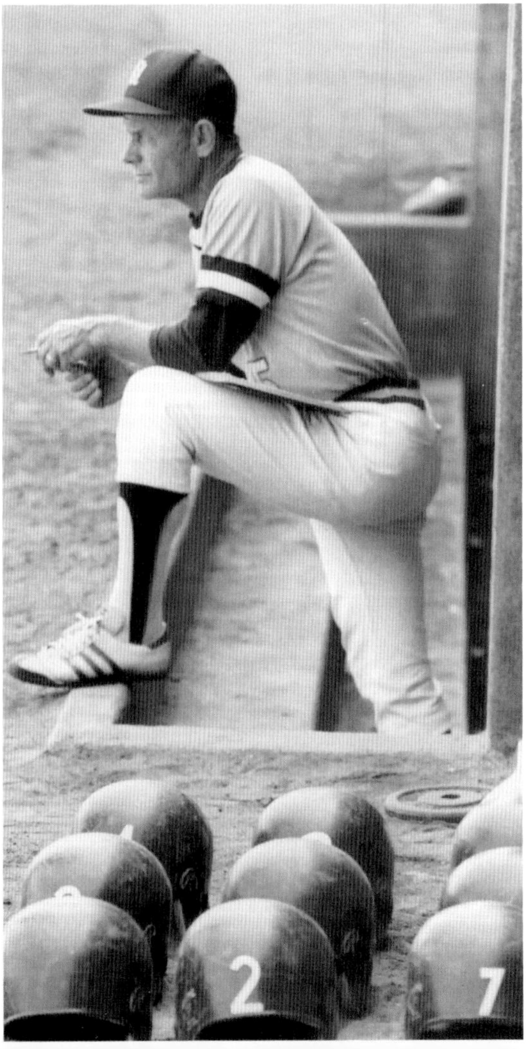

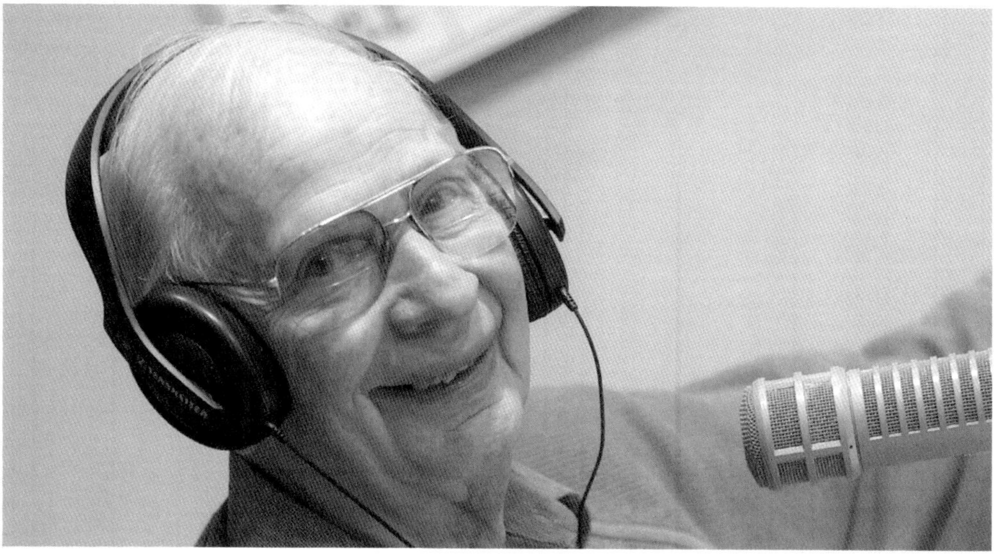

Still at the Microphone

George Hale's 60-plus years in broadcasting have set the standard for longevity. Born in 1932 when radio was in its infancy, and two decades before television arrived in Maine, Hale is a force of nature. Most people in Maine have heard his trusted voice sometime in their lives.

"I was standing in the Sea Dog [restaurant] one day and this girl came flying down from the back," Hale said in a 2014 interview. "She told me she wanted to give me a hug for so many years because when she played in the basketball tournament, I said such nice things about her."

George McHale (Hale sounded better on the air) arrived in Bangor in 1953, the same year WABI became the state's first television station. He found his niche doing commercials and live play-by-play at the Eastern Maine Basketball Tournaments, played at the Bangor Auditorium, which opened in 1955. He also broadcast seven College World Series and served on the Maine Harness Racing Commission.

Hale planned to stay in Bangor one year, but after a successful TV and radio career, and now as cohost of a WVOM-FM morning radio program, he has lingered a lifetime. (Both, courtesy of BDN.)

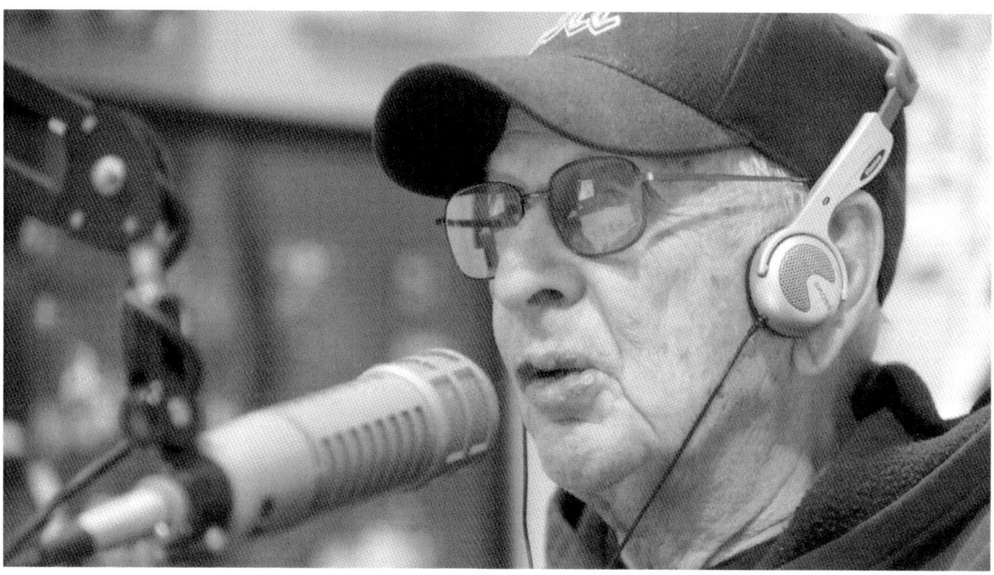

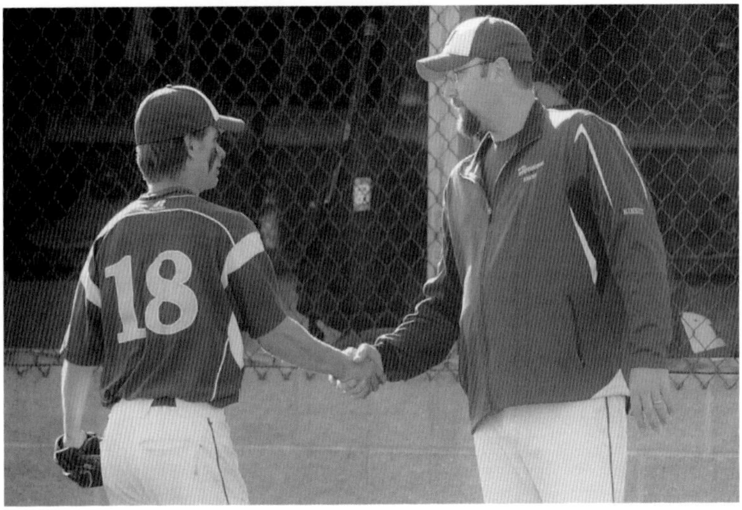

Player and Coach
Drafted by the Boston Red Sox in 1995, Bangor High School baseball star Matt Kinney (right) spent 16 years playing professional baseball in the United States and Japan before retiring in 2010. Debuting as a major-league pitcher with the Minnesota Twins in 2000, he pitched for three other MLB teams. In the winter 2014, Kinney was named varsity baseball coach at Hermon High School. (Courtesy of BDN.)

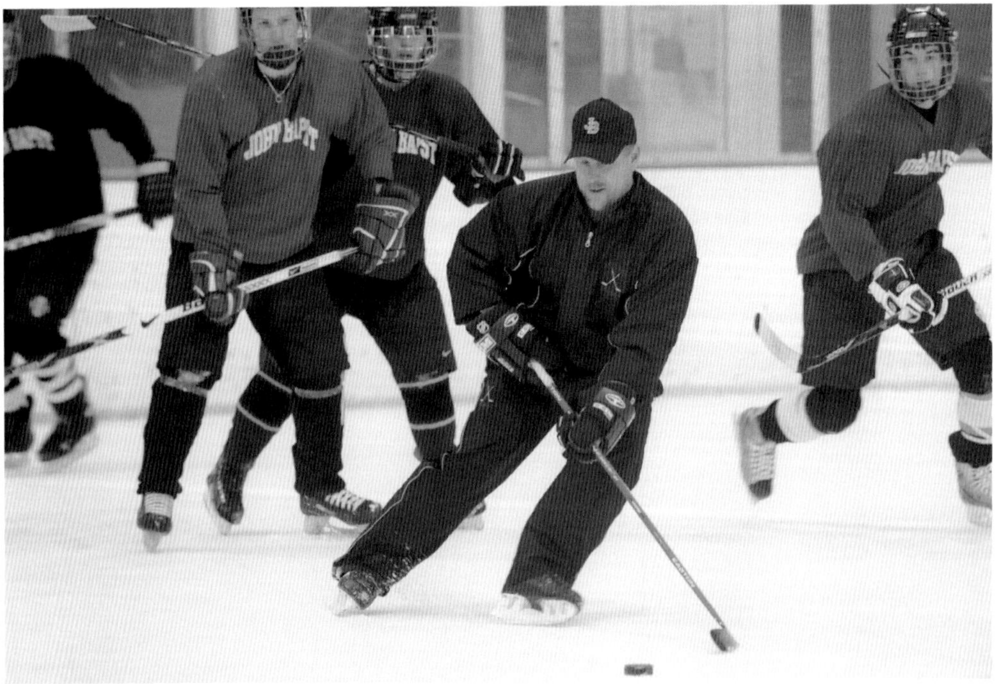

Of Spikes and Skates
Matthew Stairs played in Major League Baseball for 19 seasons and lived many years in Bangor with his family. A home run by Stairs won Game 4 of the 2008 National League Championship Series for the Philadelphia Phillies; the team won the World Series. An avid hockey fan, Stairs later served as an assistant hockey coach at John Bapst, pictured, and Bangor High Schools. (Courtesy of BDN.)

CHAPTER SIX

Feeding the Hungry

Boasting dozens of eateries and restaurants today, Bangor has a long history of feeding the hungry, including people seeking a great place to dine and folks wondering where they will find their next meals.

Sanford "Sonny" Miller and his family operated a legendary restaurant on Bangor's Main Street for more than 40 years and wove the phrase "meet me at Miller's" into Queen City lore. Everyone met at Miller's, well known for its large buffet and elegant dining.

Three members of the Soucy family (Frank Sr. and sons Frank Jr. and Joseph) started Frank's Bake Shop in Bangor in 1947. Famous for its pastries, turkey pies, and other homemade foods, the bakery is still operated by the Soucy family. And for many out-of-town residents, Frank's is a must-stop destination when visiting Bangor.

And Bangoreans are known for reaching out to the down-trodden and the hungry. Begun so long ago that no one can trace the exact date, the tradition of caring for the less fortunate continues to this day among the men and women dedicated to providing better lives for their neighbors.

Located in a Main Street brick building designed by Bangor architect Wilfred Mansur, the Bangor Area Homeless Shelter provides overnight shelter and three meals a day to Bangor-area homeless people. Under the direction of Dennis Marble and his staff, the shelter operates a food pantry and offers a day program that assists the homeless in finding permanent housing.

Bill and Karen Rae started Manna as a faith-based ministry in 1991 to assist the homeless. Manna also ministers to the working people and area residents living on fixed incomes. Besides serving a daily meal, the Manna staff operates a food pantry that supplies local food pantries in the lower Penobscot Valley. Manna also offers various counseling services for people living with mental health or substance abuse issues.

Two lay brothers of the Franciscan Brothers of St. Elizabeth, a Catholic order, opened the Friars' Bakehouse in Bangor in 1999. The popular downtown bakery sells delicious breads, cookies, muffins, and other baked goods; the brothers also minister to local residents and visitors by providing a welcoming place for them to chat and relax.

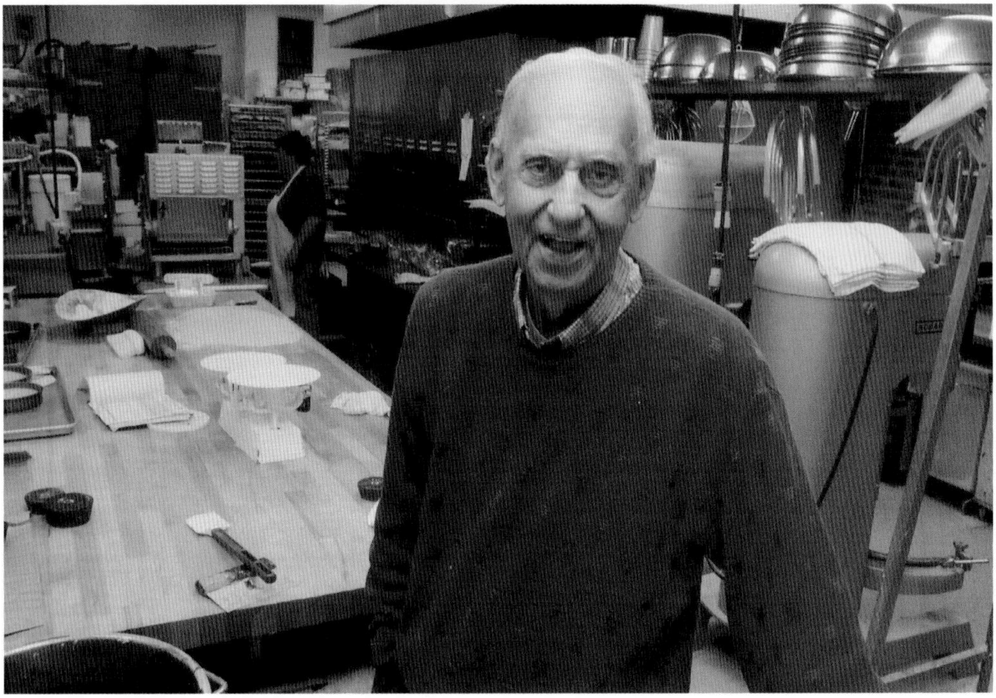

Baker to Bangor

The small bakery that Frank Soucy Sr. and his sons, Joseph and Frank Jr., opened on Harlow Street in Bangor in 1945 became a local legend in its own right—and so did Frank Jr., a John Bapst Memorial High School graduate who was only 19 when the bakery started selling breads, cakes, and cookies.

In 1945, Joseph worked as a mail sorter for a Maine-based railroad, and Frank Jr. was a civilian employee at Dow Army Air Base. He and Joseph did not enjoy their respective jobs, a fact that the brothers made clear to their father, then head baker at the University of Maine.

"My dad suggested the three of us get together and start a bakery. And we did, with $200 between the three of us," Frank Jr. (above) told the *Bangor Daily News* in October 2010. That particular week, the employees of Frank's Bake Shop honored Soucy for his 65 years with the bakery and his official retirement from the family-owned business.

"I think we've come a long way," Soucy said. "My father was the brains of the baking business. He taught us. He taught me how to decorate cakes, so I did that for over 30 years. And it just went on from one year to the next."

In 1947, the Soucys moved Frank's Bake Shop to 199 State Street in Bangor. Among the well-known bakers involved in baking cookies, pastries, pies, turkey pies, and other delicious fare were, from left to right (opposite, above), Walter Beaulieu, Ben Gunn, Joseph Soucy, Frank Soucy Jr., and Dwight Frasier, shown displaying "glazed doughnuts, cakes, and turkey pies in 1985," according to the *Bangor Daily News*.

In time, the bakery added sandwiches, meatloaf, quiches, lasagna, and baked beans to the menu. Frank's Bake Shop catered various events—and no matter the time of day, customers could call ahead to order meals for pickup.

The Soucys remodeled their bakery over the years, and passersby on busy State Street easily saw its brightly lit window displays. Even today, employees prepared baked goods from scratch, as was done in the 1950s.

Additional generations of Soucys joined the business, which was owned by five of Joseph's children—Theresa Soucy, Bernadette Gaspar, Joseph Soucy, Richard Soucy, and Fleurette Dow—when Frank Jr. retired in 2010.

He died in January 2012. (All, courtesy of BDN.)

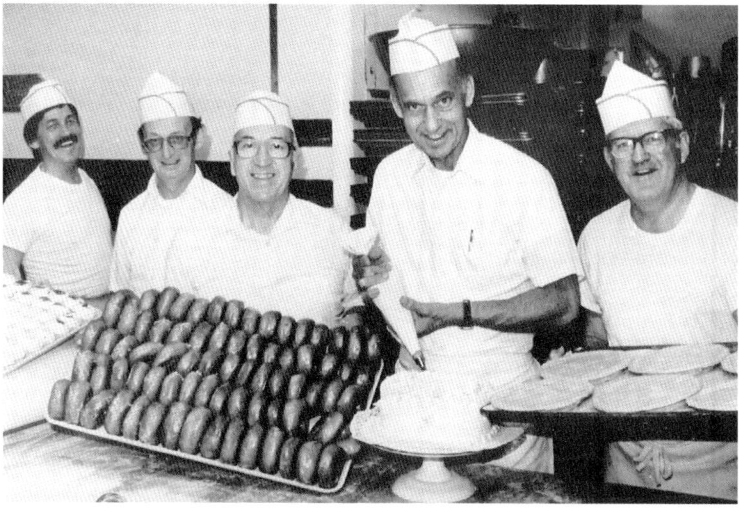

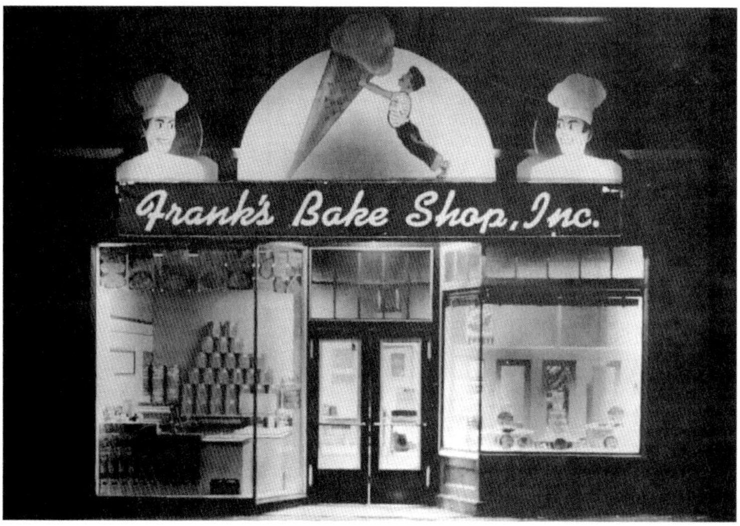
Frank's Bake Shop, Inc.

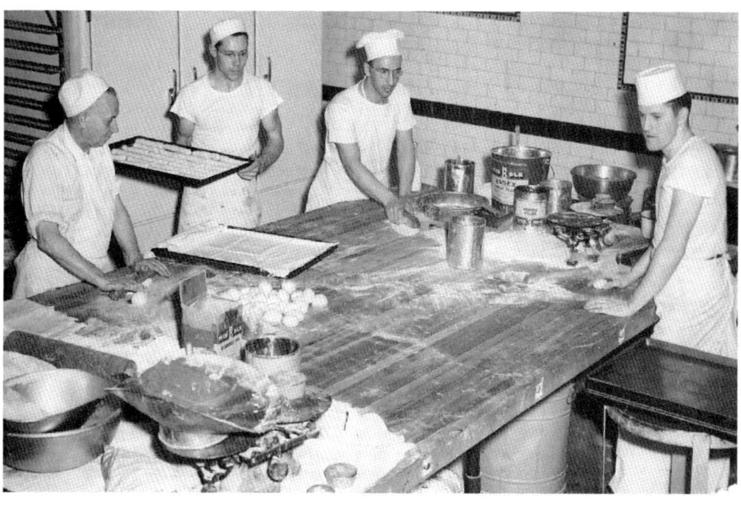

A Home for the Homeless

A committed and experienced staff helps the Bangor Area Homeless Shelter provide critical services to the region's downtrodden residents, says executive director Dennis Marble.

Born in Boston and raised in Natick, Massachusetts, Marble came to Maine after high school to earn a degree in English from Colby College. He later earned a master's degree in education and counseling at the University of Maine.

In January 1996, Marble became the executive director of the Bangor Area Homeless Shelter, which had opened on Christmas Eve 1986 at 263 Main Street, Bangor. Designed in the late 19th century by Bangor architect Wilfred Mansur and commissioned by the Catholic Diocese of Maine, the brick building once housed Catholic brothers and nuns affiliated with nearby St. Mary's Catholic Church. Businesses leased space at street level.

When the Bangor Area Homeless Shelter opened, "it was only an overnight shelter," Marble said. "It replicated the concept the Catholic church" had used by housing guests on the second floor and renting commercial space on the first floor.

Volunteers, including Mary Hale and Rev. Ansley Throckmorton (minister at Hammond Street Congregational Church in Bangor), were instrumental in creating and supporting the shelter. "The church served as the environment in which interested people started the discussion that led to the formation of the [nonprofit] agency," Marble said.

The Bangor Area Homeless Shelter provides overnight shelter, including "clean linens, showers, access to toiletries," according to Marble, to guests who are supervised by two staffers. The shelter, which had 12 beds in 1986, offers 38 guest beds today.

The day program works with guests "to help them get out of being homeless" and find permanent housing, Marble said. Staffers assist guests in finding the services they need outside the shelter.

Three meals are served daily, with breakfast and supper strictly for shelter guests and lunch open to the public. The shelter opens a food pantry to the public on Tuesdays and Thursdays and supplies such donated items as bedding and clothing. According to Marble, the food pantry helps many low-income individuals and families to lower their food costs; this lets them focus financially on staying in their homes.

Marble stressed that the shelter has a phenomenal staff. Among the dedicated staff members working with Marble (left) at the Bangor Area Homeless Shelter are, from left to right, Rowena Griffin, Sarah Brown, Megan Harrigan, and Daniel Cohen. (Courtesy of BFS.)

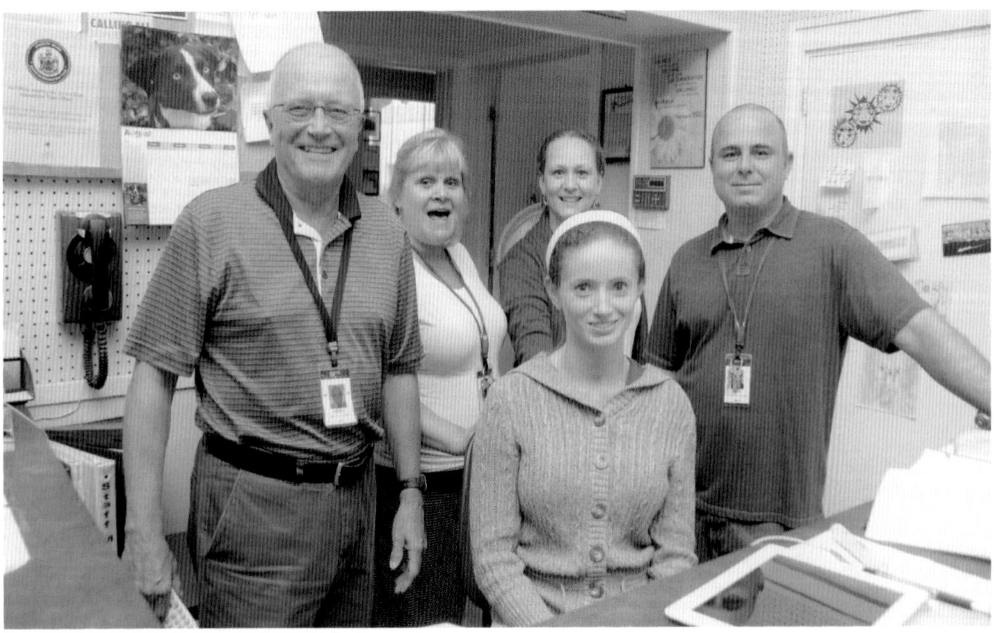

Serving the Needy

Ministering to the less fortunate has been the focus of Bill Rae and Manna for almost a quarter century. On July 5, 1991, Bill and his wife, Karen, established Manna as a faith-based ministry "to provide food and work for the homeless," he said. The Raes soon realized that ministering to "the working poor and people on fixed incomes had become our calling.

"We want to provide them with hope, the idea that there is a tomorrow," Bill said.

The Raes moved to Maine years ago as part of the "back-to-the-land" movement. "I'm a Navy brat. I moved up here from Rhode Island" in hope of "getting away from city life" and "getting back to the country and taking a deep breath," Bill said.

"Twenty-two years ago, we decided it was time to go back to work. It was time to give back," Bill said. Dedicated Christians, the Raes opened Manna on a shoestring budget, sought the less fortunate in Bangor and its surrounding communities, and helped people. From the beginning, "providing food has always been the core of our ministry," Bill said.

"We've always had a soup kitchen. I've always believed that when Jesus fed the 5,000 people, it was the first soup kitchen on the face of the earth," he said.

Manna serves 32,000 meals a year; recently Bill (left) was joined by volunteers Ryan Chabot (center) and Taylor Buotte as they prepared to serve an evening meal.

There are "tens of thousands of people we've provided food for," Bill said. Manna, which serves a Thanksgiving Day dinner at a local church, also gave away 6,800 frozen turkeys last year to people who could not afford the Thanksgiving staple.

Manna also operates a food pantry that supplies other local food pantries.

Located since 2006 at 629 Main Street, Manna offers mental health and substance abuse counseling and case management services and operates Derek House (a faith-based residential substance abuse treatment program) and Elijah's House, which provides short-term residential substance abuse treatment.

"We've planted a lot of seed in a lot of people's lives," said Bill.

Although Karen died a few years ago, son Mark is Manna's operations director; his brother, John, has worked at Manna in the past. "It's just really a joy to do this, to serve other people. My family and I really enjoy doing this," Bill said. (Courtesy of BFS.)

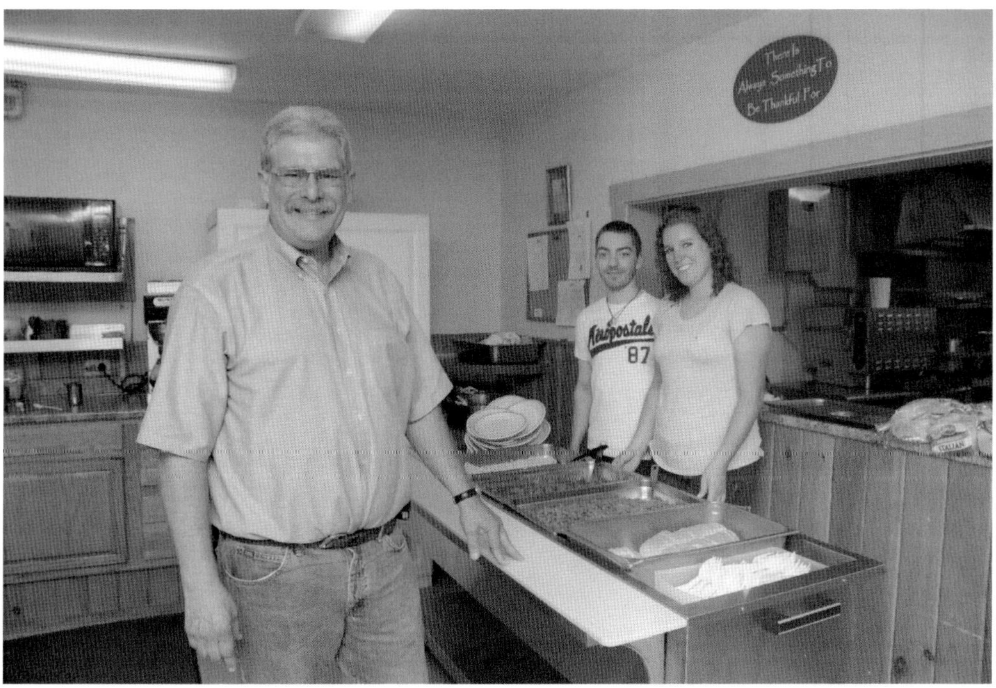

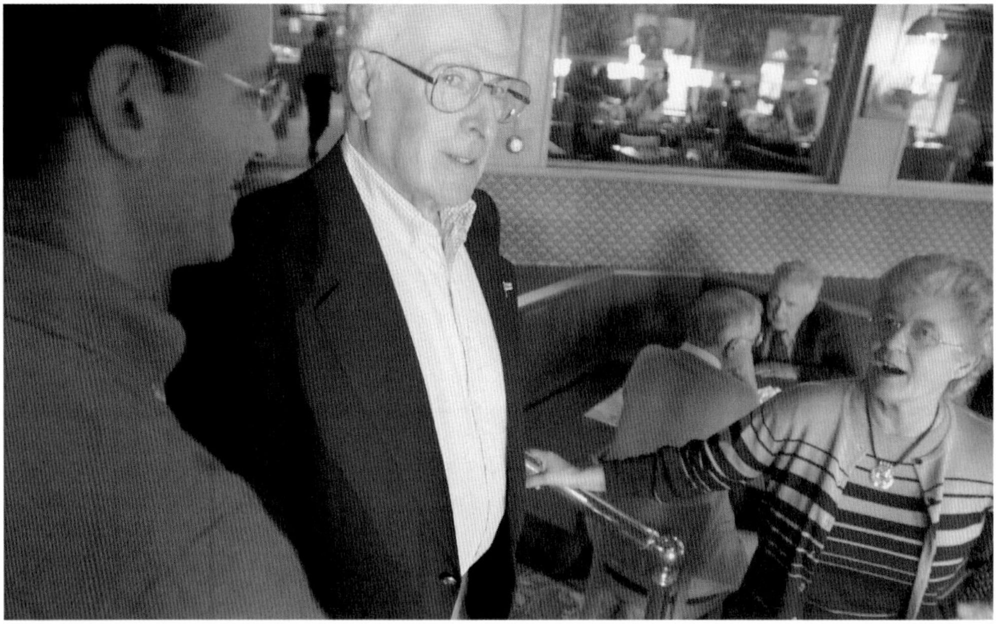

"Meet Me at Miller's"

For many years, running the popular Miller's Restaurant on Main Street in Bangor was a family affair for Sanford "Sonny" Miller (above, center), his son John (left), and wife, Joanne (right). Sonny's other children also worked at various times at the restaurant, which opened in its familiar location in 1963.

"Meet me at Miller's" was the familiar invitation to enjoy the large buffet at the restaurant.

Sonny Miller (below, center) was involved with many local organizations, including the Board of Directors for Congregation Beth Israel, the Bangor Lions Club, and the Anah Shrine. (Both, courtesy of BDN.)

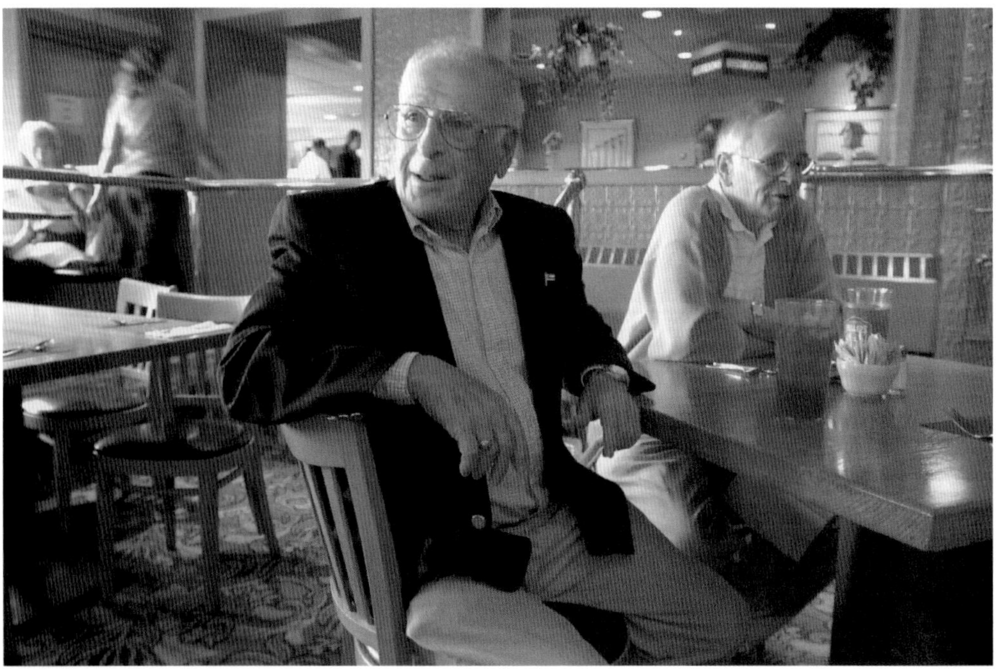

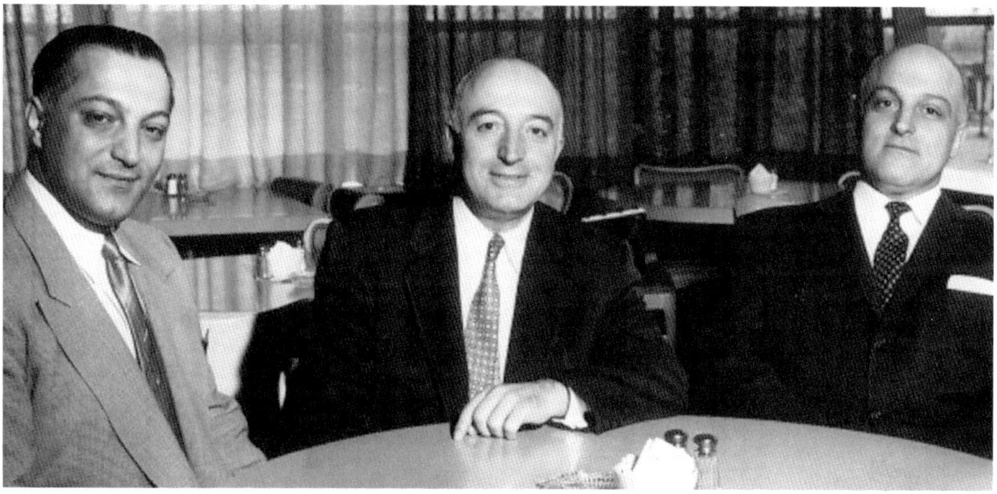

The Family behind Pilots Grill

Bill Zoidis and his daughter Paulette made every guest in their restaurant feel like family. Those guests included movie stars, politicians, traveling salesmen, and plain folk who kept returning over the years for Pilots Grill's signature steaks, seafood, and cheese dip.

Paul Zoidis, Bill's father, opened the original Pilots Grill in 1940 opposite the future Dow Air Force Base. His growing clientele of airmen and Bangor-area families required an enlarged staff, which included Paul's Armenian American brothers Peter and Ernie (above, left and right, with Paul center).

The Pilots Grill that most customers remember was established farther out Hammond Street in 1957, after the air base expanded its runway, swallowing the restaurant property. An enlarged facility included the Skyview Dining Room, Knotty Pine Room, and Rococo Banquet Room.

In 2002, after Bill and Paulette Zoidis announced that Pilots would be closing, nearly 500 people shared their memories at a local event.

"You can't win a game without good players, and we've had good players for 62 years," Bill Zoidis said, while crediting his loyal staff. (Both, courtesy of BDN.)

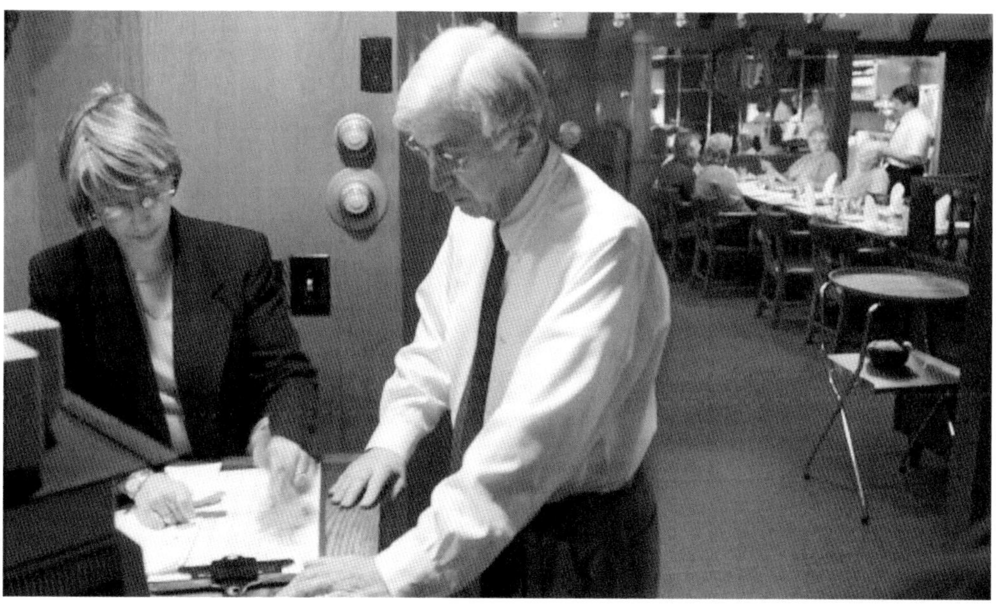

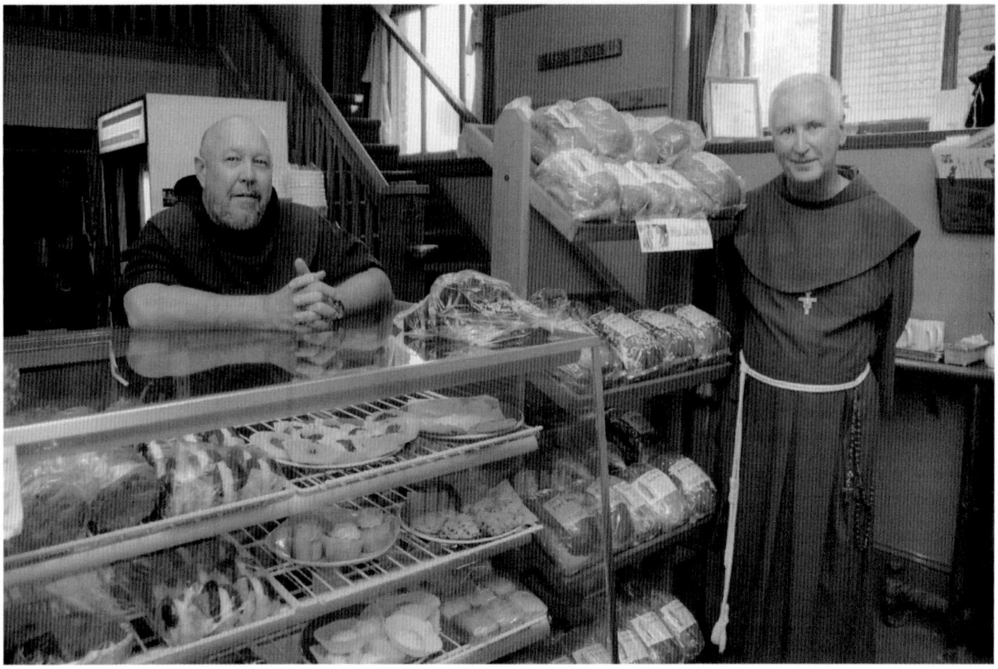

Divinely Baked Breads
Brother Kenneth Leo (right) and Brother Donald Paul (left) opened Friars' Bakehouse at 21 Central Street, Bangor on July 7, 1999. Since then, the bakehouse has become a popular place to buy various breads and baked goods, enjoy lunch, and meet people in downtown Bangor.

Members of the Franciscan Brothers of Saint Elizabeth, a Catholic order founded in Bucksport in 1996, Brothers Kenneth and Donald opened the bakehouse "as our way to become self-sufficient as a community and to outreach to people," Brother Donald said.

Before the bakehouse opened, "we sold our breads on street corners," said Brother Kenneth.

The brothers do their own baking at Friars' Bakehouse, which is open 8:30 a.m. to 2:00 p.m., Tuesday–Friday, and serves lunch 11:00 a.m. to 2:00 p.m. those same days. The bakehouse sells several bread varieties, blueberry muffins, corn muffins, chocolate chip cookies, macaroons, scones, and whoopie pies.

On Fridays, the brothers also sell bake and sell "decadence," defined by Brother Kenneth as Mortal Sin-A-Buns, Venial Sin-A-Buns, caramel walnut sticky buns, and Mexican sweet bread, also called "concha."

Beyond the foods that it sells, Friars' Bakehouse offers "a ministry of presence, just being here for people," said Brother Donald. "On those days we are here, accessibility to us is total; whoever comes through the door is ministered to."

"We meet them where they are" in terms of social, economic, or spiritual needs, he said. Friars' Bakehouse often "is the first point of contact" for people just arriving in Bangor, especially if they "need a bite to eat."

The communal seating encourages people to chat and get to know one another. Strangers become acquaintances, and "lifelong friendships have been made at these tables," Brother Donald said.

The brothers are easily identifiable in their Franciscan habits; "people approach us and ask us for prayer," Brother Donald said. During winter, the order's chaplain, Father Roland Nadeau, holds Mass in the upstairs chapel at Friars' Bakehouse; he also conducts Mass at the order's monastery in Bucksport.

The brothers, who opened a brew house at the monastery in 2013, serve one Saturday meal a month for area seniors and serve Thanksgiving dinner at their bakehouse. "We share this space with other groups that have ministries," Brother Kenneth said.

People flock to Friars' Bakehouse, which is becoming a popular eatery with a second generation of Bangor-area residents. "We're blessed, we really are," Brother Donald said. (Courtesy of BFS.)

CHAPTER SEVEN

Doing Their Jobs

Since their ancestors established settlements along a rock-bound coast in the mid-17th century, Maine Yankees have been known for their work ethic—and Bangoreans are no different.

Facing intense competition in Augusta, newspaper publisher Peter Edes spent $143 for a teamster, wagon, and oxen to haul his printing press to Bangor in 1815, when he launched the city's first newspaper. Thomas Newhall Egery learned to craft in iron and made his services indispensable for the elite of Bangor who were building large homes during the mid-19th century.

Adolf Pfaff brought his watch-making and -repairing skills to Bangor from Europe and made his name synonymous with local watch-making for a half century.

When not running his drug store in Bangor—and he established one of the first apothecary shops in the Queen City—George Washington Ladd represented Maine in the US House of Representatives and strongly supported the development of railroads in Maine. Samuel Freeman Hersey was another congressman from Bangor; he sadly died while in office.

Dr. William Gallupe introduced homeopathic medicine to Bangor. Benjamin Sproul introduced new traffic-control concepts to the Bangor Police Department as the automobile displaced the horse and buggy in the 1920s.

In the 20th century, Allie J. Cole moved his trucking company to Bangor and, along with his sons, transformed the way that freight was hauled in central and northern Maine. He did not even let Ol' Man Winter stop him; when the state could not keep Route 2 plowed north of Mattawamkeag, Cole showed how snowplowing should be done so that his Cole's Express trucks could get through to Houlton in southern Aroostook County.

Shep Hurd was running a successful sporting goods business on Central Street when on-the-lam gangsters rolled into Bangor and tried to buy a tommy gun from him in the 1930s. The resulting shoot-out thrust Hurd and Bangor into the national spotlight.

Candy-maker George F. Burton helped satisfy Maine's collective sweet tooth in the early to mid-20th century, and Marshall Frankel was a well-known Bangor businessman and city councilor a few generations later. He was made famous when a local newspaper photographer snapped a shot of the suit-and-tie-clad Frankel shoveling snow off the sidewalk outside his downtown business.

The Reverend Renee Garrett has ministered in the Queen City since 1987; today, she is passionately involved with a local street ministry. Managing Bangor's transportation hub—the busy place known as Bangor International Airport (BIA)—is the responsibility of Tony Caruso and his staff; from BIA, Maine residents and people living as far away as the Maritimes connect with destinations across the world.

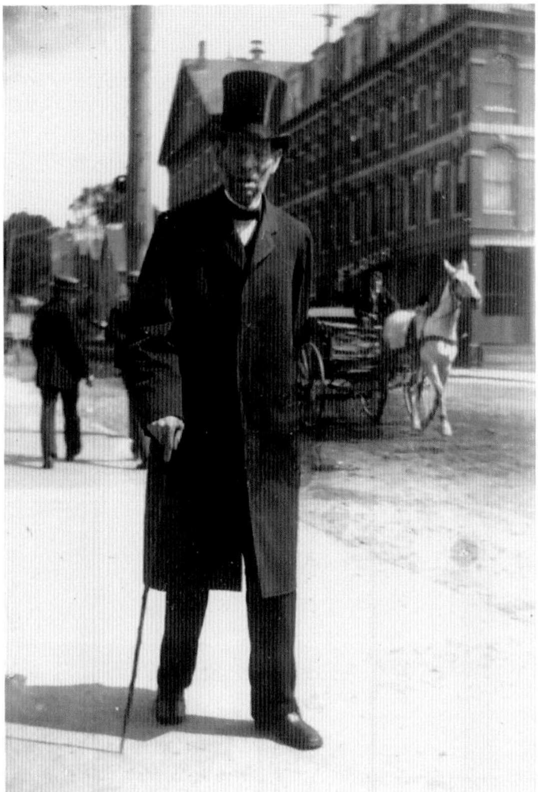

A Self-Made Man

Charles D. Bryant was seven years old when he arrived Bangor in 1820. His father later purchased a Hermon farm; starting in 1829, the inadequately educated Charles worked to pay off the mortgage and then to put himself through school. By dint of hard work, Bryant became a well-known Bangor businessman involved with real estate. "Industry and economy, combined with promptness in business, are the foundation of success in business," he believed. (Courtesy of BPL.)

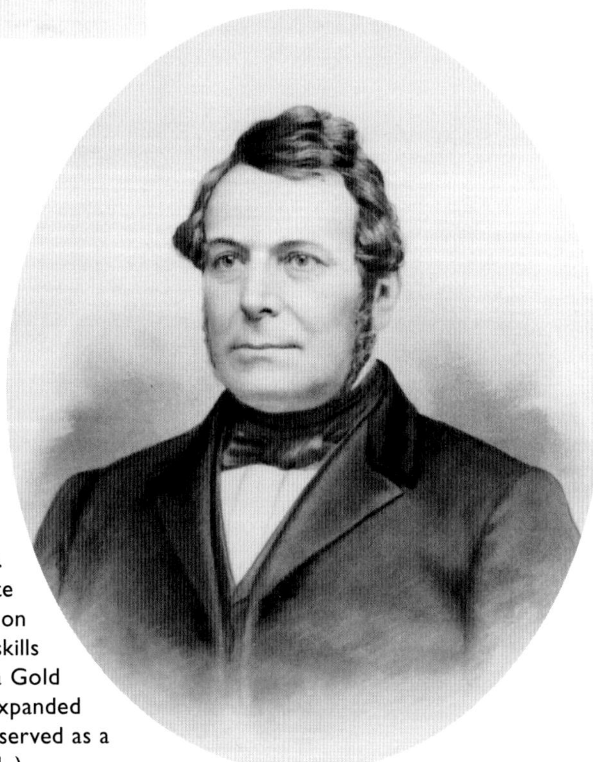

Ironworker

When Bangoreans built a new courthouse in the 1830s, ironworker Thomas N. Egery crafted the iron doors and shutters. Wealthy businessmen hired him to create fences and other iron fixtures appearing on stately homes. Taking his ironworker's skills to San Francisco during the California Gold Rush, Egery returned to Bangor and expanded his business as the city grew. He later served as a legislator from Bangor. (Courtesy of BPL.)

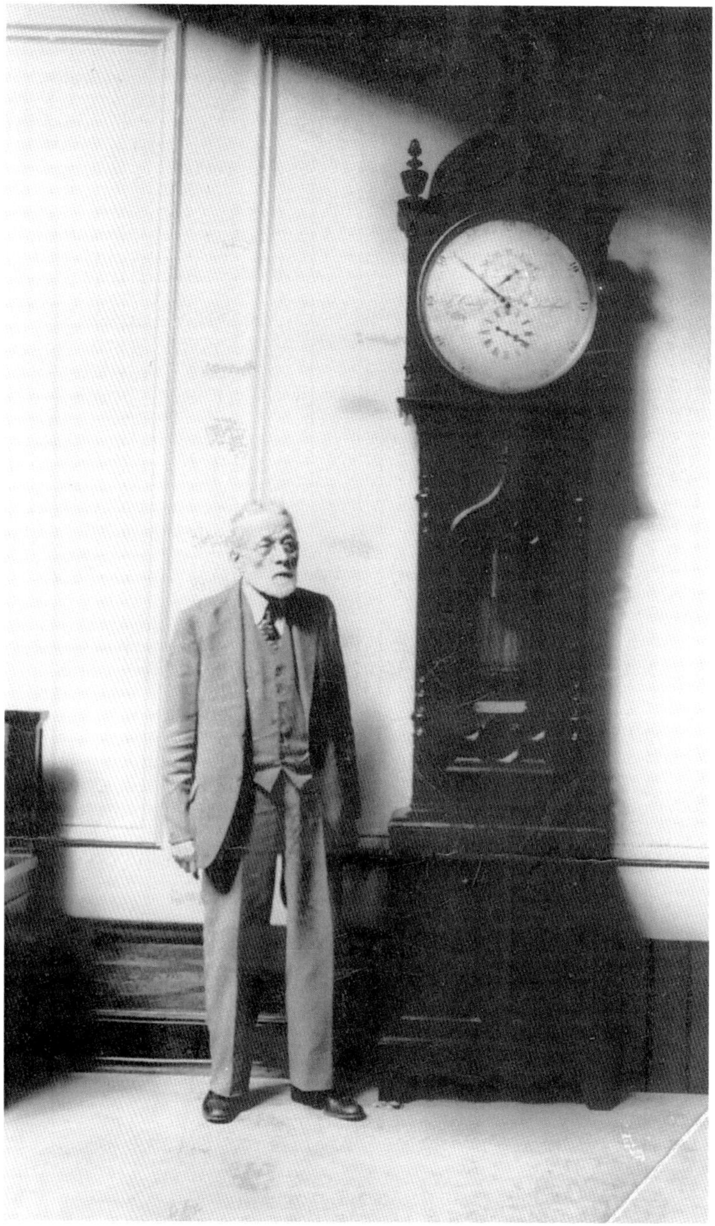

Dean of Bangor Watchmakers
When he died on July 17, 1937, Adolf Pfaff was considered to be Bangor's premier watchmaker (and repairer), and he had operated his business at the same downtown location for 63 years.

Born in Germany, Pfaff apprenticed with his clockmaker father and made his first watch at age 14. Pfaff immigrated to the United States in 1872 and arrived in Bangor in 1873.

His skills landed Pfaff employment with W.F. Weeks, a local jeweler and watchmaker located at 25 Hammond Street. An astute businessman, Pfaff joined Charles Hight in buying Weeks's shop in 1879; four years later, Pfaff bought Hight's share of the business and operated the shop until ill health forced him to retire in April 1936.

Pfaff calculated that he had repaired at least 300,000 watches before he retired. (Courtesy of BHS.)

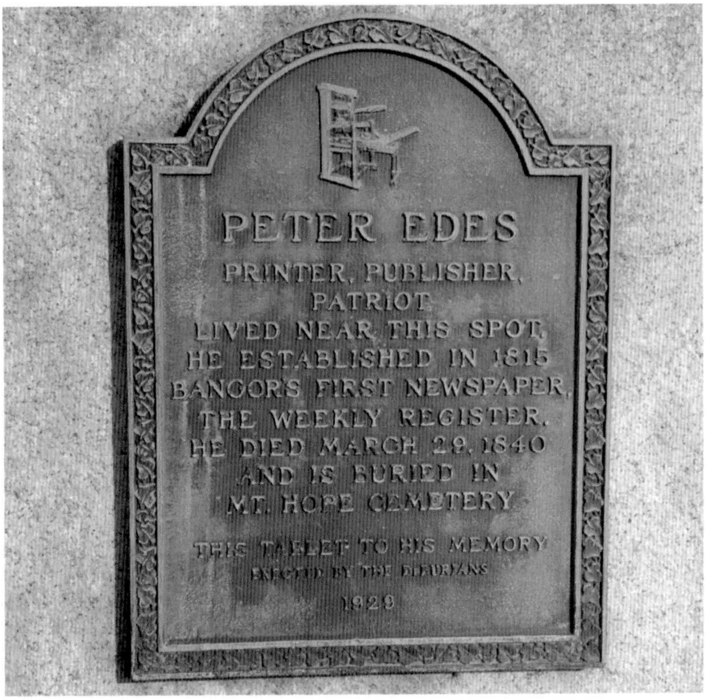

Edes Published Bangor's First Newspaper

An advertisement posted in Augusta in May 1815 kicked off Bangor's rich newspaper history.

On behalf "of several gentlemen in the county of Hancock," printer Peter Edes sought proposals for publishing a weekly newspaper in Bangor. He promised that "the work shall be executed on good paper with a fair type and shall contain all the latest news both foreign and domestic."

Edes promised the newspaper would cost $2 per year, "exclusive of postage," and "the publication will commence" as soon as 800 subscribers had signed up.

People did subscribe; the *Bangor Weekly Register* first published on November 25, 1815.

Peter Edes hailed from Boston, where he was born in 1756 into a printing family; his father, Benjamin, and John Gill jointly owned a print shop and a newspaper. Peter grew up in exciting times; several patriots intent on tossing British tea into Boston harbor changed into Indian garb at his family's home in 1773, and after Peter cheered for the patriots while watching the 1775 Battle of Bunker Hill from a distance, British authorities tossed him into prison for three months.

Edes ventured on his own into newspaper publishing in 1785, gradually working his way from Massachusetts to Rhode Island to the District of Maine. There he ran a print shop and published a newspaper in Augusta.

When two competitors brought their newer printing equipment to Augusta, Edes took apart his four-ton press and hired a teamster, a wagon, and six oxen for $143 to haul the pieces to Bangor.

Edes opened a print shop at 43 Main Street and bought a house at 23 Ohio Street. From the start, the *Bangor Weekly Register* struggled financially, probably because Edes accepted payment in "wheat, cheese, butter, eggs or cash." Family members worked diligently in the print shop or a young women's school that Edes's wife, Elizabeth, opened.

Edes sold the *Bangor Weekly Register* in December 1817. He later moved his family to Baltimore, where cholera claimed Elizabeth and the couple's son, Benjamin, in 1832.

The aging Peter Edes returned to Bangor to live with a daughter, Maria Sargent. "Had I known how affairs would have turned out with me I would never have left Bangor," Edes supposedly said, "and would have preferred wading up to my knees in snow."

A monument to Edes stands at the intersection of Hammond and High Streets. (Courtesy of BFS.)

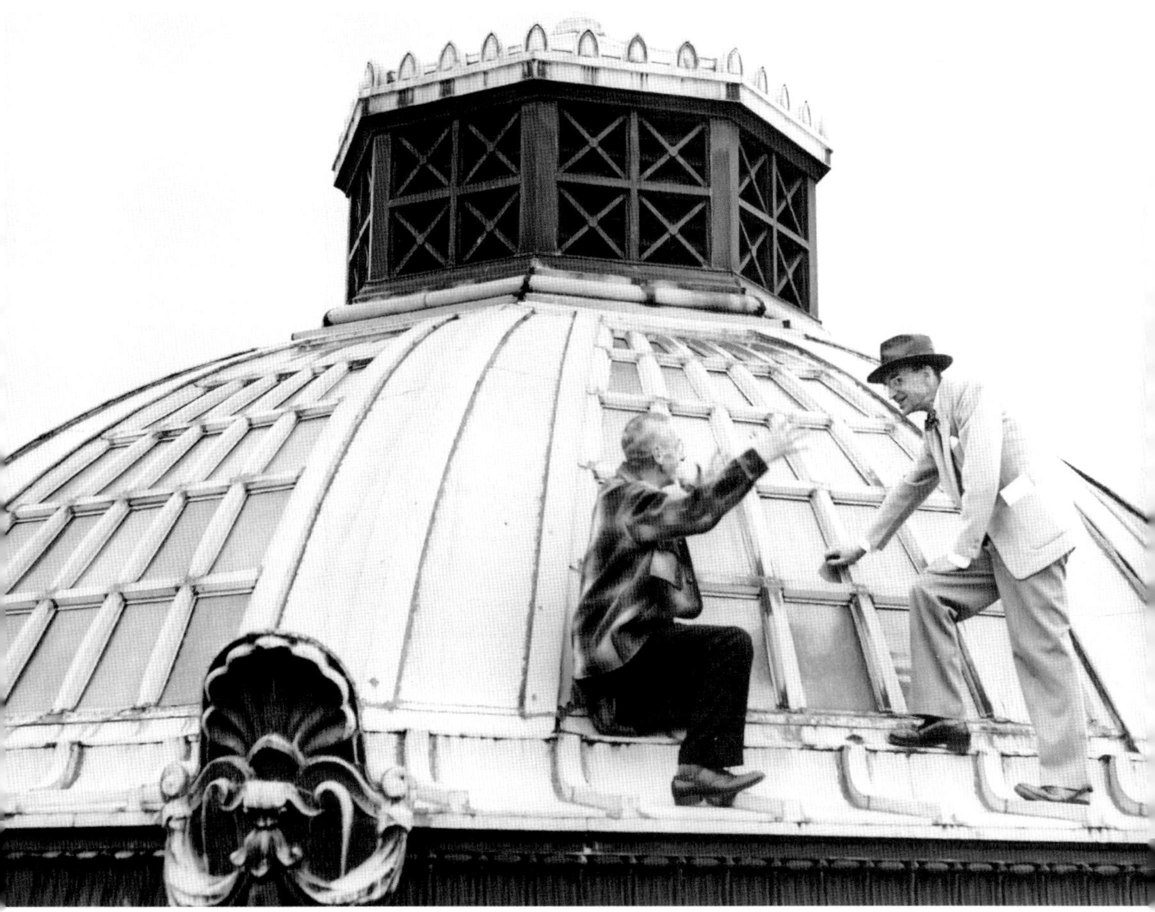

Reaching for New Heights

There was nothing standoffish about Louis Felix Ranlett. The tall, affable director of the Bangor Public Library from 1937 to 1962 loved people and the knowledge that books brought to life.

Ranlett lost an eye during World War I. He did not talk about his combat experiences unless someone asked. He would often pull out his book *Let's Go!*, written in a plain style. Years after his death, his son John and daughter Mary Mossman donated a priceless collection of his World War I posters to his hometown library.

One day in 1958, Ranlett wanted to see for himself how the 1913 copper library dome was holding up. So, dressed in a tan suit, bow tie, and fedora hat, he climbed onto the roof and had a look. The accompanying photograph shows the librarian with an unidentified worker. In 2013, after a multimillion-dollar fundraising campaign, the deteriorating dome was removed, restored, and replaced. Ranlett would have loved to witness the moment when the sparkling new dome was hoisted back onto its perch. Heights never bothered Ranlett, as proven by the many trips he and his wife, Helen, took to the mountains of New Hampshire. They climbed the White Mountain's highest peaks, returning each summer and autumn to meet old friends. Ranlett photographed every excursion.

In addition to *Let's Go!*, Ranlett wrote the 1962 booklet, "All Souls Congregational Church," which recounts aspects of the church's history and key church furnishings. It was revised in 1983 and is available on the church's website.

Felix and Helen loved children, and each Halloween beginning around 1950 they welcomed them into their 60 Montgomery Street home. Neighborhood ghosts and goblins would sign the Ranletts' guest book before proceeding into the kitchen for punch and cookies. (Courtesy of BPL.)

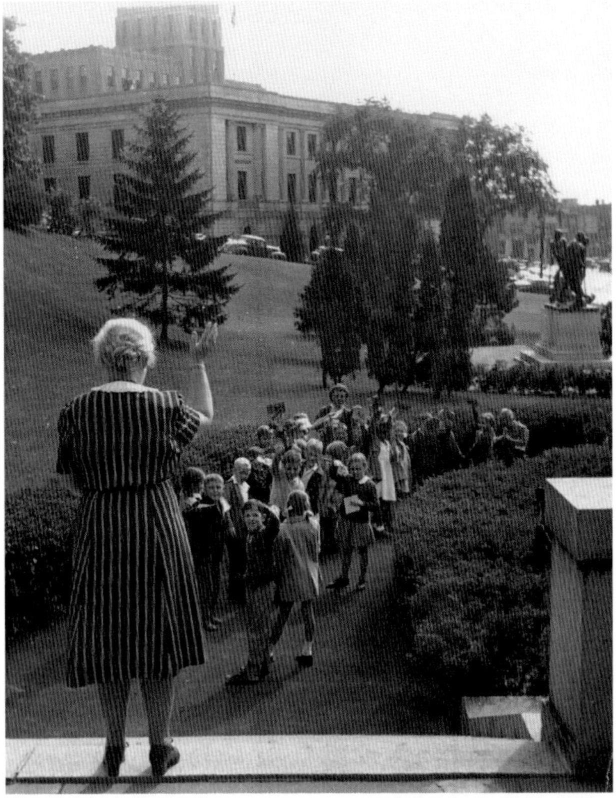

Children's Reading Companion

Many children at heart can still recall seeing Alice Wetherell, Bangor's longtime children's librarian, waving from the side entrance of the Bangor Public Library. Once inside the building's sanctuary, young readers, like the ones pictured here in 1946, would be read to by Wetherell, an expert in juvenile literature. She also helped organize boxes of books to be distributed to the city's elementary schools. (Courtesy of BPL.)

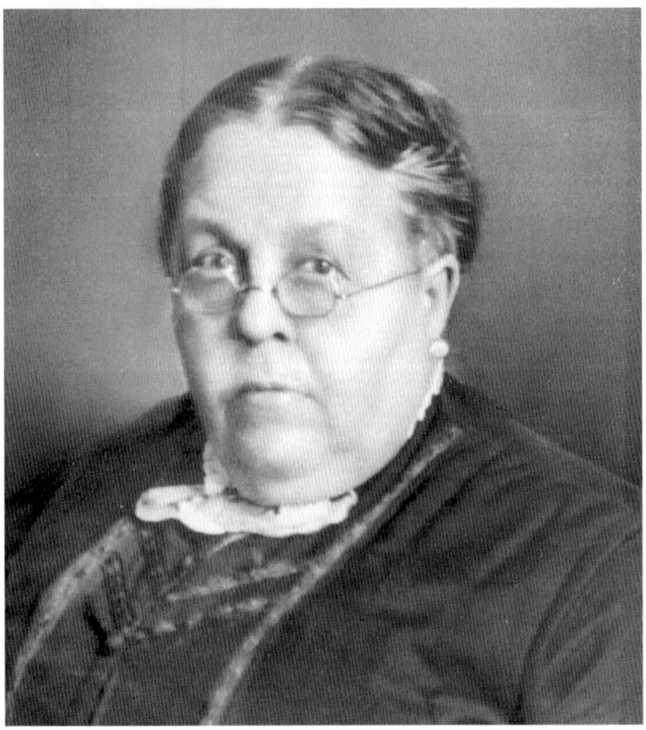

Librarian in Two Buildings

She may have had a stern demeanor, but Mary Curran was a caring librarian. Her career began at the Bangor Public Library's original State Street location. During the April 30, 1911, fire, she reportedly raced into the burning block to save priceless collections. In 1913, Curran moved to the library's new Harlow Street building, which originally housed books and Bangor Historical Society items. (Courtesy of BHS.)

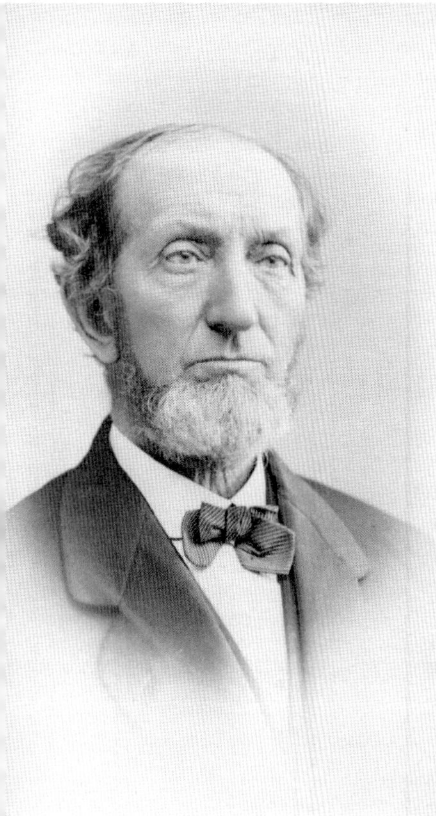

Homeopathic Physician

Born in Connecticut, Dr. William Gallupe later made his home in Bangor, where he likely was the city's first homeopathic physician. Educated in medicine at Dartmouth College, Gallupe practiced homeopathy elsewhere in New England for 14 years before moving to Bangor. Overcoming great public skepticism about his chosen medical field, he developed a successful practice and enabled other homeopathic physicians to become established in the area, too. (Courtesy of BFS.)

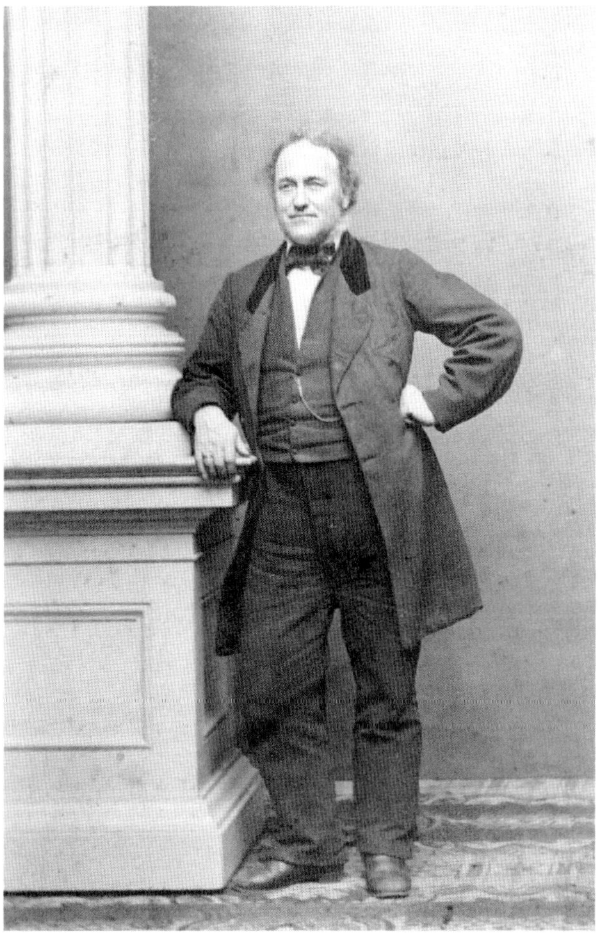

Congressman Died in Office

Bangor lost a loyal son when Congressman Samuel Freeman Hersey died in office in February 1875. Originally from Sumner, Hersey moved to Bangor in 1844 after working in business elsewhere in Penobscot County. He served in the Maine legislature, helped raise two infantry regiments during the Civil War, and, at age 60, won election to Congress for the first time in 1872. (Courtesy of BPL.)

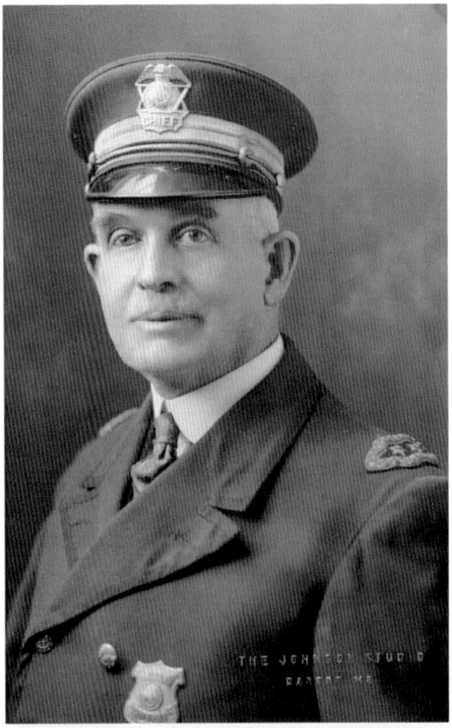

30 Years a Police Officer

Reporting as a Bangor Police Department patrolman in mid-September 1896, Benjamin Sproul made captain in seven years and chief in 1923. By then, increased auto traffic taxed Bangor's road network, especially downtown; Sproul was instrumental in creating "well directed systems in handling the hundreds of cars" and in training his men to direct traffic, according to a Bangor newspaper. Sproul retired in January 1927. (Courtesy of BPL.)

Candy-Maker's Sweet Career

George F. Burton started making candy at age 14 in Houlton. In 1944, he set up shop in Bangor, where he sold peanut brittle, flowered mints, and other treats. He worked at Lufkin's Candy and Food Shoppe, 60 Columbia Street but spent most of his 77-year career baking alone. Prior to his death in 1980 at age 97, he made candy for Doug's Shop 'n Save. (Courtesy of BDN.)

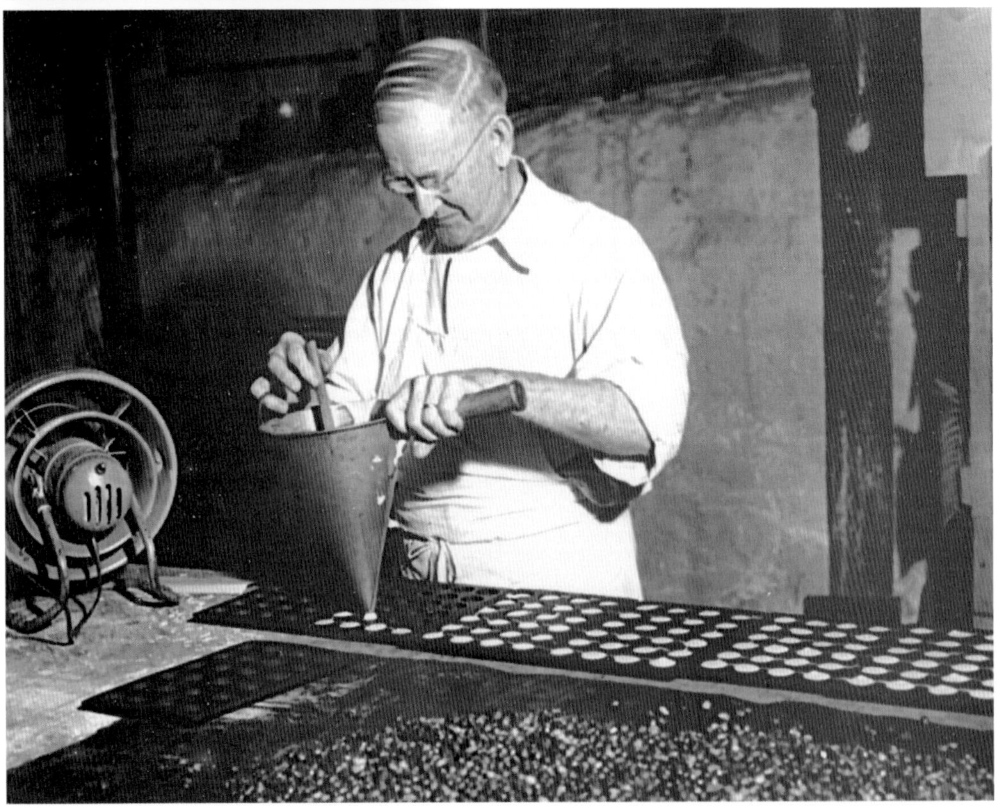

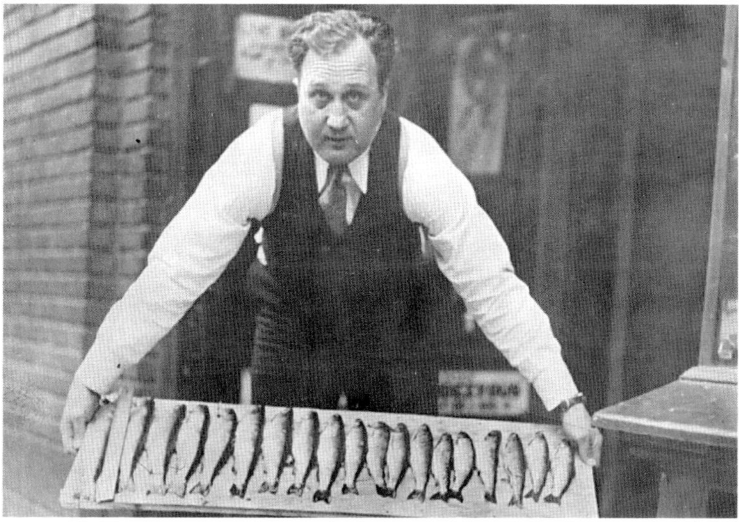

The Brady Gang's Nemesis

Everett S. Hurd was well known as the man who managed Dakin's Sporting Goods Company at 25 Central Street. But the year his path crossed with the infamous Brady Gang made him an international celebrity. It all started on September 21, 1937, when two men, James Dalhover and Clarence Lee Shaffer Jr., entered his store to buy weapons and ammunition. He and his clerks felt there was something wrong about the men, who drove a Buick Roadmaster with Ohio plates YK 747. Two weeks later, Dalhover returned to Dakin's to purchase more of the same. As he was leaving, he asked Hurd if he could get him a Thompson submachine gun.

"I can get you a used one," replied Hurd, to which Dalhover agreed. Hurd then contacted the Maine State Police, who called in an FBI agent from Boston, who visited Hurd's store with a mug shot album.

Immediately, Hurd identified Dalhover, and the rest is history. On October 12, the three gangsters drove into an FBI trap as they returned to Dakin's. Brady and Shaffer were shot dead. Dalhover was captured inside the store and, later, executed for the murder of an Indiana State Trooper. The photograph below shows Hurd in front of his bullet-riddled store window.

Up until his death in 1976, Hurd was regarded as a hero. He sold photographs of the shoot-out scene and talked to civic groups about the shootings. (Both, courtesy of RRS.)

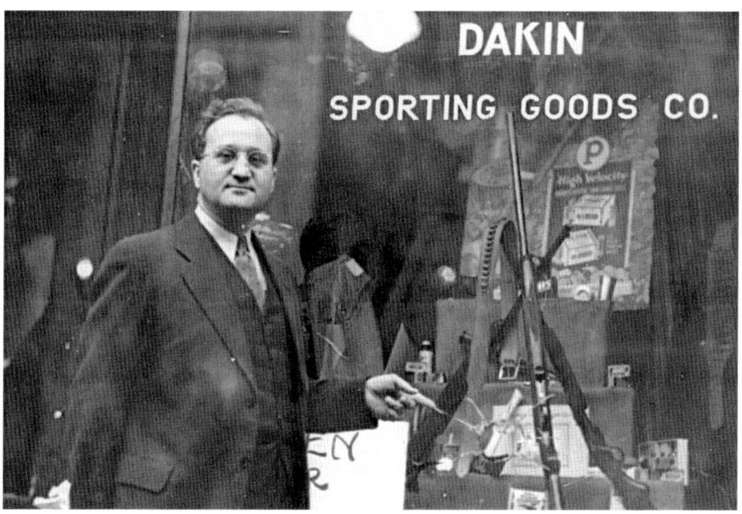

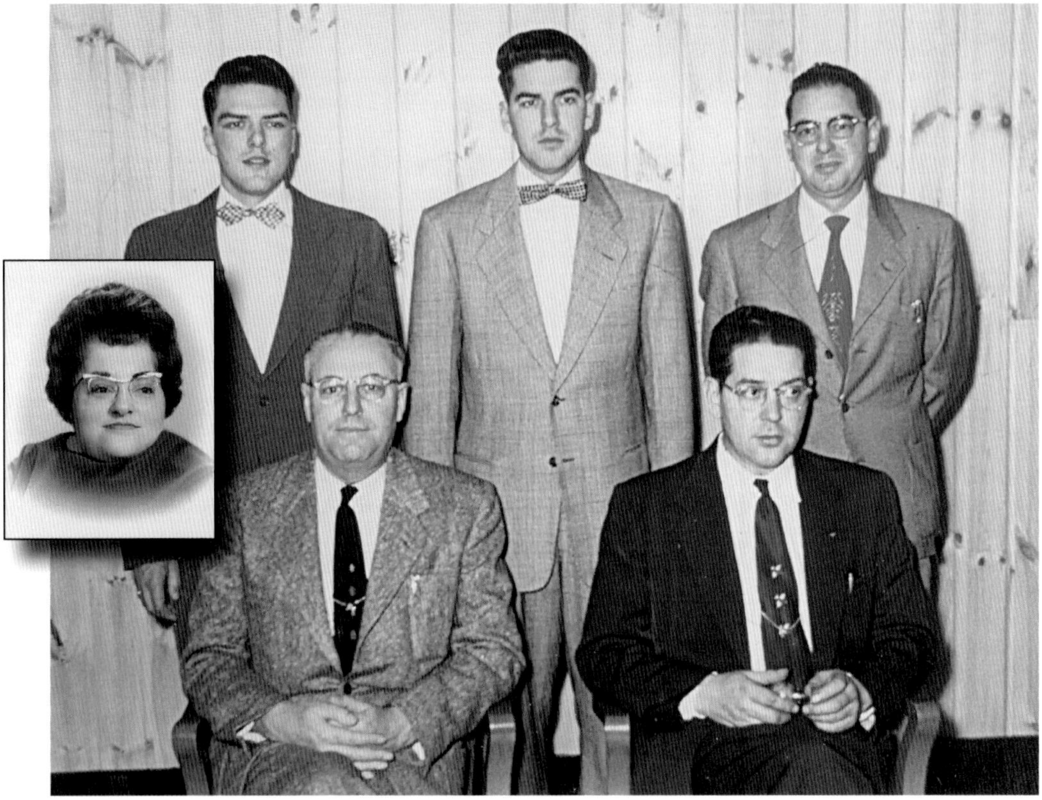

Family Kept on Trucking

If Bangor ever had a dynasty, it was the Cole family. Allie and Amy Cole moved from Enfield to the Queen City in the early 20th century, starting a family of seven along with a trucking company.

The tradition of Cole's Express began with Amy Cole, who delivered mail in a Model T Ford, driving from the Enfield train station to area post offices. By the time A.J. Cole died in 1955, the company operated terminals in Houlton, Presque Isle, Fort Kent, Portland, and Bangor. His four sons worked for the company. Pictured above clockwise from the top left are Vaughn, Galen, Chesley, Gerald, and Allie Cole.

At age 29, Galen Cole headed the business after his father's death, continuing the family tradition of hiring people of integrity. In 1989, his family's foundation opened the Cole Land Transportation Museum.

Jackie Cole (inset), the youngest of the children, was born in 1933 with a genetic disease that confined her to a wheelchair. In 1964, she married Ray Wakefield. After her death in 1973, she was remembered as an eternal optimist. A transportation museum display and a Bangor Public Library elevator are dedicated to her life's work. (Both, courtesy of Dorothy Cole Warren.)

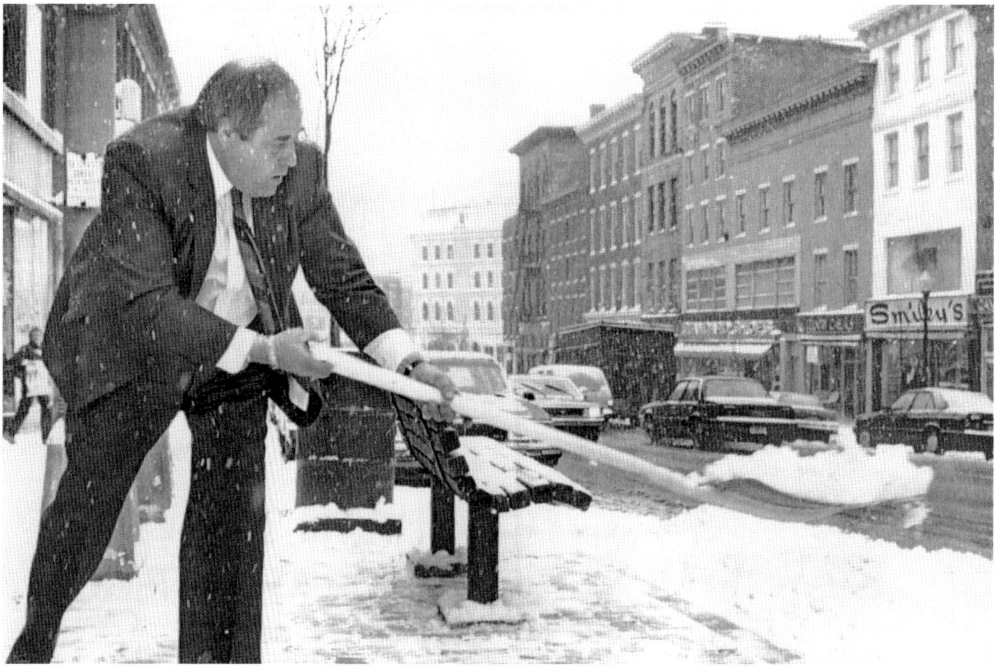

Remembering "Mister Bangor"
Marshall M. Frankel was nicknamed "Mister Bangor" because of the civic issues he cared about. During his three terms as mayor, ranging from 1985 to 1996, he fought for the restoration of Cascade Park, which had fallen into disrepair. After a snowstorm in November 1987, Frankel was photographed shoveling the sidewalk in front of G.M. Pollack and Sons jewelers, which he managed. (Courtesy of BDN.)

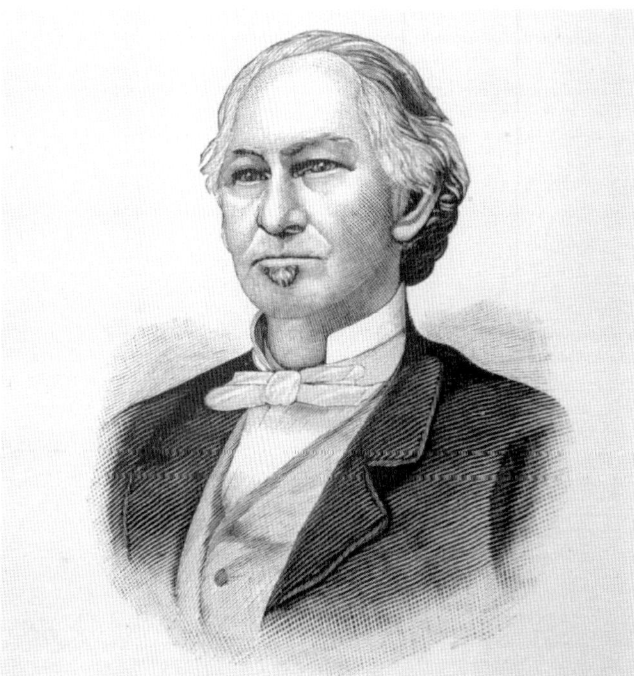

Congressman Was Nominated by Two Parties
George Washington Ladd moved to Bangor in 1838 to open a drugstore, among the young city's first. Defeated in his first try for Congress in 1868, Ladd ran again in 1878 as the dual nominee of the Democratic and Greenback parties; he won the election by 3,000 votes. That gap narrowed to 880 votes when he won reelection in 1880. (Courtesy of BPL.)

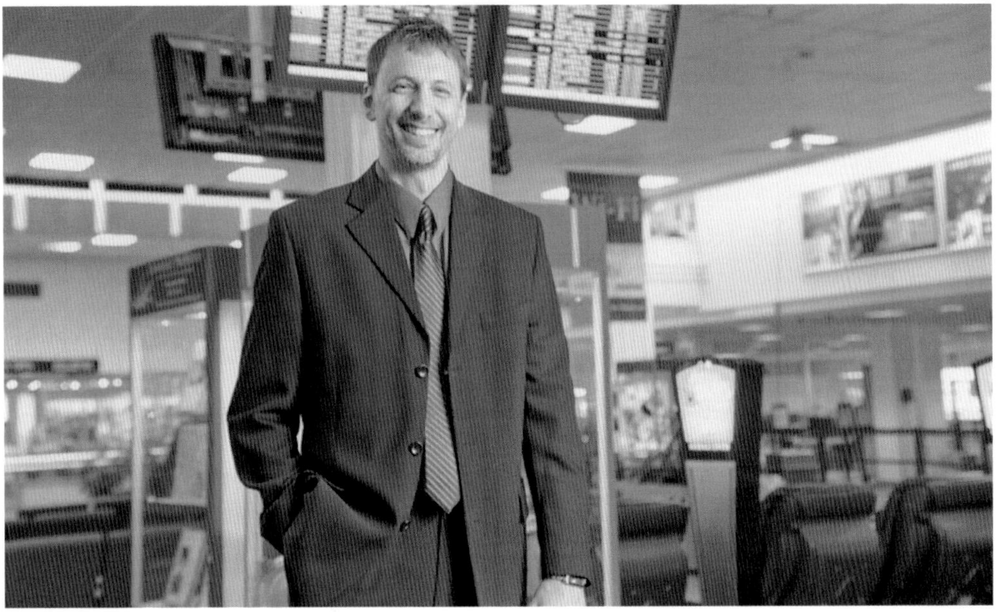

Managing the Air

If he could not be a commercial jet pilot, managing a top-notch facility like Bangor International Airport is the next best thing for Tony Caruso, airport director for the City of Bangor.

"I had wanted to be a commercial pilot," recalled Caruso (a Vermont native), but while attending Bridgewater State University (BSU) in Massachusetts, he delved into airport management. "Airports have always intrigued me," he said.

Caruso graduated from BSU with a bachelor's degree in aviation science and a concentration in airport science. He worked for various fixed-base operators and an airline before moving to Maine in 1995 and starting as the general aviation supervisor at BIA in 1996.

He left the airport briefly in 2001 but then returned in late 2002 as the assistant airport director. The Bangor City Council named Caruso as airport director in spring 2012.

The local airport known as Godfrey Field in the 1930s and Dow Air Force Base in the 1950s and 1960s has undergone "significant changes" in the past 20 years, Caruso said. Regional jets replaced the turboprops that once connected Bangor to other American airports.

"On the international side, the corporate general-aviation business has been a backbone of the airport," he said. "Overall it has been one of the most stable business segments we have had."

Today, several airlines connect Bangor with such hubs as Detroit, New York City, Philadelphia, and (seasonally) Chicago, plus two Florida destinations. "From Bangor, Maine, you're just one stop away from the rest of the world," Caruso said.

Bangor International Airport draws travelers from Augusta north and east to the Canadian border—and New Brunswick. "We have a significant number of Canadians who will utilize the airport," Caruso pointed out.

The airport, which handles "40,000 to 45,000 operations a year," is a city department supported by the Bangor City Council and Maine's Congressional delegation, he said. Caruso and his staff "work collaboratively with the city's economic development folks" and other business-focused entities, such as the Bangor Region Chamber of Commerce.

"The airport can be seen as an economic engine," Caruso said. Based at BIA, C&L Aerospace has recently expanded from 22 employees to more than 120 workers.

The Maine Air National Guard and Army National Guard operate aviation units at BIA; "they are our partners here on the airfield," Caruso said. "We have a great relationship with them." (Courtesy of Bangor International Airport.)

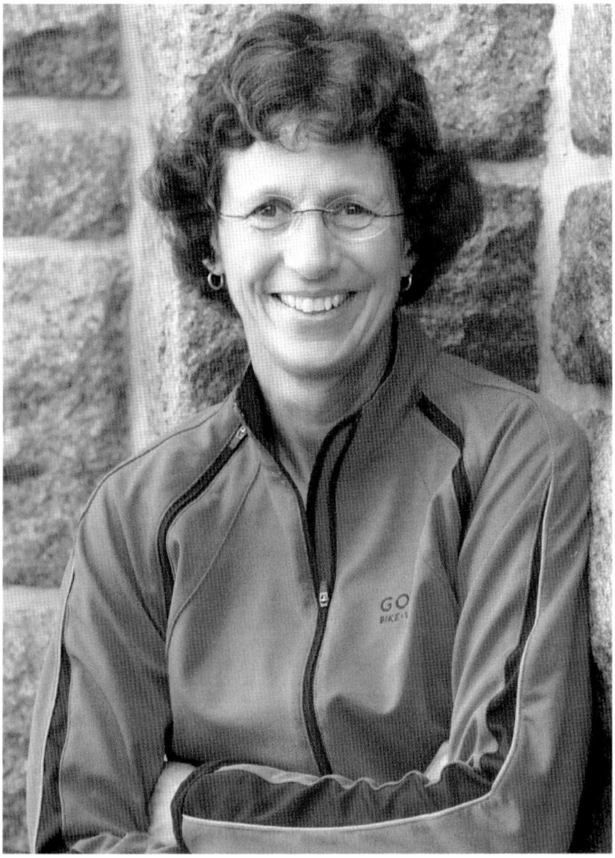

Called to the Ministry

"God has given me the invitation to serve as a Christian minister," says Rev. Renee Garrett—and she has never regretted her decision to follow a God-centered career.

A native of Lodi, California, Garrett felt called to the ministry "because I genuinely loved God. My greatest joy was being involved with things in the church." After earning a master's of divinity degree at Andover Newton Theological School in Massachusetts in May 1977, she was ordained that August at her home church, the First Congregational Church, in Lodi.

Named the minister of Christian Nurture at All Souls Congregational Church in Bangor in 1987, Garrett has been involved in various ministries, including Christian education for adults and young people, since then. Responsible for the church's mission outreach, ASSIST-JC, which includes adults and teens, she focuses on young people in particular.

"People do not realize the spiritual vacuum in which they are living," Garrett said. One goal of her youth ministry "is to help build a solid foundation there so the teens will have faith underpinnings as they go on to live their lives. They need to understand that God is bigger than the difficulties and challenges they face." To this end, a collection of her original children's stories, *One Man's Roses—Tales From Uncle Sol's Neighborhood*, was published in 2011.

She recently helped bring the Street Pastors Initiative, an interdenominational ministry initially established in London, to the streets of Bangor.

The program's trained volunteers meet and chat with people in downtown Bangor on weekends and try to help meet the needs of individual people. Several churches are involved with Street Pastors, joining their efforts with other local churches that have previously established specific ministries to serve Bangor's street people.

"Right now in Bangor, there is this upwelling of churches that see the need to help these people," Garrett said. "We're finding so many interesting ministries that are going on. God is stirring up the churches to say, 'We've got to get outside our buildings and love our neighbors.'"

"There is an awakening in our churches to make an impact in Bangor," she said. "We're reaching out across denominational lines. We have a message to share with our community, and it's filled with hope."

"I think it's beautiful," Garrett said. "I can only see good coming from this." (Courtesy of Rev. Renee Garrett.)

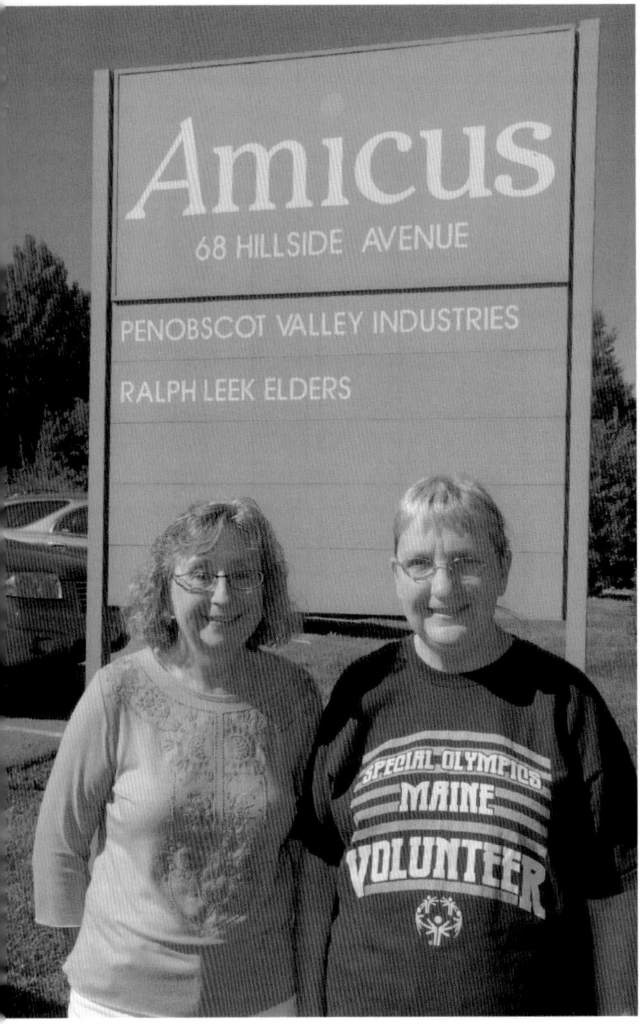

Caring Teacher

Edna "Eddie" Taber (right) always wanted to be a teacher. English was her intended subject, but when Taber worked part-time in a Madison nursing home during her teens, her planned career took an entirely different path.

For 28 years, Taber has worked as a program specialist for Penobscot Valley Industries (PVI), a division of Amicus. Taber teaches various subjects—cooking and music, among others—to special needs and intellectually challenged individuals.

Back at the nursing home, "my favorite patients were those just coming out of Pineland [Hospital]," Taber said. She also had a cousin who, because he had cerebral palsy, "had to fight for each new step in his life."

Her work at PVI involves "finding out what's important to the folks we serve and finding ways to make it happen," she said. Class participants range in age from 18 to their 60s; according to Pamela Colson Power (left), the PVI program director, Taber teaches approximately 90 people.

"They are such wonderful people," said Taber, who is always amazed at their "incredible sense of humor" and by "how curious they are and how much they want to learn. They are concerned for one another."

For Taber, the two most favorite aspects of her job are Special Olympics and "the things we do in the community." She has "seen Special Olympics grow into something more than just sports" over the years, and she coaches such Special Olympics sports as basketball, bocce, soccer, and winter games. Taber, who introduced the TRAIN program at PVI for individuals wanting to participate in Special Olympics, has volunteered for World Games held in such countries as China, Greece, and Ireland.

"We remember her planning and organizing the first Special Olympic event in Maine in Newburgh in the wintertime," Power said.

The people who come to PVI "are constantly doing something to give back to the community," Taber said. They work on joint projects with various local organizations.

"They are so enthusiastic about what they do," Taber said.

Years ago she helped write a grant that started Penobscot Area Housing (PAH), with the goal "to create a family-atmosphere home" for individuals who come to PVI or similar agencies. Taber is the current PAH board chair.

"Her lifelong career serving this population is a testament to her personal and professional devotion in making a difference in the quality of their lives," Power said. (Courtesy of BFS.)

CHAPTER EIGHT

A Ripe Old Age

Longevity is a way of life in Bangor, where many residents have thrived well into their 70s, 80s, and 90s—and occasionally into a second century. From the Hammond Street Senior Center in the heart of the downtown to the seniors' groups organized by local churches and other organizations, older Bangoreans enjoy many ways to socialize and to serve their community.

Among the 19th-century legends long associated with Bangor was "Molly Molasses," a Penobscot Indian officially named Mary Pelagie upon her birth in 1775. A frequent traveler on the ships that connected Bangor with towns along Penobscot Bay, Molasses was a shrewd trader in Native American crafts and medicines.

Born to wealthy parents in Bangor in 1884, Waldo Peirce became a famous artist decades before his death 86 years later. His life spanned two world wars; Peirce volunteered his services as an ambulance driver in France during World War I. He spent much time in France and elsewhere as his painting career developed in the 1920s. Peirce became an artistic legend during his lifetime, and to this day, few people realize that he was a Bangor boy.

After studying for three years at the Maine School of Commerce in Bangor, educator Clara Swan later returned to that school to teach. Soon named Husson College (and recently Husson University), the college was where Swan taught business classes, coached the women's varsity basketball team, and served as vice president. A longtime resident of next-door Hampden, Swan retired from Husson in the 1970s.

Bernard "Doc" Mann was another Bangor resident who reached the century mark. Often known by the nickname he gained as a Boy Scout, Mann taught in the Bangor School Department for more than four decades. He strongly supported the Scouts and other youth organizations throughout his life and belonged to such organizations as the Knights of Columbus.

Lillian Katherine Towle was the daughter of *Bangor Daily News* publisher J. Norman Towle. She later married Fred D. Jordan, became known as Lillis Jordan, and was the newspaper's publisher for some years. Her grandson Richard J. Warren publishes the modern *Bangor Daily News.*

There are other Bangor legends who served their community while living many years. Veteran Bill Knight became synonymous with the Maine Troop Greeters, the dedicated volunteers who welcome military personnel flying through Bangor International Airport. Dr. Eugene Sanger, who lived in another time, honed his surgical skills while caring for sick and wounded soldiers during the Civil War.

And then there is Paul Bunyan, the Bangor legend whose life has spanned three centuries as he cut the tall trees growing from Maine to the upper Midwest. Today, he smiles from his vantage point outside the new Cross Insurance Center in Bangor.

Molly Molasses

The Native American woman known throughout the Penobscot Valley as "Molly Molasses" was officially named Mary Pelagie upon her birth in 1775. A member of the Penobscot Nation, she was skilled in the traditional tribal arts; her people also believed that Molly had the gift of *m'teoulin* (magic).

The Penobscots' way of life gradually changed as more settlers moved to Bangor and other nearby towns. Penobscots had to learn nontraditional ways to support their families.

Molly Molasses became a shrewd trader by selling Native American crafts and medicines for food and other necessities. A familiar figure in Bangor, she proudly represented her people in an era when too many whites viewed Native Americans as inferior.

Often the only Native American whom local settlers encountered on a regular basis, Molly died in 1867. (Courtesy of BPL.)

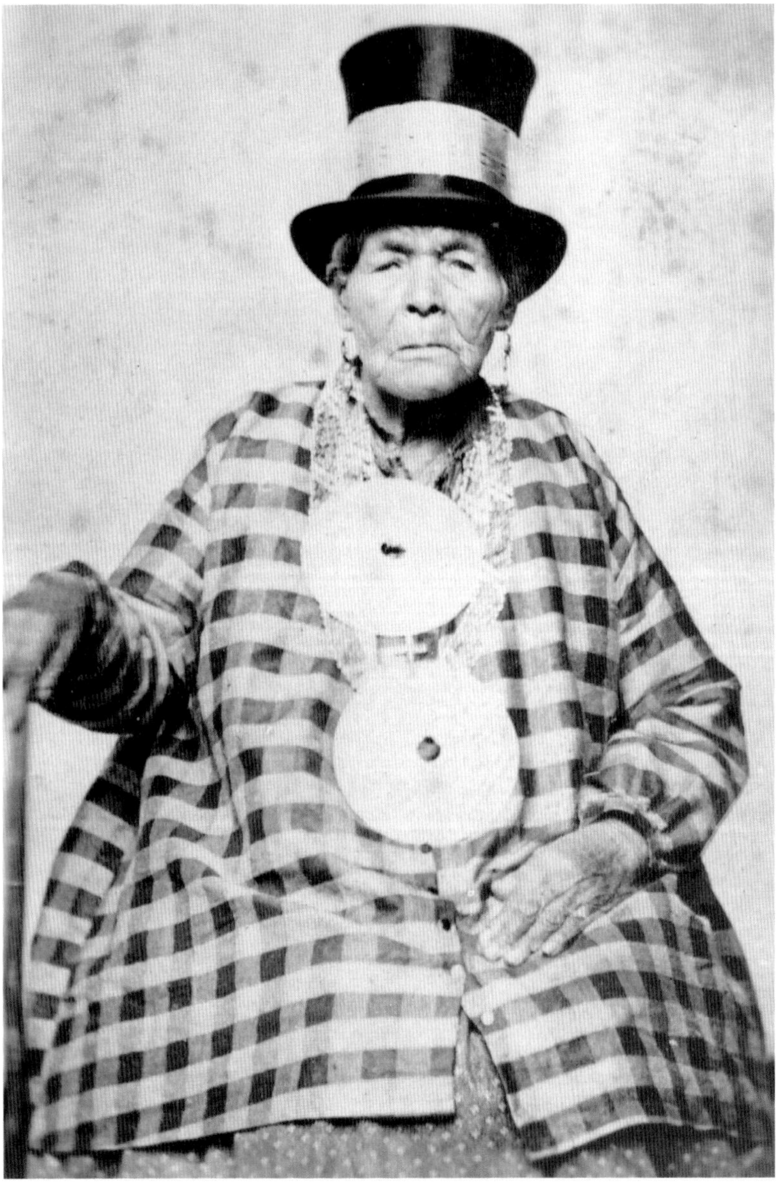

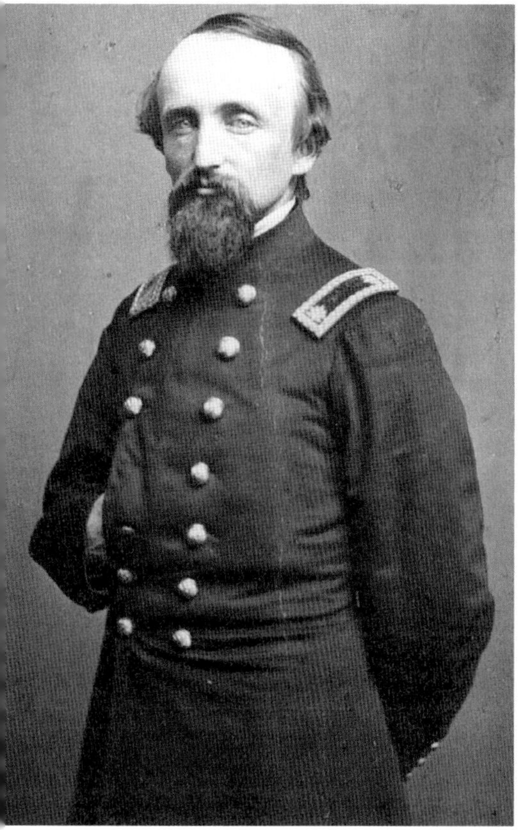

An Experienced Surgeon

When Dr. Eugene Sanger, MD, arrived in Bangor in 1857, he had already honed his medical skills at American and European hospitals.

Named surgeon of the 6th Maine Infantry Regiment in June 1861, Sanger later served in Virginia and the Mississippi Valley, where under a flag of truce he crossed Confederate lines to care for wounded Union soldiers in Louisiana. Sanger held the position of "medical director" at other Union posts, including a prison camp in Elmira, New York.

Resuming his Bangor medical practice in autumn 1865, Sanger was soon in demand across eastern Maine. Focused on specific surgical procedures and medical topics, including malpractice, his papers were published by medical journals, such as the *Transactions of the Maine Medical Society*.

Sanger became president of the State Medical Association in 1876. (Both, courtesy of BPL.)

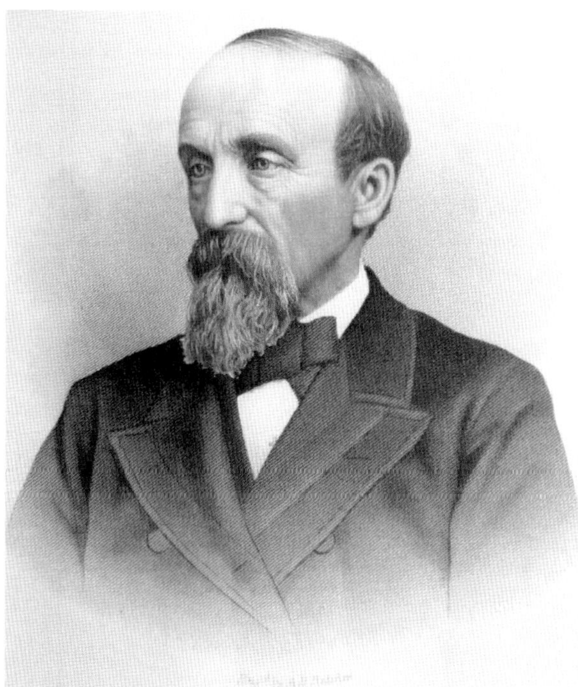

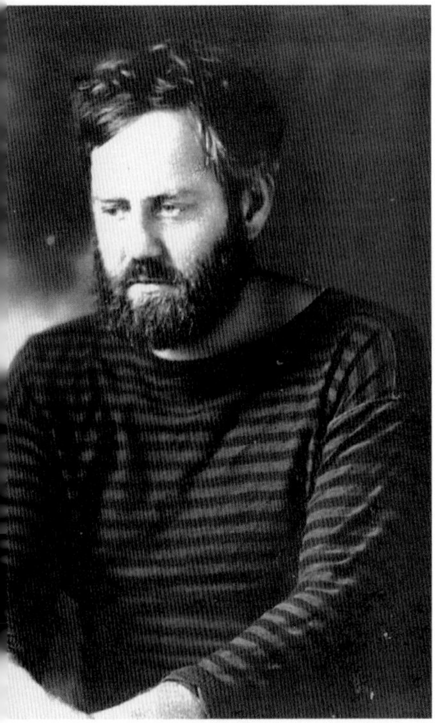

Joie de Vivre

Born in Bangor on December 17, 1884, Waldo Peirce became a world-renowned painter who lived until he was 85. And during those intervening years, he lived an adventurous life.

Peirce's parents were Bangor lumber baron Mellen C. Peirce (a name well known in the late 19th-century economies of Maine and New England) and Anna Hayford Peirce; her family's surname lives on in Bangor's Hayford Park. Family wealth allowed Waldo Peirce to attend Phillips Academy in Andover, Massachusetts; from there, he studied at Harvard University—and although his actual graduation date remains hazy, Peirce always identified with the class of 1907.

Art, specifically painting, may have been his calling. Peirce could have followed his father into the world of business and finance, but instead he decided to travel to Europe to study with Spanish artist Ignacio Zuloaga and at a famous art school in Paris. Peirce initially focused on Impressionism; his career as an artist was starting to develop when the Great War engulfed Europe.

In 1915, two years before the United States officially entered the war on the side of the Allies, Waldo Peirce volunteered his services as an American Field Service ambulance driver. He often ventured close to the front lines to retrieve wounded Allied soldiers, especially during the slaughter at Verdun. (Left, courtesy of Gary W. Woolson; below courtesy of BPL.)

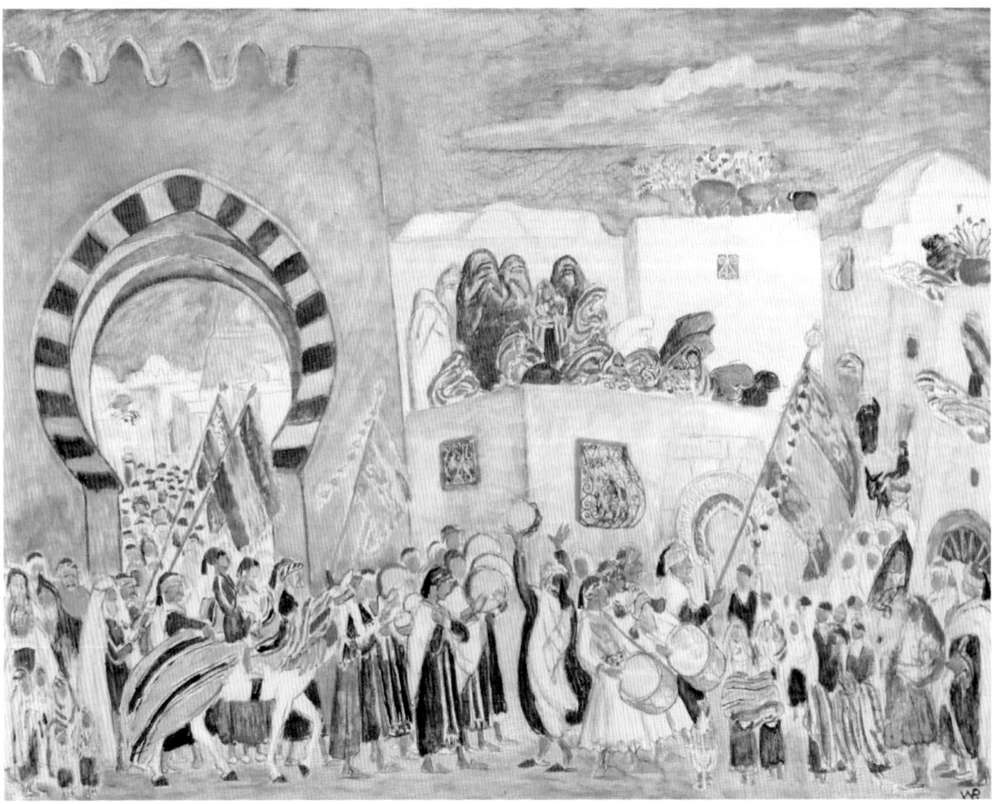

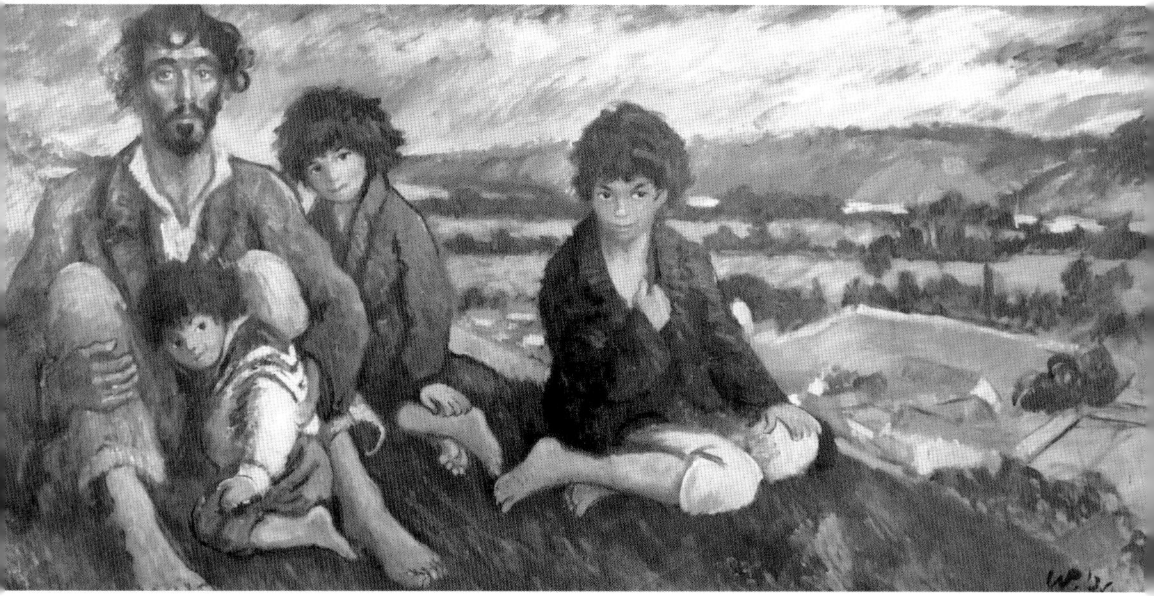

Prolific Artist

In honor of his heroic work, the French government later awarded Peirce the Croix de Guerre.

Close friends with writer Ernest Hemingway, Peirce saw his art career blossom after the war. He traveled extensively with Hemingway; places that they went often appeared in Peirce's paintings. Both men shared a love of life that individually spilled over into their respective callings.

Among Peirce's paintings were *Baptismal Procession in Tunisia* (left, below), *Gypsies* (above), and *Portrait of Walter Manley Hardy* (right).

Styled during his lifetime as the "American Renoir," Peirce was a prolific artist whose works often involved his extensive family. He was married four times (Dorothy Rice, Ivy Troutman, Alzira Boehm, and Ellen Antoinette Larson), and his children were often the subjects of his paintings.

Peirce moved back to Maine in the 1930s. His work often reflected the people and scenes around him in Maine.

Peirce died at Newburyport, Massachusetts, in early March 1970. He is buried at Mount Hope Cemetery in Bangor. (Both, courtesy of BPL.)

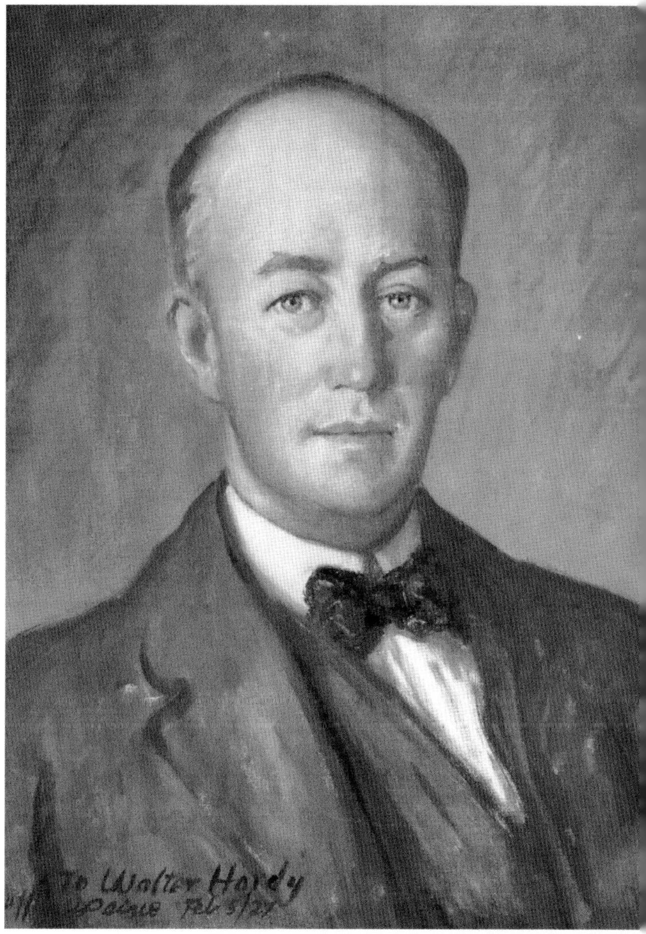

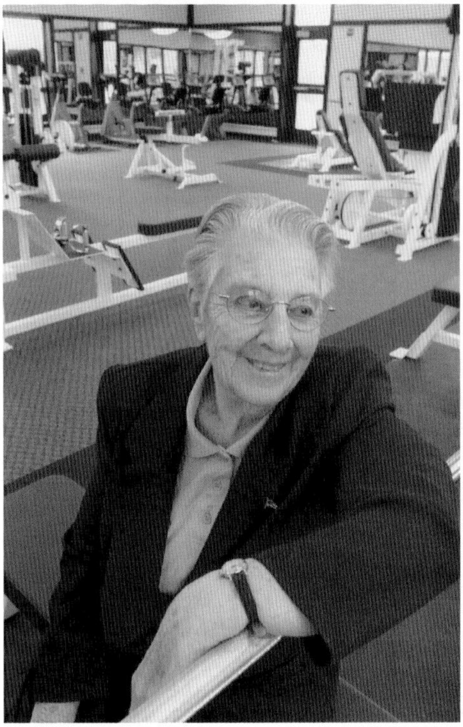

Dedicated to Higher Education

Clara Swan has a warm place for Husson University in her heart; after all, that's the school to which she dedicated much of her professional career.

Born in Princeton in 1912, Swan (above) was valedictorian of the Brewer High School class of 1930. After attending the Maine School of Commerce (Husson's earlier name) for three years, she taught for two years at Mexico High School in Oxford County and three years at Foxcroft Academy in Piscataquis County. Swan also coached women's basketball at both schools.

In 1939, she graduated from American International College in Springfield, Massachusetts, with a bachelor's degree in education. "I trained to be a business teacher," she said; her degree and training led her back to Husson College that year.

Established in 1898 as the Shaw School of Business, Maine School of Commerce was acquired in the mid-20th century by Chesley H. Husson Sr. and was renamed for him. "Mr. Husson was young when he came here," Swan said. "He was a smart man."

Husson College was small in the early 1940s; one of only five teachers, Swan taught such business courses as bookkeeping, shorthand, and typing. Having played women's basketball in high school and college, Swan coached the Husson women's team for many years. Her basketball teams could be quite large; Coach Swan stands at the far left in the third row (opposite page, above).

Swan recalled with pleasure when Chesley Husson relocated his school's classrooms to a large building atop Park Street hill in Bangor and, later, established a campus on Griffin Road in the Queen City. "It was Mr. Husson's dream to have a college there," she said. "He devoted his life to it."

Husson officially became a college in 1953 and a university in 2008. "I've enjoyed seeing it grow," said Swan, who has lived in Hampden for more than 50 years. "It's a university of every sense of the word." In time, Swan became a dean, headed a Husson department, and served as the vice president.

Swan retired from Husson in the 1970s and, along with two other women, purchased Casco Bay College in Portland. Swan was that school's president from 1975 to 1981. Today, she lives with her cat at the home that she built in Hampden more than 50 years ago. (Clockwise from top left, courtesy of BDN; courtesy of RRS; courtesy of BFS.)

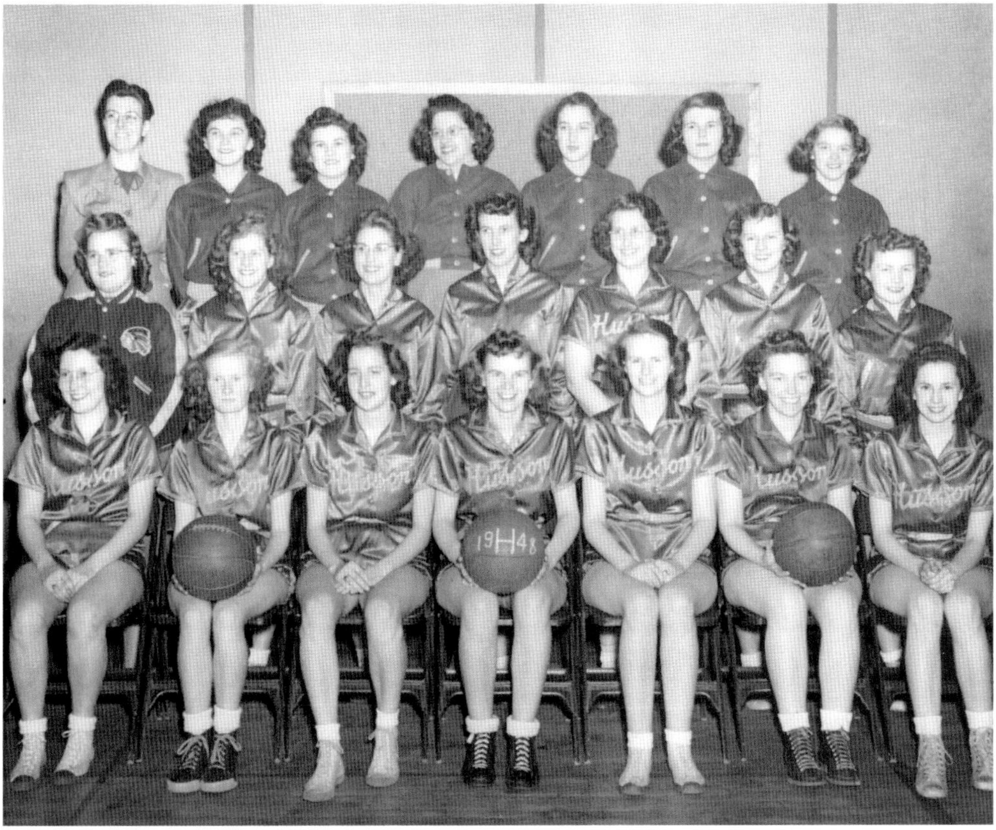
19H48

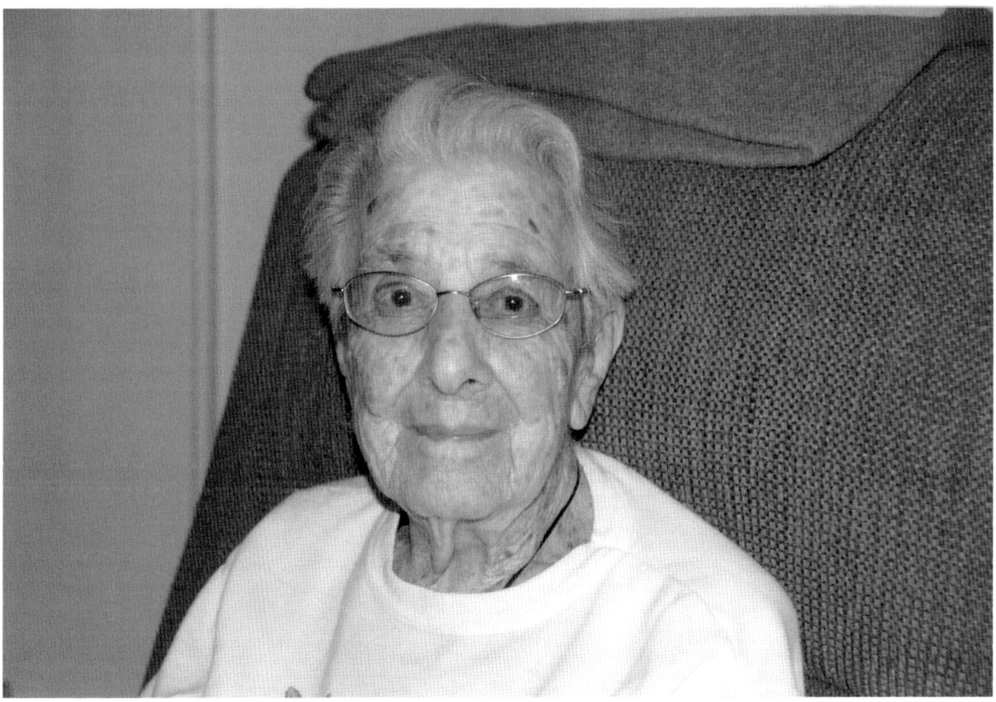

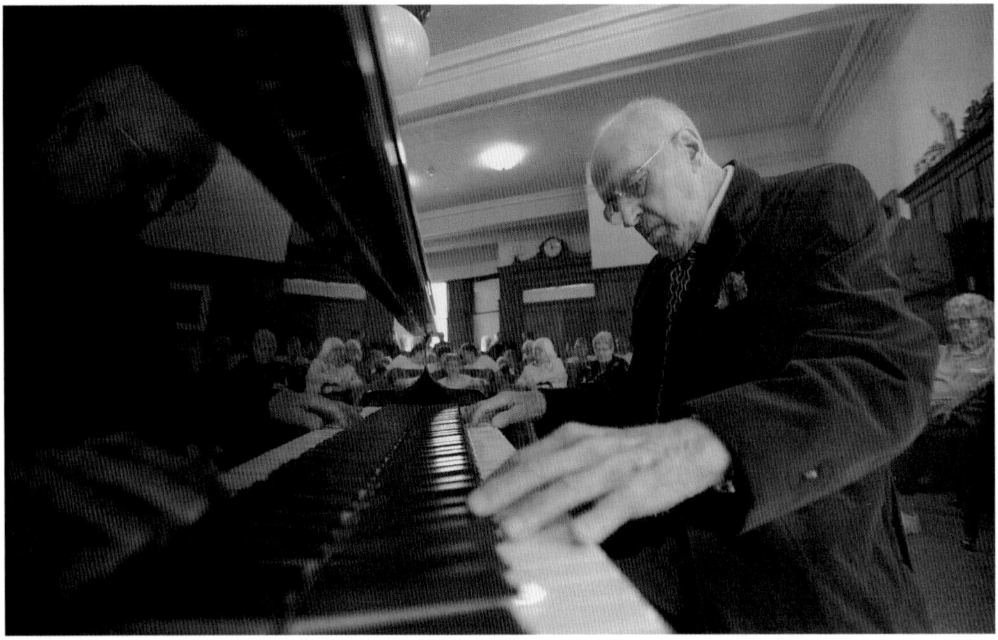

Piano Man

A teacher in Bangor schools for more than 40 years, Bernard "Doc" Mann devoted his time to many local youth organizations, especially the Boy Scouts of America.

Born in Bangor in 1909, Mann started teaching in Bangor in 1935 after earning a bachelor's degree in languages and a master's degree in French. He later worked at Eastern Maine Community College.

Among the members of the Maine Association of Football Officials meeting in Bangor in November 1953 were, from left to right, (first row) Harry Dalton, Henry Cameron, and Merle Finley; (second row) John Roberts, Bob Clukey, Bowdoin College Coach Adam Walsh, and Bernard Mann.

In his retirement, Mann was active in the Hammond Street Senior Center, where in May 2009 he tickled the ivories as listeners sang "Happy Birthday" to him a month shy of his 100th birthday. (Courtesy of BDN.)

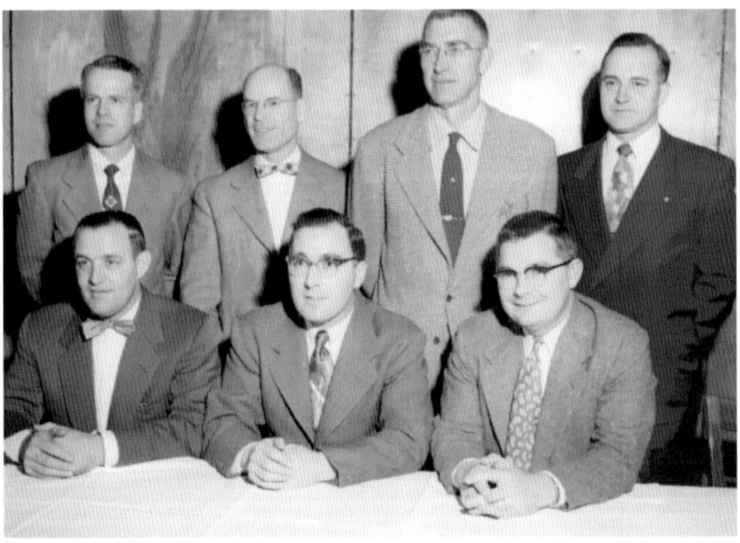

An Unforgettable Woman

Catherine "Kay" Lebowitz was an unforgettable woman. Well coiffed and wearing designer eyeglasses, she turned heads when she walked into a room. When she died in 2010 at age 94, the former city councilor and state legislator received many accolades. Perhaps the rarest was the dimming of the lights in her honor on the Thomas Hill Standpipe.

Lebowitz served on local committees, boards, and groups, including the Bangor Museum and History Center, Eastern Maine Community College, Maine Center for Aging, St. Joseph Hospital, and the Eastern Maine United Way. Lebowitz also made her mark as a Maine Troop Greeter. Group president Tom Kohl said, "She was just a very warm person, and it came out. The troops really responded to her. She will be sorely missed by the entire community, and she was a major part of our community here [at Bangor International Airport]."

She was born in Massachusetts and moved as a girl to Searsport. She moved back to Boston at one point, but returned to Maine in 1955, at which point she became active in the community. In 2008, the Bangor Region Chamber of Commerce renamed its Public Sector Service Award the Catherine Lebowitz Award for Public Service. That service included volunteering at the Bureau of Motor Vehicles, where she tactfully made sure each customer had his or her paperwork in order.

Lebowitz was married to Murray Lebowitz, who predeceased her. (Courtesy of BDN.)

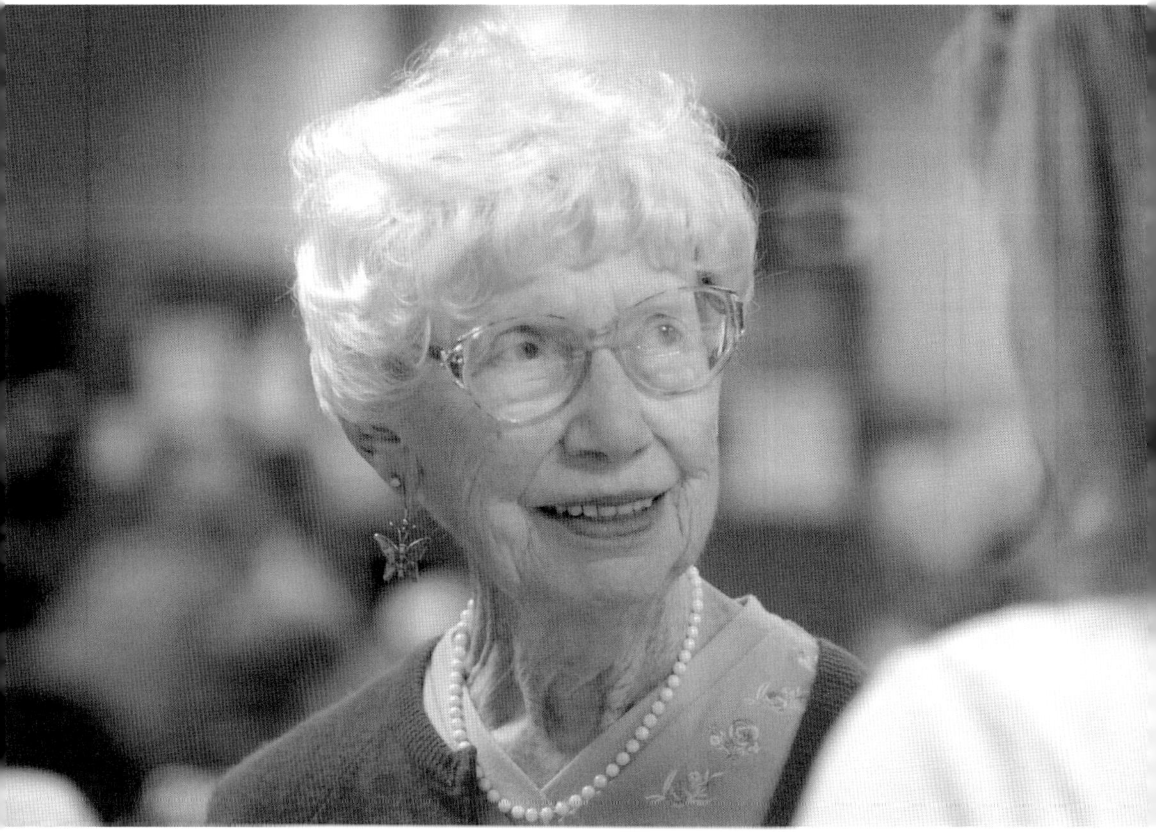

Maine Troop Greeter

After William Franklin Knight, age 91, died at the Maine Veterans' Home on Christmas Day 2013, the media reported on the various ways he had served his country.

Knight was best known as the unofficial head of the Bangor-based Maine Troop Greeters. The 32-year US military veteran estimated in 2011 that he had shaken hands with more than a half-million military personnel leaving or returning from the Middle East. He liked to attend parades in his Navy dress blues. "[He] outlived two daughters and wives," reported the *Bangor Daily News*, "lost his farm and was close to homelessness before hearing from a friend two years ago about the Veterans Aid and Assistance program, a little-known benefit that pays qualified wartime veterans and their surviving spouses up to $1,949 a month in aid and living assistance." Such stories formed the basis of the 2009 documentary, *The Way We Get By*, produced by Gita Pullapilly and her husband, Aron Gaudet. Fellow greeters Jerry Mundy and Joan Gaudet, Aron's mother, costarred in the film. (Right, courtesy of BDN; below, photograph by Sean Carnell, courtesy of The Way We Get By Productions.)

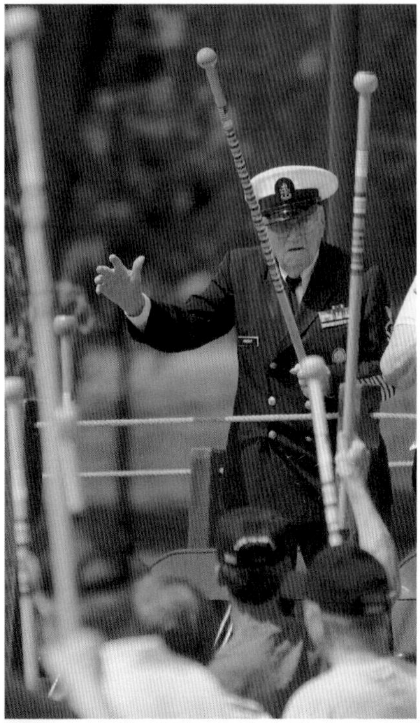

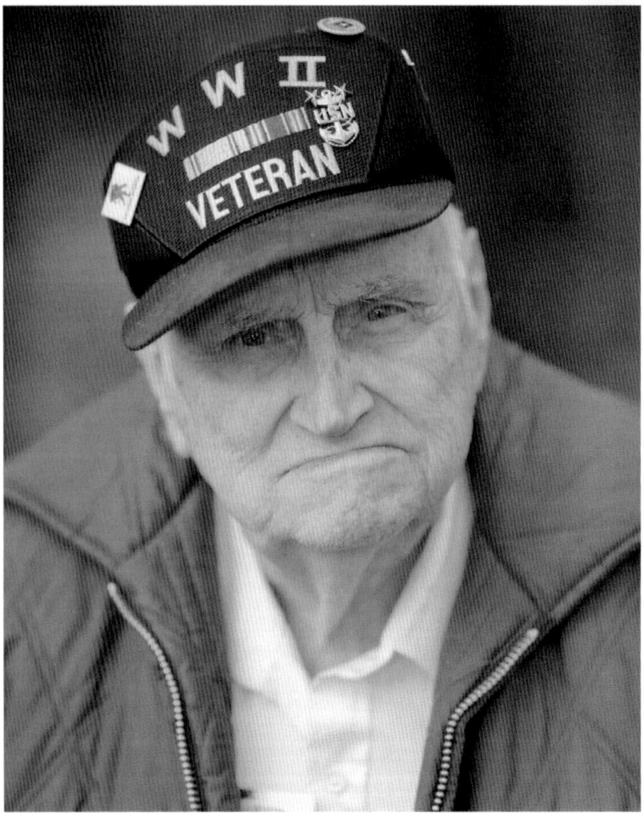

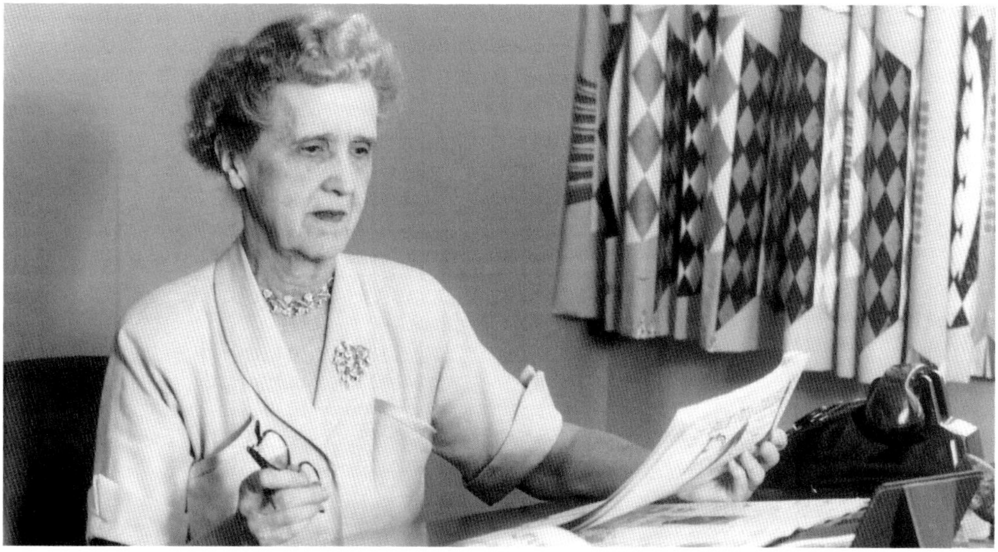

Fearless Newspaper Publisher

The Bangor publishing world may never see a woman like Lillis T. Jordan again. She lived most of her life in Bangor, where she was born in 1893 to grain merchant J. Norman Towle and his wife, Mary. After her father purchased the *Bangor Daily News* in 1895, her life was all about newspapers.

As the paper's chairman of the board, Jordan was a wealth of history. In an interview conducted not long before her 1986 death, she recalled the great fire of 1911, which charred buildings near the newspaper's Exchange Street plant. "[The paper] was set by oil lamp . . . and by hand," she said. "All the electricity was turned off."

One day in 1947, her husband, publisher Fred Jordan, died of a stroke. Soon afterward, she was acting as publisher. "I had all kinds of people . . . wanting to buy," she recalled. "I never talked to them, so I don't know what they would have paid."

Jordan's grandson Richard J. Warren was named publisher in 1984, following in the footsteps of his father, Jordan's former son-in-law, Richard K. Warren. (Above, courtesy of BDN; below, courtesy of RRS.)

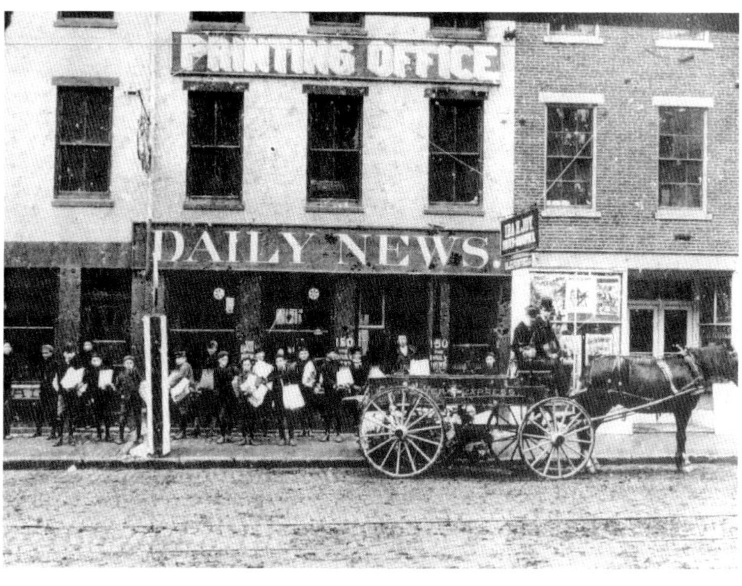

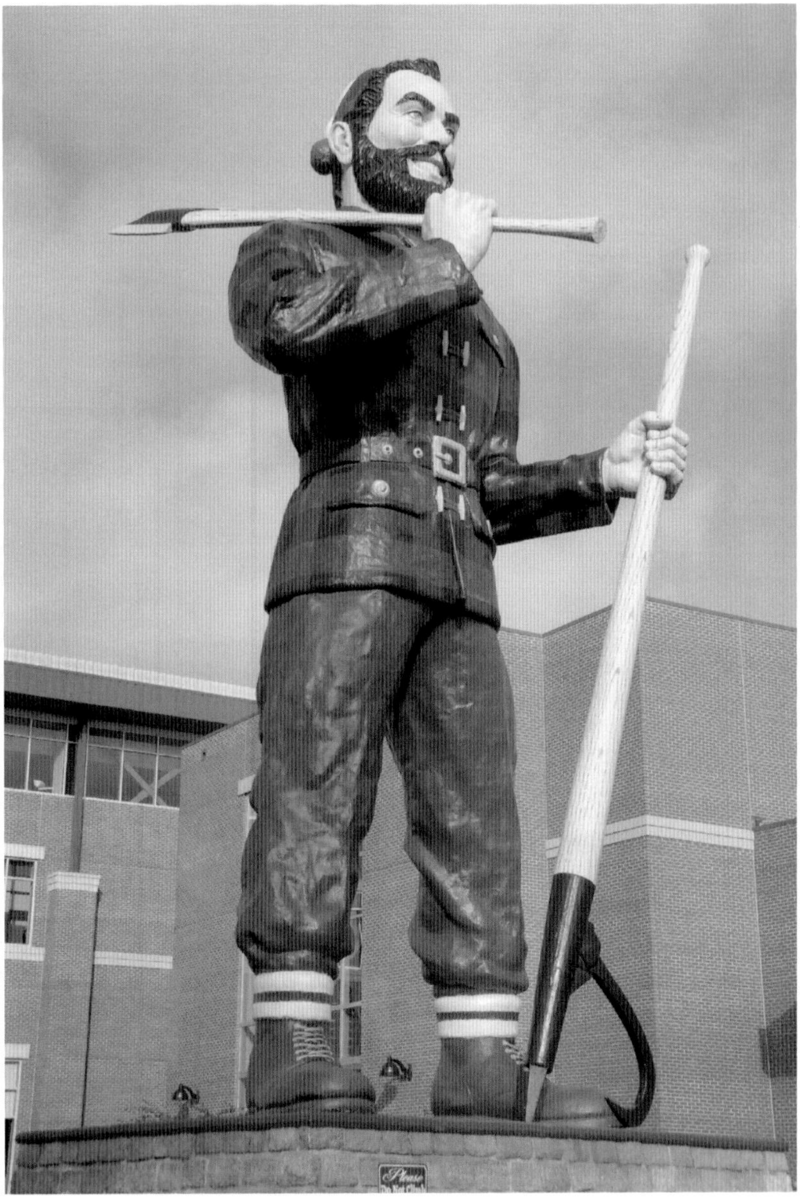

Lumberjack

One famous Bangorean who has not aged with time is Paul Bunyan, the perennially smiling lumberjack who has stood beside lower Main Street since 1959.

But the actual Paul Bunyan is much older.

Bangor lore claims that Bunyan was born in the Queen City sometime in the 1830s, 1840s, or 1850s, during the city's heyday as the world's lumber capital. Tall, tall trees stood in the forests upriver from Bangor in that era; harvesting the virgin timber by broadax and crosscut saw required tall, hardy men, and Paul Bunyan was the biggest of them all.

Designed by J. Normand Martin (see page 73), the 37-foot Paul Bunyan went up on his pedestal in 1959. With his peavey at his left side and double-bladed ax slung over his right shoulder, Bunyan weighs 3,700 pounds. (Courtesy of BFS.)

BIBLIOGRAPHY

Bourne, Annie Nettleton, trans. *The Voyages and Explorations of Samuel de Champlain.* New York: Allerton Books, 1904.

Godfrey, Hon. John E., Esq. "The Ancient Penobscot or Panawanskek." *The Historical Magazine and Notes and Quarters concerning The Antiquities, History, and Biography of America, Third Series, Volume I, No. 2.* Morrisina, NY: Henry B. Dawson, February 1872.

Gold, David M. *Cyrus Hamlin's Civil War: Letters of the Vice President's Son on the Civil War and Reconstruction.* Westminster, MD: Heritage Books, 2011.

Hatfield, Mark O. *Vice Presidents of the United States, 1789–1993.* Washington, DC: US Government Printing Office, 1997.

History of Penobscot County, Maine, with Illustrations and Biographical Sketches. Cleveland: Williams, Chase & Co., 1882.

Otis, Charles Pomeroy, and Rev. Edmund F. Slafter. *Voyages of Samuel de Champlain.* Boston: Prince Society, 1880.

Porter, J.W., ed. *The Bangor Historical Magazine, Volume 5.* Bangor: Benjamin A. Burr, printer, 1980.

The History of Madison County, Ohio: Containing a History of the County, Its Townshops, Towns, Churches, Schools, etc. Page 1025. Chicago: W.H. Beers & Co., 1883.

Reilly, Wayne E. *Remembering Bangor: The Queen City Before the Great Fire.* Charleston, SC; The History Press, 2009.

———. *Hidden History of Bangor: From Lumbering Days to the Progressive Era,* Charleston, SC; The History Press, 2009.

Scee, Trudy Irene. *City on the Penobscot: A Comprehensive History of Bangor, Maine.* Charleston, SC; The History Press, 2010.

Shaw, Richard R. *Bangor.* Dover, NH; Arcadia Publishing, 1994.

———. *Bangor, Vol. II.* Dover, NH; Arcadia Publishing, 2001.

———. *Bangor in Vintage Postcards.* Charleston, SC; Arcadia Publishing, 2004.

Zoidis, Marilyn, and Abigail Ewing Zelz. *Woodsmen and Whigs: Historic Images of Bangor, Maine.* Norfolk and Virginia Beach, VA: the Donning Company, 1991.

INDEX